AF718615

Women, Economic Development, and Higher Education

Diane E. Eynon

Women, Economic Development, and Higher Education

Tools in the Reconstruction and Transformation of Post-Apartheid South Africa

palgrave
macmillan

Diane E. Eynon
Graduate School of Education
University of Pennsylvania
Philadelphia, Pennsylvania, USA

ISBN 978-3-319-53143-4 ISBN 978-3-319-53144-1 (eBook)
DOI 10.1007/978-3-319-53144-1

Library of Congress Control Number: 2017939174

© The Editor(s) (if applicable) and The Author(s) 2017
This work is subject to copyright. All rights are solely and exclusively licensed by the Publisher, whether the whole or part of the material is concerned, specifically the rights of translation, reprinting, reuse of illustrations, recitation, broadcasting, reproduction on microfilms or in any other physical way, and transmission or information storage and retrieval, electronic adaptation, computer software, or by similar or dissimilar methodology now known or hereafter developed.
The use of general descriptive names, registered names, trademarks, service marks, etc. in this publication does not imply, even in the absence of a specific statement, that such names are exempt from the relevant protective laws and regulations and therefore free for general use.
The publisher, the authors and the editors are safe to assume that the advice and information in this book are believed to be true and accurate at the date of publication. Neither the publisher nor the authors or the editors give a warranty, express or implied, with respect to the material contained herein or for any errors or omissions that may have been made. The publisher remains neutral with regard to jurisdictional claims in published maps and institutional affiliations.

Cover illustration © Rawpixel / Alamy Stock Photo

Printed on acid-free paper

This Palgrave Macmillan imprint is published by Springer Nature
The registered company is Springer International Publishing AG
The registered company address is: Gewerbestrasse 11, 6330 Cham, Switzerland

Lorretto Higgins

Preface and Acknowledgements

In September 2009, I traveled to South Africa for the second time in just two months. What brought me to the country was my interest and desire to learn more about how the government had been constructing a new post-apartheid South Africa and the tools it was using to build a nation based on equality, justice, and opportunity. In particular, I wanted to learn how women were contributing to and potentially benefiting from such efforts.

My interests focused on economic development and growth, higher education, and gender-equality policies. My decision to concentrate specifically on those areas was shaped by my continuing work in emerging economies and countries, as well as by my desire to understand how certain political, economic, and educational policies influence, create, and support women's opportunities.

I also wanted to know if those policies had accomplished what they had been meant to do. Did they contribute to and advance the transformation of South Africa? Policies are, of course, formulated, negotiated, and implemented with specific intentions, yet it is often unclear how well they will meet their stated objectives—let alone what unintended consequence they might have.

In my research for this book, I gathered material through archival data sources; government statistics, reports, and policies; and newspaper, magazine, and journal articles from a variety of institutions and organizations. During my doctoral studies at the University of Pennsylvania, I also conducted interviews with leading government officials who served in executive positions in the South African Department of Education, the

Council on Higher Education, and Ministry of Education. In addition, I interviewed professors at the University of Cape Town, University of Johannesburg, University of Pretoria, University of Western Cape, and Witwatersrand University, as well as the then deputy vice chancellor of the University of Cape Town. To gain external perspective on the South African higher education system, I also spoke with the executives at the Organisation for Economic Co-Operation and Development and the South Africa Qualifications Authority, and an African scholar from the University of California, Santa Cruz.

I selected those individuals based on their deep knowledge, understanding, and experience in economic growth and development, higher education, and gender issues in South Africa. They reflect multiple perspectives, both as a group and individually. They include people who have been in the nation's higher education system during and after apartheid; educators and administrators who have experienced first-hand the changes in higher education in a post-apartheid South Africa; activists who view the economic growth and development polices of the government through a political, social, and gender lens; outside experts in academe and international development organization; and citizens of South Africa.

This book examines the current relationships and connections between three key areas—economic development, higher education, and women—and seeks to understand how they have contributed to the reconstruction and transformation of South Africa. It also identifies the ways that advances in areas such as women's rights, poverty alleviation, and access to education have been stymied—fallen victim to corruption or social prejudices, or simply overwhelmed by the enormity of the problems.

Much has been written about the topics of politics, the economy, education, and women in South Africa, but this book offers a new and comprehensive understanding of how they interrelate. It recognizes the tension in South Africa between serving the global economy and increasing equality through social justice interventions. Perhaps most important, instead of framing the major issues confronting the country in racial terms, as other books and studies have, it examines them through the lens of gender. And, as part of that, it brings to light the importance of a higher education degree for women if they are to have a voice and place in South Africa's future.

The writing of this book has been a journey. It has taken time, patience, and effort, and not just on my part, to complete. Many thanks to Marybeth Gasman for her support from the very beginning, when she gave me the space and confidence as her doctoral advisee to pursue the research, all the way through to her encouragement to write and publish this book. I also owe much to Sarah Hardesty Bray for her careful and thorough editing, which has improved the text. To my friends and colleagues at the Graduate School of Education at the University of Pennsylvania, thank you for all your support and encouragement. Thanks, as well, to Ruthann and George Riggs, my wonderful and loving grandparents, who always encouraged and supported me, even when I drew outside of the lines. Finally, once again I must thank Lorretto Higgins, for her patience, care, and love throughout the process.

Contents

CHAPTER 1

Introduction

This is a story about South African women. It examines how South Africa's patriarchal culture, the apartheid system, and the 1996 constitution and other government gender-specific initiatives have influenced the lives of those women, especially black South African women. It is also a story about the role that women can and should play in the future of the South African nation. And it is a story about how a country marked by racism, segregation, and oppression can fulfill its promise as a model for the rest of the continent—and indeed the world.

This is by no means an exhaustive study. What this book does is to bring understanding as to why, despite one of the world's best-designed policy frameworks for women's empowerment and gender equality, a significant number of women still live in poverty, have higher incidences of HIV/AIDS, are increasingly victims of rape and violence, and continue to experience low college graduation rates. By recognizing and understanding why women continue to face significant challenges, 20 years after the establishment of a national framework for women's empowerment and gender equality, we can chip away at the poverty, low graduation rates, and violence that still pervade South Africa.

Well-written policies, speeches, and theoretical papers, while important, can only do so much. If women are to live in the kind of world set forth in the South African constitution, an honest assessment—one based on the testimonies of those involved—of the challenges facing women and why they still exist must be made. Until that happens, the women of South

© The Author(s) 2017

D.E. Eynon, *Women, Economic Development, and Higher Education*,
DOI 10.1007/978-3-319-53144-1_1

Africa will continue to carry the burden of poverty, illness, violence, and illiteracy.

South Africa's Promise and Progress

Of all the continents in the world, Africa remains the poorest and has borne the greatest brunt of colonialism, famine, disease, persistent poverty, and civil unrest. Yet one country, South Africa, has emerged as the exception. In just 22 years, it has rewritten its constitution, revised its macroeconomic growth and development policies, restructured its higher education system, and made a commitment to provide opportunity for all its citizens, specifically those who have historically been marginalized, such as women and blacks.

Indeed, South Africa has come a very long way since the time that the African National Congress (ANC) and Nelson Mandela came into power in 1994. Mandela and his party inherited the economic and social legacies of apartheid. Under apartheid, a great numbers of workers were unskilled or unemployed. Poverty was widespread and deep. Most people had limited access to education, health care, and other basic public services. On top of all that, the new government had to labor under the economic sanctions and political isolation that many countries around the world had imposed on South Africa in protest to the apartheid government. In essence, when the ANC came into power, the country was economically cut off from the rest of the world.[1]

For many African countries, independence from colonial rule allowed for the first generation of black African politicians. These politicians were responsible for the construction of legal, social, and political structures during the state-building process. According to N'Dri T. Assie-Lumumba, professor of African and Diaspora Education in the African Studies and Research Center at Cornell University, "It was during this process that they were able to articulate the intended social development and national reconstruction of their country after extensive and intensive colonial rule. Many of these politicians imagined a government and citizenry to include all the African populations, males and females."[2] That promise was especially true for South Africa in 1994, when the white minority apartheid government transferred political power, without massive civil unrest or violence, to the black majority through the ANC under the leadership of Mandela.

It was in 1994 that the term "Rainbow Nation" became a symbol of South African unity. The Archbishop Desmond Tutu[3] first used the rainbow symbol during the march of church leaders to Parliament in Cape Town in 1989 and again at ANC leader Chris Hani's funeral in 1993. The rainbow symbol gained widespread popularity in 1994 when Tutu led a televised Thanksgiving service to celebrate the peaceful elections and announced to the crowd: "We are the rainbow people of God. We are free—all of us, black and white together!"[4]

The symbol of the rainbow is the Old Testament symbol of reconciliation that affirms God's covenant with Noah after the flood. At the Thanksgiving ceremony, Tutu spoke not of a covenant with a chosen people but of one with all South Africans, irrespective of origin, religion, or color.

Nelson Mandela again referred to the symbol of the rainbow at his inaugural address on May 9, 1994, in Pretoria: "We enter into a covenant that we shall build a society in which all South Africans, both black and white, will be able to walk tall, without fear in their hearts, assured of their inalienable right to human dignity—a rainbow nation at peace with itself and the world."[5]

Gender equality and women's empowerment and education were considered to be key drivers to South Africa's transformation. In a March 2008 Global Economics Paper, Goldman Sachs stated that education is key to gender equality:

> Educating girls and women leads to higher wages, a greater likelihood of working outside the home, lower fertility, reduced maternal and child mortality, and better health and education. The impact is felt not only in women's lifetime but also in the health, education, and productivity of future generations. The economic growth that results from higher education feeds a virtuous cycle, supporting continued investments in education and extending the gains to human capital and productivity. [6]

No other country has undertaken such transformation in such a relatively short period of time. What have been the results for South Africa? Has the country been able to engage and compete in the global economy? Does the education system contribute to and support the country's social and macroeconomic policies? Can or does a significant percentage of the country's population, specifically women, benefit from this transformation? No other country in the world provides such a rich and complex landscape to research and explore these issues.

This book is structured as a critical policy analysis employing historical methods. It examines how the post-apartheid government's economic growth and development polices have informed the higher education system and how those in turn have changed women's financial, occupational, political, social, and educational prospects in South Africa. Through the telling of this history, the book explores the relationship among economic growth and development, higher education, and women within the social, cultural, and political context of the country from 1994 to the present.

As noted earlier, women are essential to the future of the country for a number of reasons. At the macroeconomic level, the education of women has been identified as a key source for long-term economic growth—and linked to higher productivity, higher returns on investment, higher agricultural yields, and a more favorable demographic structure.[7] The 2002 UN Population Fund Report states that one of the most effective ways to increase and sustain development is through the "improvement of women's skills and their access to tools such as credit, training, and technology."[8] In South Africa, it is well understood that women can and do make significant contributions to the economic development and growth in their communities and country. The challenge is to make sure that policies and decision-making reflects and supports that understanding.[9]

This book attempts to demonstrate the complex and significant ways South Africa's governmental, economic growth, and higher education policies intersect to influence women's lives. These policies, like any, are formulated, negotiated, and implemented with specific intentions in mind yet without real foreknowledge of how they will resolve those intentions—let alone the effects they will have outside their stated objectives. That may be particularly true for South Africa, as the influence of that country's policies has played a key but little understood role in the country's transformation since the end of apartheid rule.

The overarching question guiding this book is: what have been the consequences for the higher education system and the prospects for women of the macroeconomic growth and development policies, as well as the gender-equality and empowerment policies, that the post-apartheid South African government has pursued since 1994? This question comprises two sub-questions:

- *What have been the implications for the country of the macroeconomic growth and development policies adopted in 1994 by the post-apartheid government?* These neo-liberal economic policies have been widely debated and were a factor in the recent national election. While the country has experienced economic growth and a strong black middle class has emerged since 1994, South Africa has also seen an increase in unemployment, poverty, and violence against women. How have those consequences influenced the higher education system and the prospects for women? Will the recently elected government move the country toward economic policies that are more redistributive and equitable in an effort to curb poverty, reduce unemployment, expand access to higher education, and improve the social and economic conditions for the majority of South Africans?
- *How have the prospects for South African women changed since 1994?* The laws, bills, and commissions focused on gender equality and the empowerment of women in the post-apartheid government have served an important purpose. The government established the Commission on Gender Equality, National Gender Forum, and the Office on the Status of Women to support efforts by higher education leaders to become more inclusive and equitable. The question now is how effective have these laws, bills, and commissions been in achieving their objectives? Do patriarchal, cultural, and social norms still have a strong influence on women? If so, how do women balance that with the progressive gender framework set forth by the government? How does that balance influence their decision and ability to access higher education? Have higher education systems become more supportive, inclusive, and equitable for female students and faculty members? What challenges do women experience in accessing the higher education system, and what barriers do they face once in it? What are the employment opportunities for female graduates? And, what influence do race, class, and geography have on women when it comes to enrolling in and graduating from college, as well as obtaining good jobs afterward?

This book does not attempt to find the answers or solutions to the pressing economic, education, and gender issues facing South Africa today. The primary focus is on understanding the relationship between economic growth and development and higher education policies and how they have changed women's prospects. Although scholars, journalists, and others have usually framed their examinations of the country's opportunities and challenges around race, this study takes a different perspective and looks at the country through the lens of gender. Doing so sheds new light on how half of South Africa's people—women—have faced the country's complexity, opportunities, and challenges over the past several decades.

While this book focuses on post-apartheid South Africa, it important to understand the final years of apartheid rule, the key political players, and the conditions and terms under which the ANC came to power. Chapters 2 and 3 provide the background information necessary to appreciate and understand the transformation of the country. That understanding will allow the reader to contextualize the challenges and opportunities facing the country today. These chapters review the early 1990s, at the beginning of the end of apartheid rule. They focus on the people who were instrumental in engineering the end of apartheid and provide a glimpse into the political landscape, the economic challenges, the condition of the higher education system, and the role of women at the time.

South Africa is a country that has gone through significant changes since 1994. The new government, led by the ANC, set out to transform the country. Chapter 4 looks at the key initiatives that new government undertook to rebuild the country: the writing of a new constitution, the development of macroeconomic growth and development policies, the dismantling and restructuring of the higher education system, and the building of a national framework for gender equality and the empowerment of women. The chapter also highlights key debates and questions that arose during the creation and adoption process of these policies—which continue to play out today.

The aim of Chapter 5 is to illustrate the far-reaching influence of the macroeconomic policies adopted by the ANC—and in particular their effect on the higher education system. Such policies have played a significant role in the country since the 1994 election campaign. What started as a strategy of redistribution and equity during the election campaign gave way to a Western, neo-liberal market-based approach with the introduction of the Growth, Employment, and Redistribution Policy (GEAR) in 1996. That policy shift had a tremendous impact on the country economically, socially, politically, and culturally.

Chapter 5 focuses on the influence of GEAR on economic growth and development, higher education, and the prospects for women since its inception in 1996 to today. It also explores the potential for changes in these macroeconomic policies, given South Africans growing discontent with the economic direction of the country and the pressures facing the government under the leadership of Jacob Zuma. Those people who supported the candidacy of Zuma—including the poor, trade unions and the South African Communist Party (SACP)—have expected the government to re-examine GEAR policies and shift to a more redistributive model with increased government intervention. The chapter ends with an examination of what, if anything, the government is proposing as it relates to economic growth and development initiatives.

The South African government and its citizens view the higher education system as one of the main vehicles for fulfilling the promise of the country, and that system has undergone unprecedented change since 1994. Three key policies have been implemented that provide the foundation for higher education in the country. The first is the 1995 White Paper, which called for increased access to higher education, development of a single coordinated system, and expansion of distance learning. The second is the 1997 White Paper, which abandoned equity goals and managerial efficiency. The government released a third White Paper in 2004 that called for the reorganization and merger of higher education institutions. The high expectations and rapid changes brought forth from these policies have put tremendous stress on the higher education system —sometimes perpetuating problems from the past as well as creating new ones —which Chapter 6 describes.

Specifically, the chapter discusses the need to provide a higher-quality education, improve the preparation of students, raise the graduation rates of black and underrepresented groups, overcome language barriers, and meet the country's need for skilled workers who can contribute to the global knowledge-based economy. In addition, Chapter 6 examines the distinct challenges associated with merging into one system multiple universities with historically different curricula, students, language, and standards. The chapter ends with an analysis of how the organizational and structural changes to the Ministry of Education were designed to alleviate some of the challenges facing the system.

Chapters 7 and 8 analyze how women's prospects have changed since the end of apartheid rule. They bring understanding to the role and relationship between economic growth and development, higher education, and gender in post-apartheid South Africa—as framed by the cultural, social, and political context in which the country operates. Since higher education is considered key to gender equality, a greater likelihood of working outside the home, higher wages, lower fertility, and reduced maternal and child mortality, the discussion in Chapter 7 starts by examining the role higher education has played in improving women's prospects, the gains they have been made, and the challenges that remain. It explores issues related to access, retention, and field of study, along with the roles that race, class, geography, and social and cultural norms have played in either increasing or decreasing the likelihood of women's success in the higher education system. The discussion then turns to the prevalence of rape, sexual harassment, pregnancy, and HIV/AIDS on campuses and how they influence a woman's ability to graduate from college.

Chapter 8 then highlights the gains women have made, the challenges that remain, and how race, class, geography, cultural and social norms, and education continue to influence their lives. While South African women have in general been making enormous strides, most black women remain in the poorest socioeconomic sector of the population—the service and agricultural sector—and occupy a small percentage of those in the professional sector. In addition women are paying a price for the gains they have made, as reflected in the level of violence against them, including rape, and the high incidence of HIV/AIDS. There is a general sense of a backlash against women from men in the country, including its leaders, and it is palatable. The chapter ends by examining these disturbing trends and attempts to explain why they are happening.

The concluding chapter will discuss the challenges that remain for women, suggestions for moving forward, and thoughts about what the future may hold given the current trends and conditions in the country.

A significant amount of literature—research studies, articles, and books —has discussed, examined, and debated from a political and economic perspective the merits of the GEAR that the post-apartheid government adopted. It is my hope that this book provides a deeper understanding of the implications of the policy by focusing on its effect on the higher education system—a topic about which less has been said—and on women, where little to no literature exists. This book fills a void by examining how GEAR has influenced two key elements necessary for meeting the economic growth and development initiatives of the country: (1) higher education and (2) the full and active engagement of women. It was anticipated that the presidency of Jacob Zuma would bring political, economic, and social change to the country, and in that regard, this book takes into account the social, cultural, and political context of current conditions and events to offer a distinct perspective on South Africa's future.

South Africa is a country whose history has been told as a racial story. But new ways of telling the story are slowly emerging. This book is an attempt to show that race is not the only guiding force in South Africa's past, present, and future. Other crucial factors and events—including those related to gender—are shaping and giving character to its story.

This book tells the story of South Africa in gendered terms so as to better understand the complexity of the country today and to analyze it in a more comprehensive way. It weaves economic growth and development, higher education, and gender together to create a new way of viewing the country and envisioning it going forward.

Notes

1. Michael Nowak and Luca Antonio Ricci, eds., *Post-apartheid South Africa: The First Ten Years* (Washington, DC: International Monetary Fund, 2005), 1.
2. N'Dri T. Assie-Lumumba, "Educational and Economic Reforms, Gender Equity, and Access to Schooling in Africa," *International Journal of Comparative Sociology* 41, no.1 (2000): 91.
3. Archbishop Desmond Tutu is a leading figure in South Africa. He is an activist who rose to worldwide fame during the 1980s as an opponent of apartheid. Tutu was the first black South African Anglican Archbishop of Cape Town, South Africa, and primate of the Church of the Province of Southern Africa (now the Anglican Church of Southern Africa). Tutu chaired the Truth and Reconciliation Commission. He received the Nobel Peace Prize in 1984, the Albert Schweitzer Price for Humanitarianism, the Gandhi Peace Prize in 2005, and the Presidential Medal of Freedom in 2009.
4. Helga Dickow and Valerie Moller, "South Africa's Rainbow People National Pride and Optimism: A Trend Study," *Social Indicators Research* 59, no. 2 (2002): 180.
5. Adam Habib, "South Africa—The Rainbow Nation and Prospects for Consolidating Democracy *African Journal of Political Science* 2, no.2 (1997): 17
6. Goldman Sachs, "Global Economics Paper No: 164, Women Hold up Half the Sky," Goldman Sachs Global Economic Website, Economic Research for the GS Institutional Portal (2008), 6, http://portal.gs.com (accessed March 4, 2008).
7. Ibid., 2.
8. Boko, *Women in African Development*, 3.
9. Ibid.

CHAPTER 2

South Africa Today: Trends and Indicators

On March 31, 2016, the constitutional court in South Africa ruled that President Jacob Zuma had violated the constitution. While the court had ruled against other post-apartheid presidents—Nelson Mandela (1994–1999), Thabo Mbeki (1998–2008), and Kgalema Motlanthe (2008–2009)—their cases were related to technical legal matters, whereas Zuma's involved the misuse of public funds.[1] Two weeks before the court ruling, Zuma's son, Duduzane, had resigned from his non-management director position at Oakbay Resources, a mining company owned by Atul Gupta, amid ongoing allegations of Gupta's influence over Zuma as the company sought political decisions favoring its holdings.[2]

The allegations of misuse of public funds began in 2014, when the Public Protector's Office, responsible for investigating public misconduct and corruption, conducted an investigation and concluded that President Zuma had in fact improperly benefitted from extensive state-funded upgrades to his homestead. It ordered him to repay a portion of the approximately $16.7 million used to upgrade his home (swimming pool, chick coop, amphitheater), although it did not specify the amount. Zuma ignored the order while the National Assembly, composed mostly of members of the ANC, Zuma's party, concluded that the expenses were legitimate security-measure costs and publicly criticized the Public Protector, Thulisile Madonsela, who is well regarded and has been noted for her contributions throughout her seven-year term. That was followed

© The Author(s) 2017

D.E Eynon, *Women, Economic Development, and Higher Education*,
DOI 10.1007/978-3-319-53144-1_2

by a report by the national police justifying the expenses, including the pool, as a "firefighting safety measure." [3]

Over the next two years, Zuma continued to defend and justify the upgrades to his home as legitimate government expenses used to make security improvements, all the while ignoring the Public Protector's order to repay a portion of the costs. That is, until February 2016, when he unexpectedly announced he would repay some of the expenses. Some weeks later, the National Executive Committee, a group known to be supportive of the president, voted full confidence in him.

Since the constitutional court ruling, people within and outside the ANC have called for the president's resignation and impeachment. But opposition leaders don't have the necessary votes in the National Assembly to be successful, and only a limited number of ANC members are willing to oppose the president as they seek to protect their own interests—including reelection.

President Zuma is a colorful and controversial figure. His past legal problems, including accusations of illegal arms trading and a highly publicized rape case, both of which were dismissed, were well known during his 2009 election bid. Yet he was overwhelming elected in 2009 as the fourth post-apartheid president and, at the same time, members of his ANC party were also elected to the National Assembly. This latest scandal over his misuse of public funds reflects the Zuma presidency and the ANC's arrogance and acceptance of corruption.

Meanwhile, the majority of South Africans continue to live in poverty, suffer high unemployment, lack adequate housing, and experience increasing university tuition rates. Most people continue to struggle and fight for basic government services in a poorly performing economy.

It has been 23 years since the end of apartheid rule and the beginning of a new democratic South Africa. There is no question the country was vulnerable economically, socially, and politically in 1994. Still, South Africans were hopeful and believed in the promise of a Rainbow Nation and the prospects of a better future. But where, in fact, is South Africa today? While significant changes have occurred, the conditions, challenges, and prospects now facing the majority of South Africans are in many ways similar to those several decades ago.

This chapter will provide a quick overview of where the country has come since the end of apartheid—both before Zuma was elected in 2009 and afterward—outlining key trends in the economy, employment, public safety, public health, higher education, gender, and other areas. Those trends, here briefly outlined, will be explored in greater depth throughout the rest of the book.

A New Democratic Nation: Economic and Social Conditions, 1994–2009

Despite the good intentions of the new leaders who took the helm at the beginning of the post-apartheid years, South African and its people have seen mixed results when it comes to the economy, employment, public safety, public health, and infrastructure. What follows are some of the key conditions and challenges that the country grappled with during the 15-year period immediately after the end of apartheid until 2009, when Zuma took power.

The Economy

The macroeconomic policies that the ANC adopted in 1996 stabilized a weak economy and led to considerable achievements. Between 1993 and 2000, the fiscal deficit was reduced from 9.1 percent to less than 2.5 percent. By 2004, the inflation rate had also dropped to the lowest rate since 1959, and interest rates were brought down to levels last seen in the 1980s. The country's credit ratings improved, allowing the finance minister to raise debt at better rates. And, by 2005, the central bank's reserves had grown to US$15.1 billion.

The growth rate in the country increased steadily after 1994, as well, giving the country its most consistent growth performance ever. Yet it remained lower than that of most developing countries—and more in line with that of advanced economies where[4] average per capita income is six to seven times higher than South Africa's.[5]

Unfortunately, the South Africa economy took a hit, as did every other country in the world, after the 2008–2009 global recession. Yet the country fared much better than other countries, due in part to government policies that prohibited banks from investing in the kind of credit derivatives that fueled the crisis in America and Europe. The government's massive public investment in preparing for the 2010 World Cup, plus a government stimulus package of 690 billion rand over the next three years, also helped improve the country's economic picture.[6]

Employment

Areas of concern still remained, however, including a decreased demand for South African exports and rising unemployment. Indeed, unemployment continued to be a persistent problem in the country—one often attributed to the shrinking demand for workers in the traditional mining sector and an education system that had failed to prepare poor students for the workplace.[7]

In January 2009, despite an annual growth rate of 5 percent over the previous five years, the fastest in South African history, unemployment remained at 23.2 percent, and it increased to 23.6 percent that June. While the unemployment rate stabilized around that time, it was estimated to be as high as 30 percent if one included those who have given up looking for employment. The number of people who stopped looking for employment in June 2009 jumped by 302,000 to 1.5 million people.[8]

Such unemployment problems spurred poverty and dissatisfaction. More than half of all South Africans, or 57 percent, were living below the poverty line in 2001. Moreover, the problem was only growing. People were sinking deeper into poverty, making it more difficult to get out of it. In addition, the gap between rich and poor had widened.[9]

By October 2008, researchers from the South Africa Human Science Research Council found that 52 percent of 3,321 people surveyed were unhappy with the state of the economy. The survey also showed that 65 percent of those identified as economically disadvantaged were unhappy with democracy, as well.[10]

Public Safety

Unemployment also contributed to rising crime and violence against women. South Africa had one of the world's highest murder rates—six times higher than America's rate and 20 times higher than Britain's; between 1994 and 2009, 275,000 murders occurred in the country. In 2009 alone, around 50 murders, 100 rapes, 700 burglaries, and 500-plus violent assaults were officially recorded every day. (Moreover, while the murder figures were believed to be accurate, it was estimated that only 1 in 10 rapes was reported to the police.)

That is not to say that the government ignored the problems and that no improvement in some of the crime rates occurred. A police report in September 2009 showed the crime rate for serious offenses had fallen by a fifth, the murder rate by half, and rape by a third over the 15 years since

1994. However, violent house robbery doubled between 2004 and 2009, and armed robbery at businesses also increased significantly.[11]

Public Health

One of the gravest public health issues in South Africa has long been the prevalence of HIV/AIDS. It is well-known fact that former President Thabo Mbeki denied the existence of HIV/AIDS, as defined by medical experts, and suppressed the widespread use of the drug AZT. Mbeki believed the root cause of HIV/AIDS was poverty, allowing him to ignore the pandemic in his country. That was when South Africa became the country with the largest number of AIDS victims for a middle-income developing country. Indeed, all of the poorest African countries at that time reported lower AIDS rates; the only country with a higher AIDS rate was Botswana.[12]

Harvard University researchers have since estimated that 365,000 premature deaths due to AIDS could have been prevented had the government acted sooner and provided antiretroviral drugs. By 2008, the overall death rate related to HIV/AIDS had increased to 756,000 from 573,000 in 2007. At that rate, policy makers predicted, deaths in South Africa could eventually outnumber births.[13]

Infrastructure

The government's commitment to social services was reflected in the 22 percent increase in government expenditure on such services from 1994 to 2009. The government also improved the physical infrastructure—including water, sanitation, housing, electricity, and communication—of a greater number of South Africans. In 2004, it offered housing subsidies to two million people. Meanwhile, the number of households with electricity more than doubled between 1994 and 2000, from 32 percent to 70 percent. More than four out of 10 South Africans, however, still lacked modern sanitation.[14]

The Recession's Aftermath: Economic and Social Conditions, 2009–2016

On April 22, 2009, South Africans went to the voting booths to elect a new government. The mood of the country differed significantly from past elections, with increasing discontent among South Africans who had traditionally supported the ANC. Yet while the ANC failed to gain a two-thirds majority for the first time since coming to power, Zuma won the presidency, and the ANC was victorious in the election, gaining 66 percent of the vote.

Zuma was re-elected to a five-year term in 2016—despite corruption charges, high unemployment, and increasing income gaps. The ANC again won the election, as well, with 62 percent of the vote.

How has South Africa fared under the Zuma presidency? How have the nation's economic and social indicators changed, if at all? And what implications, if any, can be drawn, given the great global recession in 2007–2008, falling commodity prices worldwide, and the worst drought in South Africa in 30 years in 2015—which forced 50,000 South Africans into poverty?

The following section will provide a brief overview of South Africa's economic and social conditions—and its persistent and continuing challenges—since Zuma took office.

The Economy

As has been the case since the end of apartheid, the country's current growth rate of 1.9 percent has remained lower than that of most developing countries, including the BRIC nations (Brazil, Russia, India, China), of which South Africa is now a member. After the global recession, South Africa's growth rate reached 3.2 percent before slowing to 1.5 percent in 2014. The fall in global commodity prices since 2011 has certainly been a contributor, as have been continued infrastructure issues related to power generation and distribution and the railways. In April 2016, the government lowered the predicted growth rate for 2017 from 2.6 percent to 0.8 percent. [15]

The monetary policies that the government has adopted have had mixed results. By 2008, before Zuma became president, the inflation rate had hit an all-time high of 9.35 percent. The next few years saw a significant decrease—to as low as 3.37 percent in 2010. Yet that rate had risen to 7 percent in February 2016, the highest since 2009, due in part to drought-induced rising food prices and the depreciation of the rand (30 percent against the US dollar). [16]

Meanwhile, the fiscal deficit dropped from 3.85 percent in 2009 to 2.9 percent in 2011, only to increase to 4.07 percent in 2014.[17] Looking ahead, the government projects a 3.2 percent deficit in fiscal year 2017–2018.

In addition, government debt in the period since 2009 has mushroomed—from a record low of 28.3 percent of GDP in 2007 to a record high of 50.1 percent in 2015. [18] The combination of the bigger deficit and greater debt, along with sluggish growth and the president's decision in December 2016 to sack the finance minister (only to name three different finance ministers in one week), has put the country's credit rating at risk. Standard and Poor's and Fitch have now downgraded South Africa's sovereign rating to one level above speculative grade, making it increasingly difficult for the finance minister to cover debt at reasonable interest rates.[19]

Employment

The portion of South Africans living in poverty, defined as living on less than $1.25 a day, decreased from 57 percent in 2009 to 46 percent in 2011 (the latest data available), yet the gap between rich and poor has continued to widen.[20] Unemployment remains a persistent problem, stuck at around 25 percent since 2010, and it is estimated to be as high as 35 percent if people who have given up looking for employment are included. In September 2015, an estimated 5.4 million of working-age South Africans were unemployed, of which 40 percent were new to the labor market.[21]

Public Safety

Persistent unemployment, poverty, inequality, and slow government reform continue to contribute to the level of violence in the country. In fact, South Africa remains one of the world's most criminally violent countries—with a crime rate five times higher than the global average, as reported in the South African Police Services 2015 report. While bank robberies, robberies of cash in transit, and commercial crimes have decreased, the number of murders increased by 4.6 percent from 2014 to 2015.[22] The number of sexual offenses rose by as much as 34 percent in that same single year, the largest increase across the 27 crime categories in the police report.

Meanwhile, frustration related to lack of service delivery, strikes, and conflict between political groups has led to growing protests throughout the country. According to statistics from the South African Institute of

Race Relations, the number of protests in the country has jumped a whopping 96 percent since 2010.[23]

Public Health

Today, a little more than 1 in 10 South Africans are living with HIV, or about 11.2 percent of the estimated 54.95 million people in the country. Yet South Africa has made progress in its fight against HIV/AIDS due to the rapid expansion of the use of antiretroviral drugs. The number of deaths in the country that were AIDS related has dropped significantly—from 51 percent in 2005 to 31 percent in 2015. In addition, infection rates for 15- to 49 year olds have also been decreasing. As a result of the progress made against HIV/AIDS, life expectancy has risen to 62 years, after falling to a low of 53 years in 1992.[24]

Infrastructure

The government has continued to extend physical infrastructure— water, sanitation, housing, electricity, and communication—to many South Africans, accounting for 60 percent of government spending in 2014.[25] The percentage of South Africans receiving housing subsidies rose from 10.1 percent in 2010 to 15.3 percent in 2014, and the number of households with electricity increased from 82 percent in 2010 to 86 percent in 2014. The number of South Africans with access to modern sanitation has also grown significantly.[26]

In addition, the government has spent much more on social services since 2009. Two-thirds of the elderly receive grants, and the number of grants for the elderly and disabled has held steady. Meanwhile, the number of grants for childcare increased from 10 million in 2009 to 12 million in 2014, reflecting the country's relatively young population.

All in all, however, despite some undeniable progress, the economic and social conditions of South Africa several decades after the end of apartheid remain cause for concern. During a speech to Parliament last year, Pravin Gordhan, South Africa's finance minister, spoke of the need to cut government spending to reduce the deficit. He also announced tax increases in certain areas and predicted the nation's growth rate would drop from 1.7 percent to 0.09 percent. And he acknowledged continuing challenges: corruption in the system, high unemployment, and widespread poverty. Indeed, before the speech, he warned, "There is no doubt about the fact that we are in crisis."[27]

Economic Growth and Development in a Global Economy

The post-apartheid South African government's macroeconomic and growth policies were created at a time when globalization, as we know it today, had just taken hold. The collapse of the Berlin Wall and Russia's move away from communism marked the beginning of this era. Today, in the decade following one of the worst economic downturns since the 1930s, the extent to which nations are interconnected and driven by a global knowledge-based economy is quite apparent. No longer is any country isolated or insulated from what happens in another part of the world.

Globalization—the removal of barriers to free trade and the pursuit of greater integration of nations' economies—changed the way the world communicated, engaged, and operated. The most powerful and developed countries, along with international organizations such as the World Bank (WB) and International Monetary Fund (IMF), encouraged, persuaded, and pressured other nations to play in the global arena.

Yet even before the global economic downturn, developing countries and their allies in nongovernmental organizations (NGOs) were questioning the merits of globalization. For many developing countries, especially those in Africa, the benefits have been questionable. In fact, some observers would argue that such countries have been marginalized and are now even poorer than they were several decades ago.

What are some of the key characteristics of developed countries that allow them to benefit from today's global economy? One is they take a neo-liberal[28] approach to economic growth and development, resulting in minimal state involvement or intervention in the economy since the market—unfettered by any national political objectives or domestic concerns—is expected to perform better than the state. Second, they have a well-developed educational system that is also well matched to the country's economic needs. And third, a significant percentage of the country's population has a high standard of living.

South Africa has tried to cultivate those characteristics in its attempt to transform itself. Crucial elements in that transformation include, in particular, the restructuring of the higher education system and the pursuit of gender equality and women's empowerment. South Africa has pursued initiatives in such key areas with an eye on the potential benefits they could bring to the country. What follows is a brief introduction to each of those elements and the prevailing thoughts and opinions about their role and value in today's South Africa.

Higher Education as an Engine of Advancement

The global economy is increasingly knowledge intensive, putting pressure on nations and their higher education systems to produce highly skilled labor as well as to teach people how to access, produce, and use knowledge.[29] International agencies, governmental policy makers, and leaders in the private sector view higher participation rates in postsecondary education as a key factor in achieving greater economic and social development, creating wealth, and reducing poverty.[30]

Today's global knowledge-based economy is prompting international development organizations and institutions like the WB to focus more than ever on the role higher education can play in the development and growth of emerging economies.[31] Such institutions previously viewed higher education as an expensive and inefficient public service that largely benefited the wealthy and privileged. Now, however, they consider it to be an essential engine for successfully boosting a country's productivity, competitiveness, growth, innovation, and performance across key economic sectors.[32]

Policy makers increasingly recognize that both private and public benefits can be gained from higher education. For individuals, those benefits include better employment prospects, higher salaries, and a greater ability to save and invest. Such benefits may also result in better health and an improved quality of life, creating a virtuous cycle in which life-expectancy improvements enable people to work more productively over a longer time—further enhancing lifetime earnings.

In a knowledge economy, higher education also provides broad public benefits, helping less-developed national economies keep up or catch up with more advanced ones. Higher education graduates are likely to be more aware of and better able to use new technologies than those without postsecondary degrees. They are also more likely to develop new tools and skills. In addition, their knowledge may generate entrepreneurial ventures, with positive effects on job creation, as well as improve the skills and understanding of nongraduate coworkers.[33]

In 1998, UNESCO and the World Bank Task Force on Higher Education and Society issued a report that concluded that, in the present globalized knowledge economy, higher education was necessary.[34] Two years later, the bank acknowledged the "need to embrace a more balanced, approach to the entire lifelong education system, irrespective of a country's income level."[35] In fact, in their book, *Stratification in Higher Education A Comparative Study*, Yossi Shavit, professor of sociology at Tel Aviv University; Richard Arum, professor of sociology and education at New York University; and Adam Gamoran, professor of sociology and educational policy studies at the University of Wisconsin at Madison, state the "most significant" reason that low-income countries began to focus on improving participation rates in higher education at that time was the WB's policy reversal on higher education.[36]

Less than a decade later, in 2007, the WB[37] released its new strategic report specifically for Africa, "Expanding the Possible in sub-Saharan Africa: How Tertiary Institutions Can Increase Growth and Competitiveness." In that report, the bank stated that a more knowledge-intensive approach to development was essential for African countries. It held that education was the only path that could lead to sustained outward-oriented development, given the circumstances in Africa and the global economy. And it maintained that a knowledge-intensive strategy required a greater focus on tertiary education and research.[38]

How has South Africa fared after apartheid when it comes to higher education? According to N'Dri T. Assie-Lumumba, a professor at Africana Studies & Research Center at Cornell University, for decades, educational reform has been a symbol of "freedom and self-determination for African countries."[39] And in South Africa, as in many postcolonial African nations, education has become a vehicle to redress past inequalities and a tool for training the labor force to meet the country's economic plans. Since the end of apartheid, the number of students attending universities has grown tremendously. The most recent data show that the number of students enrolled in public higher education has more than doubled from 495,356 students in 1994 to close to one million (968,890) in 2014.

In particular, greater numbers of historically disadvantaged students have been attending college. Just 12 years after the end of apartheid rule, in 2006, the number of black and mixed-raced students attending university had risen by 268 percent.[40] As of 2013, black students made up 68 percent of all students in public higher education institutions, with colored students representing 7 percent and Indian students making up 5 percent.[41]

But while the numbers are impressive, they don't tell the whole story. Of those students enrolled today in higher education, 55 percent are not expected to graduate.[42] In fact, in 2013, graduation rates were lower than targets set by the National Plan for Higher Education (NPHE), with just 15 percent of undergraduates, 21 percent of masters students, and 13 percent of doctoral students graduating.[43] Those numbers are high for countries in sub-Saharan Africa but low compared to other parts of the world.

The fact is that the increase in access has also meant an increase in the financial burden that students and their families carry. The overall budget for higher education in 2007–2008 was R13.3 billion, representing 0.65 percent of GDP, and that figure increased to 0.075 percent in 2011. Since 1994, however, the proportion of the national budget going to higher education has declined—which has meant that students and their families must pay more. Government contributions decreased from 49 percent in 2000 to 40 percent in 2012, for example, while students' share increased from 24 percent to 31 percent during the same period.[44]

As a result, dropout rates for first-generation students from low-income, less-well-educated families have been high, and less than one in three students have graduated on time. The participation rates have often broken out along racial lines, as well, since many more black students continue to be from low-income families than whites. For example, in 2007, of all students with a low socioeconomic status, 73 percent were black compared to just 12 percent who were white. Similarly, only 9 percent of black students came from a family with a high socioeconomic status, whereas 47 percent of white students did.

In fact, while people recognize the crucial role that higher education plays in a global knowledge-based economy, questions remain as to who truly benefits from its expansion. Despite the progress many countries have shown in increasing the participation rates of less-privileged groups, the majority of students still come from affluent segments of society. In the words of Shavit, Arum, and Gamoran, "It is debatable whether educational expansion reduces inequality by providing more opportunities for persons from disadvantaged strata, or magnifies inequality by expanding opportunities disproportionately for those who are already privileged."[45]

Government policies in South Africa, especially since Zuma took office, have been put in place to expand access to higher education and support low-income students. Many of the poorest students receive financial aid through the National Student Financial Aid Scheme (NSFAS), which was expected to spend $180 million on loans and scholarships in 2016—or double the amount awarded two years earlier.[46] In 2015, close to 500,000 university students received a state loan, versus just 7,240 in 1991.[47] Further, student loan allocations are expected to rise from R5.1 billion in 2013 to R6.6 billion in 2016–2017. And there is no doubt the government's focus on access has been somewhat successful.

Yet, in the end, higher education is still primarily a place for those with resources and social capital, with a high cost of attending university and low retention rates. Moreover, because higher education is an important element in the process of state building,[48] some observers have argued that any educational reform has been largely for show. They believe it should be considered as just one more of a number of "symbolic gestures designed to indicate governmental awareness of problems and sympathetic intentions, rather than serious efforts to achieve social change," in the words of N'Dri T. Assie-Lumumba.[49]

We'll explore these and other issues, such as recent student protests and the government's reaction to growing concerns about its higher education system, in Chapter 6.

Sidebar: Higher Education and Economic Development and Growth

A key concept in understanding the relationship between higher education and economic development and growth is the concept of human capital. Human capital is the skills and knowledge available to participate in labor, which results in economic value.[50] A well-known application of the idea can be found in Gary Becker's book, *Human Capital*. According to Becker, human capital is similar to physical assets (factories and machines) in that one can invest in it via education and training. One's output as a worker depends on the human capital one possesses. In this model, additional investment yields additional output.[51]

The role of education as an input in the production process and its contribution to economic growth can be looked at in a variety of ways. One way is to consider the level of education of each worker as an efficiency unit. This view holds that if you keep the number of workers the same and increase the number of years of schooling per worker, you increase the efficiency unit, generating greater output. Growth in the number of years of education per worker increases the growth output per worker.[52]

Another view holds that an uneducated worker has a different input than a worker with a higher level of education. That difference in input requires different production processes for each type of worker. If a country relies more heavily on exports, it will focus on production processes such as those found in the apparel industry—which do not require a high level of education. If it relies more on technologically oriented goods, it will require a labor force with a higher level of education.[53] Researchers have found evidence that, as developing countries increase their education levels to those of developed countries, they can move from an export-based economy that relies on less-educated workers to an economy based on the export of more technologically advanced products and participate more fully in the knowledge economy.[54]

Historically, studies measuring the return on higher education have been limited to the traditional financial rewards that individuals accrue and the tax revenues they generate. Today, studies are examining the broader benefits of higher education, such as entrepreneurship, job creation, good economic and political governance, improved health, and social benefits. In particular, there is growing interest in understanding the speed at which an emerging country can adopt technology and what impact that has on the rate of its economic development and growth.[55]

Women and South Africa's Future

Women account for half of the world's population and talent. The costs associated with not developing this talent are significant for any country. By enabling and encouraging women to be active participants in economic growth and development, many emerging countries can increase their potential to participate in the global economy while, at the same time, boost their capacity at home.[56]

At the macroeconomic level, female education has been identified as a key source for long-term economic growth. It has been linked to higher productivity, higher returns on investment, higher agricultural yields, and a more favorable demographic structure.[57] The 2002 UN Population Fund Report stated that one of the most effective ways to increase and sustain development is through the "improvement of women's skills and their access to tools such as credit, training, and technology."[58]

South Africa has long recognized the vital role women can play in its rebuilding and future success, across all sectors. After the end of apartheid, it began creating bills, passing laws, and establishing policies, commissions, and frameworks to promote and ensure gender equality and empowerment. Since that time, the government has established the Commission on Gender Equality, National Gender Forum, and the Office on the Status of Women, to name just a few initiatives, to support efforts to become more inclusive and equitable. It is well understood and recognized that African women can and do make significant contributions to the economic development and growth of their communities and country as a whole.

But the challenge going forward is to make sure that policies and decision-making reflect and support the South African government's understanding and recognition of women as a vital force in the nation's future.[59] Thus far, such efforts have often been thwarted by social and cultural norms. South Africa remains extremely patriarchal. In this culture, women are expected to take care of the home and family while men are encouraged to focus their attention outside the home to establish a career. The issue is not so much the duties they each perform, but rather that those duties are rewarded and valued differently and unequally.[60] The widespread and persistent inequality of women and girls is especially prevalent when it comes to higher education, as women are often not encouraged to attend to improve their education and skills.

What's more, access is an issue for those women who do wish to attend college, which has been denied to the majority of Africa's women and girls, a troubling trend that we will analyze in depth in future chapters. This lack of access to advanced education for women and girls is an economic and political issue with socioeconomic consequences.[61] As author Mariam Williams says, "Lost learning opportunities, especially in today's globalized world and what is also referred to as knowledge-based society, constitute a loss of full participation in the development of families, communities, countries, sub-regions, the continent as a whole, and global Africa."[62]

A countervailing force to the country's deeply entrenched paternalism has been the women's movement in Africa, often referred to as "African Feminism." African Feminism has played a key role in the transformation of gender relations in South Africa and the movement toward gender equality.[63] African Feminism is multidimensional in that it focuses on the politics of gender and the power relations between men and women; it is pragmatic, group oriented, and action-oriented. It concentrates on creating independence and dignity out of the oppression created by colonial, western patriarchal and African patriarchal cultures. Philip Higgs, formerly a research professor at the University of South Africa and now an emeritus professor and research fellow at UNISA, has observed of the movement that women are committed to developing their own voice, which they feel, has often been silenced by Western and European feminists who spoke for them, thereby denying them the opportunity to voice their own thoughts.[64]

As we'll explore in Chapter 7 and Chapter 8, South African women have made gains across all sectors, yet significant and serious challenges remain. In the future, the key question will be how effective the laws, bills, and commissions that the government has established will be in achieving their objectives. Do patriarchal, cultural, and social norms still have a strong influence on women? If so, how do women balance this with the progressive gender framework set forth by the government and the African Feminism movement? How will that influence their decision and ability to access higher education, employment opportunities, and political participation? And, what role do race, class, and geography play in women's access to and success in higher education and employment opportunities?

The answers to these questions—and the concepts, issues, and challenges introduced in this chapter regarding economic development and growth, higher education, and women's empowerment—continue to unfold in a very complex country, one that continues to find its footing in a post-apartheid era. Thus, without venturing too far into the past, it is important to take at least a step back and examine such issues as they existed and emerged in 1994 when Nelson Mandela and the ANC were elected to govern the country. By doing so, we can better understand how and why the nation has come to the place it finds itself today.

BOX: Eight Key Reasons for Gender Equality in Higher Education
In *Advancing Development: Core Themes in Global Economics* (Palgrave Macmillan, 2007), Mark Blackden, Sudharshan Canagarajah, Stephan

Klasen, and David Lawson present eight arguments, supported by theoretical literature, that show that gender inequality in education and employment reduces economic growth:

1. Gender inequality in education reduces the average amount of capital in a society and, as a result, creates market distortion and harms economic growth. In many countries, including South Africa, women account for half the total population. Therefore, if women lack the educational knowledge and skills necessary to participate in the formal economy, economic growth is hampered.
2. The failure to promote female education or earnings negatively affects other benefits. These benefits include reduced fertility rates and child mortality levels, as well as the likelihood of education for the next generation.
3. Gender gaps in employment artificially diminish the talent pool, thereby reducing the average ability of the workforce.[65]
4. The competitive advantage of large gender gaps in pay is erased when there are also large gender gaps in education and employment—that is, when women are not trained and hired in large numbers.
5. Female employment and earnings increase women's bargaining power at home, leading to greater investments in the health and education of children. Without those earnings, the potential for improvement in the next generation is diminished.
6. When women's productive activities are under-resourced and capitalized it reduces the overall aggregate and production levels of a country.
7. The work that women perform at home and for their family is not measured in income growth or poverty statistics and, as a result, is not counted in GDP growth.
8. Women are less prone to corruption and nepotism. By increasing the number of women in the workplace and in decision-making bodies, there is a better chance of improving governance in business and government.[66]

Profiles of South African Women

Profile 1: Thulisile Madonsela—South African Public Protector

In 2009, newly elected President Jacob Zuma appointed Thulisile Madonsela as the third Public Protector of South Africa. She had been recommended by Parliament and received full support from all parties when her appointment came to vote.

During her tenure she has been praised for her efficiency and professionalism and for exhibiting qualities of integrity and commitment to public service, as reflected in the number of cases her office has taken on and the number of investigative reports issued covering all levels of government, including the presidency. And it is for this work that she has come under fierce fire, including threats of arrest, anonymous allegations, and personal attacks.

In an article written for *The Sunday Independent* in 2014, Madonsela wrote

> Regardless of where we are, we need to guard jealously our treasured constitution, which is a road map to who we wanted to become when we embarked on this road in 1994. This we can do by playing our part honestly and diligently in taking a stand against bad governance and maladministration, thus ensuring an accountable state that acts with integrity while ensuring there is responsiveness to the needs of all our people.

Madonsela is also a strong advocate for women, having authored and coauthored numerous publications on gender management and gender mainstreaming. In addition, she is a member of the South African Women's Lawyer Association and Business Women's Association of South Africa. In 2012, she received South Africa's most Influential Women Award and, in 2014, she was identified as one of *Time* magazine's top 100 influential people in the world.

She was also one of the drafters of South Africa's constitution in 1994.

Source:

Thulisile Madonsela, *The Sunday Independent*, "Why I Value My Role as Public Protector," April 27, 2014, http://www.iol.co.za/sundayindependent/why-i-value-my-role-as-public-protector-1680954#.U1-dKlWSznh, accessed June 8, 2016.

Notes

1. Norimitsu Onishi, "Jacob Zuma Violated Constitution, South African Court Rules," *New York Times*, March 31, 2016, http:nyti.ms/22RsU8m (accessed March 31, 2016).
2. Mahr Krista, "Zuma Ruling Exposes Deep ANC fissures," *Financial Times Weekend International*, April 9/10, 2016, 3.
3. Onishi, "Jacob Zuma Violated Constitution, South African Court Rules".
4. Krista, "Zuma Ruling Exposes Deep ANC fissures," 3.
5. Alan Hirsch, *Season of Hope: Economic Reform Under Mandela and Mbeki* (University of KwaZulu-Natal Press, Scottsville, South African and International Development Research Centre, 2005), 235–238.
6. "Briefing South Africa's Elections: Voting for the People's Man. *The Economist,* April 18–24, 2009, 23–25.
7. Celia W. Dugger, "South Africa's Jobless Hope Zuma Delivers Work," *New York Times*, June 11, 2009, http://www.nytimes.com (accessed June 11, 2009).
8. Richard Lapper, "Slowdown Punctures South Africa's Optimism," *Financial Times,* January 20, 2009, http://www.ft.com (accessed January 21, 2009); and Nasreen Shea, "South African Jobless Give Up Hope as Economy Shrinks," *Bloomberg*, June 28, 2009, www.bloomberg.com (accessed August 28, 2009), 102.
9. Southern African Regional Poverty Network (SARPN), "Fact sheet: Poverty in South Africa," *Human Sciences Research Council*, (2004), http://www.sarpn.org.za/documents/d000090/ (accessed October 17, 2009).
10. Matthew Richmond, "Finance Labor: South Africans Are Unsatisfied," June 2, 2009, http://www.iol.co.za (accessed June 2, 2009).
11. "Crime in South Africa: It Won't Go Away," *The Economist*, October 1, 2009, World: Middle East and Africa Section, http://www.economist.com/world/middleeast-africa (accessed December 17, 2009).
12. R. W. Johnson. 2009, *South Africa's Brave New World: The Beloved Country Since the End of Apartheid* (New York: Penguin Group, 2009), 36.
13. Celia W. Dugger, "Zuma Rallies South Africa to Fight AIDS," *New York Times,* November 1, 2009, http://www.nytimes.com (accessed November 2, 2009).
14. Organisation for Economic Co-Operation and Development (OECD), *Country Background Report: South African Education* (Paris, France: OECD, 2008), 31.
15. Catriona Mary Purfield, Marek Hanusch, Yashvir Algu, Tania Priscilla Begazo Gomez, Martha Martinez Licetti, Sara Nyman, *South Africa Economic Update: Promoting Faster Growth and Poverty Alleviation*

Through Competition. South Africa economic update; issue no. 8 (Washington, DC: World Bank Group, 206).

16. National Treasury, South Africa, May 2016, http://www.tradingeconomics.com/south-africa/inflation-cpi (accessed June 9, 2016).
17. *Government at a Glance*, OECD National Accounts at a Glance Data, July 6, 2015, http://dx.doi.org/10.1787/gov_glance-2015-en (accessed June 07, 2016).
18. National Treasury, South Africa, June 2016, http://tradingeconomics.com (accessed June 9, 2016).
19. Purfield et al., *South Africa Economic Update*.
20. Statistics South Africa, *Poverty Trends in South Africa: An Examination of Absolute Poverty Between 2006 and 2011* (Pretoria: Statistics South Africa 2014), 12.
21. Organisation for Economic Co-Operation and Development (OECD) *Economic Surveys, South Africa Overview* (Paris, France: OECD, 2015), 8 OECD, *Paris, France, OECD* July 2015.
22. South African Police Service, Annual Report 2014/2015, August 31, 2015, http://www.saps.gov.za/about/stratframework/annual_report/2014_2015/SAPS_AR_2014-15_for_viewing.pdf (accessed June 10, 2016).
23. South African Institute of Race Relations, *Service Delivery Protests Are on the Rise in South Africa,* Video—IRR research analyst Gabriela Mackay and Mienke Steytler talk about the rise of social protests in South Africa, May 26, 2015, http://irr.org.za (accessed June 10, 2016).
24. Statistics South Africa, *Mid-year Population Estimates*, July 23, 2015, http://www.statssa.gov.za/publications/P0302/P03022015.pdf (accessed June 09, 2016), 7.
25. World Bank, "South Africa Economic Update: Fiscal Policy and Redistribution in an Unequal Society," *South Africa Economic Update*, No. 6, World Bank Group (Washington, DC: National Treasury, 2014).
26. Statistics South Africa, General Household Survey, May 27, 2014, http://www.statssa.gov.za/publications/P0318/P03182014.pdf (accessed November 11, 2015), 34.
27. "South Africa's Economy in 'Crisis', *BBC News*, February 24, 2016, http://www.bbc.com/news/business-35650701 (accessed June 8, 2016).
28. The neo-liberal model is based on (1) minimum state involvement or intervention; (2) market is not only a substitute for the state but also preferred because it performs better; (3) resource allocation and utilization is based on market prices; and (4) national political objectives, domestic economic concerns or boundaries should not act as constraints. Gerald Meier and James Rauch, *Leading Issues in Economic*

Development, 8th edition (New York and Oxford: Oxford University Press, 2005), 184.

29. Teboho Moja, T., "Politics of Exclusion in Higher Education: The Inadequacy of Gender Issues in the Globalization Debates," in *Women and Higher Education in Africa: Reconceptualizing Gender-Based Human Capabilities and Upgrading Human Rights to Knowledge*, ed. N.T. Assie-Lumumba (New York: CEPARRED, 2007), 70.
30. Louise Morley, Fiona Leach, and Rosemary Lugg, "Democratising Higher Education in Ghana and Tanzania: Opportunity Structures and Social Inequalities," *International Journal of Educational Development* 29 (2009): 56–64.
31. David Bloom, David Canning, and Kevin Chan, "Higher Education and Economic Development in Africa," *World Bank, Human Development Sector, Africa Region* 102 (2006), 1.
32. Ibid., 3.
33. Ibid., 4.
34. World Bank Task Force on Higher Education and Society, *Higher Education in Developing Countries: Peril and Promise* (Washington, DC: World Bank, 2000), 6.
35. Ibid., 6.
36. Yossi Shavit, et al., eds., *Stratification in Higher Education: A Comparative Study* (Stanford, CA: Stanford University Press, 2007), 57.
37. World Bank, *Expanding the Possible in Sub-Saharan Africa: How Tertiary Institutions Can Increase Growth and Competitiveness* (Washington, DC: World Bank, 2007), 7.
38. Ibid., 8.
39. N'Dri T. Assie-Lumumba, "Educational and Economic Reforms, Gender Equity, and Access to Schooling in Africa," 89.
40. Karen MacGregor, "South Africa: Debate Moves on from Access to Success," *University World News*, March 15, 2009, http://www.universityworldnews.com (accessed March 24, 2009).
41. Higher Education and Training, *Statistics on Post-School Education and Training in South Africa:2013,* Department of Higher Education and Training, Republic of South Africa; March 2015, 11.
42. Council on Higher Education, *A Proposal for Undergraduate Curriculum Reform in South Africa: The Case for a Flexible Curriculum Structure* (Pretoria: Council on Higher Education; 2013), 41
43. Higher Education and Training, *Statistics on Post-School Education and Training in South Africa:2013,* Department of Higher Education and Training, Republic of South Africa; March 2015, 6,9.

44. OECD, *Education at a Glance 2014: OECD Indicators* (OECD Publishing, 2014), http://dx.doi.org/10.1787/eag-2014-en (accessed June 10, 2016), 230.
45. Shavit, et al., eds., *Stratification in Higher Education*, 1.
46. MacGregor, "South Africa: Debate Moves on from Access to Success:" and Karen MacGregor, "South Africa: Student Drop-out Rates Alarming," *University World News*, October 28, 2007, http://www.universityworldnews.com (accessed November 17, 2009).
47. Nicky Falkof, "South Africa's Student Revolt," *The New York Times*, October 25, 2015, http://www.nytimes.com/2015/10/26/opinion/south-africas-student-revolt.html (accessed June 10, 2016).
48. N'Dri T. Assie-Lumumba, 89–120.
49. Ibid., 5.
50. N'Dri T. Assie-Lumumba, ed., *Women and Higher Education in Africa: Reconceptualizing Gender-based Human Capabilities and Upgrading Human Rights to Knowledge* (Ithaca, NY: CEPARRED, 2008), 56.
51. GaryBecker, *Human Capital: A Theoretical and Empirical Analysis, with Special Reference to Education*, 3rd edition (Chicago: University of Chicago Press, 1993), 17.
52. Ibid., 187.
53. Ibid., 188.
54. John Romalis. "Factor Proportions and the Structure of Commodity Trade, *American Economic Review* 94 (2004), 67–97.
55. Mariama Williams, *Financing for Gender Equality and the Empowerment of Women: Some Theoretical and Practical Issues from a Trade and Macroeconomic Policies Perspective* (New York: United Nations Division for the Advancement of Women, 2007), 4.
56. Ibid., 4.
57. Ibid., 9.
58. Sylvain Boko, Mina Baliamoune-Lutz, and Sitawa R. Kimuna, S.R., eds., *Women in African Development: The Challenge of Globalization and Liberalization in the 21st Century* (Trenton, NJ: Africa World Press, 2005), 3.
59. Ibid., 10.
60. Malehoko Tshoaedi. "In the Union . . . Women Union Officials Speak Out," *South African Labour Bulletin* 22, no. 2 (2000): 55.
61. N'Dri T. Assie-Lumumba, ed. *Women and Higher Education in Africa*, 60.
62. Williams, *Financing for Gender Equality and the Empowerment of Women*, 1.
63. Philip Higgs, "Current Status of, and Legislation to Redress, Gender Inequalities in South Africa," in *Women and Higher Education in Africa: Reconceptualizing Gender-Based Human Capabilities and Upgrading*

Human Rights to Knowledge, ed. N'Dri. T. Assie-Lumumba (New York: CEPARRED 2007), 128.

64. Ibid., 128.
65. Mark Blackden et al., "Gender and Growth in Sub-Saharan Africa: Issues and Evidence," in *Advancing Development: Core Themes in Global Economics,* ed. G. Mavrotas, and A. Shorrocks (New York: Palgrave Macmillan, in association with the United Nations University-World Institute for Development Economics Research, 2007), 70–72.
66. Ibid., 73.

CHAPTER 3

Before the End of Apartheid

The Shifting Political Tide

In 1924, the National Party became South Africa's first governing party. Several decades later, in 1948, it passed sweeping racial legislation designed to ensure white supremacy in the country—naming its racial policy "apartheid." Under apartheid, the nation developed policies that systematically institutionalized racism and the segregation of people according to the color of their skin.

By the time F.W. de Klerk campaigned as the presidential candidate for the National Party in the 1989, however, he promised voters it would be the last time blacks would be excluded from an election. He and the National Party knew the days of the apartheid system were numbered. Due to years of pressure from the international community in the form of boycotts and sanctions, along with the impact of a global recession in the early 1980s, that system could no longer be maintained.

The global recession was challenging for many countries, but it was particularly so for South Africa. As a result of growing antiapartheid attitudes,[1] it had become increasingly difficult for multinational companies to justify doing business in the country. For example, in 1986, Gavin Reilly, the chairman of Anglo-America, the largest company in South Africa, made public remarks calling for the dismantling of apartheid, the freeing of political prisoners like Nelson Mandela, a leader in the fight against apartheid; and a lifting of the ban on political parties such as the antiapartheid ANC. [2]

© The Author(s) 2017

D.E. Eynon, *Women, Economic Development, and Higher Education*,
DOI 10.1007/978-3-319-53144-1_3

By that time, limited trade, commercial sanctions, and the demand for repayment on outstanding international bank loans had cost South Africa an estimated $32–40 billion and an additional $3.7 billion in capital flight. The country was in a recession, and state debt was escalating, forcing the government to use domestic savings to fund development and pay off creditors.[3]

In addition to economic challenges and pressure from the global community to end apartheid, social strife was also erupting throughout the country. That unrest, in the form of mass strikes and protests against local administrations, grew as the trade-union movement gathered in strength. In addition, emerging community organizations of women became powerful forces in their local communities as they rallied around "bread and butter" issues that affected their daily lives, such as the price of food, health, and education.

The South African government's immediate response was to declare a state of emergency and call in the army to occupy and heighten repression in black townships.[4] Yet the apartheid system could no longer hold against the discontent and fury of the people. In many parts of the country, outright civil war broke out. As the pressure built, something had to give: the apartheid system itself.

On February 2, 1990, in a speech before Parliament, President de Klerk lifted the state of emergency and the ban on political parties such as the ANC, the Pan-Africanist Congress, the SACP, and 31 other previously illegal organizations. He also announced the release of many political prisoners and detainees, including Nelson Mandela.[5] President de Klerk and the leaders of the National Party were prepared to dismantle apartheid and negotiate a power-sharing arrangement with the ANC. The president's intention was not to give up the National Party's position, but rather to ensure it had a legitimate role in a majority government.

Several political factors had also contributed to de Klerk's announcement in February. They included a lack of commitment on the part of younger Afrikaner leaders to maintain the apartheid system as well as increasing pressure to end apartheid from South African business leaders, who realized the country's economy was suffering as a result of international boycotts.

In 1991, the government began dismantling the apartheid system by repealing key laws. One was the Group Areas Act, which assigned racial groups to different residential and business sections in urban areas as a way to exclude non-whites from living in developed areas. Another was the

Population Registration Act, which required South African to be classified and registered in accordance with their racial characteristics.

Government leaders next entered into formal negotiations with several opposition parties, including the ANC, and acknowledged their commitment to move forward with a new constitution and democratic rights for all South Africans.[6]

As negotiations began between the government and the ANC, it became clear that de Klerk's proposition of power sharing was a non-starter for the ANC. The ANC and Nelson Mandela insisted on a system of "one person, one vote democracy."[7] In response to growing pressure from within South Africa and Western nations, de Klerk decided to drop the power-sharing proposal in order to keep the talks moving and to avoid an outright conflict with the ANC and potential bloodshed. Both parties agreed to work together to form the Convention for a Democratic South Africa (CODESA), whereby the ANC, National Party, and other political parties—such as the Inkatha Freedom Party (IFP), a liberation movement founded in 1975—would come together to discuss, create, and negotiate a plan for moving the country forward.

Although matters were progressing toward a democratic South Africa, not everyone welcomed the turn of events. In a 1991 poll conducted of white South Africans, only 15 percent believed they would be "better off" in a new South Africa.[8] There was also a significant level of discontent and rumbling among conservative Afrikaners. The Afrikaner Conservative Party and other right-wing organizations referred to de Klerk's speech in February as the start of the Afrikaners' "third war of liberation."[9] They tried to organize and disrupt the negotiations but had little success.

In fact, a number of difficult moments occurred during the negotiation process. Perhaps the most contentious one came when Nelson Mandela accused de Klerk of not doing enough to curb the violence that had broken out in the country. He and the ANC were convinced, and publicly stated, that within the security forces of the national government, a "third force" was provoking intra-black violence.

At that point, the ANC was coming to the end of its role of leading a liberation movement and moving on to a position of governing. It had black labor on its side, represented by the Congress of South African Trade Unions (COSATU). But there was also friction within the liberation movement, particularly between the ANC and the IFP. Over the years, that friction had become violent, resulting in the deaths of a number of black South Africans. Things came to a head in 1990 when violence broke out in the province of Natal between the ANC and the IFP, resulting in many deaths.[10]

Mandela insisted de Klerk had to do more to end the violence and demanded he call off the security forces in black townships, which he believe had incited the unrest. The president countered that the security forces were not involved and he, too, wanted to see the violence come to an end. It was a difficult moment, and some people feared it would derail the negotiations. But in the end, Mandela and de Klerk were able to keep negotiations alive as they continued to transition the country away from apartheid rule.

A New Democratic State

In December 1991, the first session of CODESA was held at the World Trade Centre in Johannesburg. As many as 228 delegates representing 19 political groups attended. The purpose of the gathering was to discuss the transition from apartheid rule and the constitutional process for change. At the end of the meeting, all parties agreed to support the Declaration of Intent, which called for the writing a new constitution for South Africa.

That was followed by a referendum in March asking white South Africans if they supported the continuation of negotiations with the ANC for a democratic government. Based on an 89 percent turnout, 69 percent of those voting said they supported the negotiations.[11] At that point, it became clear the country was moving forward with the constitutional process.

All was not settled, however. When CODESA met again at the World Trade Centre on May 15, 1992, agreement had been reached on the basic principles for a constitutional document, but the ANC and National Party differed strongly on how to define a majority when it came to adopting a new constitution. The ANC wanted a two-thirds majority and the National Party a three-fourths majority.

At the end of that meeting, the ANC and the black trade unions decided to begin a "rolling mass action" consisting of strikes, demonstrations, and boycotts. They chose the date of June 16 to coincide with the anniversary of the 1976 SOWETO uprising, when students took to the streets in protest over a ruling mandating half the curriculum be taught in Afrikaans—an incident during which police confronted and killed several students.[12] On June 17, violence erupted in the township of Boipatong, resulting in 46 deaths. Once again, Mandela and the ANC accused de Klerk's government of complicity and the security forces of instigating the violence, and the ANC suspended talks.[13]

Negotiations resumed in early February 1993, however, and it was agreed that a general election would be held in April 1994, with the outcome based on the ANC's definition of majority (two-thirds). It was also agreed that an interim constitution, lasting for two years would be drawn up, including the constitutional principles that would guide the Constitutional Assembly in the writing of the final document. All the parties concurred that if the final constitution did not encompass all those principles, then the constitutional court would not be able to certify it.[14]

Over the course of three days in 1994, from April 27 to April 30, close to 20 million South Africans waited peacefully in long queues to cast their ballots in the general election. It was the first time all South Africans were eligible to vote. The end result, after delays and accusations of election fraud, was a majority win for the ANC, which received 63 percent of the vote. Yet that was still short of the 66 percent needed to write the final constitution without other parties' involvement. The National Party won 20 percent of the vote, ensuring de Klerk a role in the new government as one of the two deputy presidents, with the other position going to ANC's Thabo Mbeki.[15]

The end of apartheid rule and the transformation to a democratic state was the result of intense bargaining and compromise. Despite predictions throughout the international news media that widespread violence would erupt, the transition of power from the National Party to Mandela and the ANC came to a peaceful conclusion. In 1993, Nelson Mandela and F.W. de Klerk were jointly awarded the Nobel Peace Prize "for their work for the peaceful termination of the apartheid regime, and for laying the foundations for a new democratic South Africa." [16]

The Economic Challenges Facing the Country

At the time Nelson Mandela was elected as president in 1994, the economic picture in South Africa was bleak. From the 1980s until the mid-1990s, domestic investment as a proportion of GDP had fallen from 27 percent to 15 percent, and domestic savings had dropped from an average of 23.5 percent of GDP to 17 percent. Government expenditures exceeded revenues.[17] Further, 40–45 percent of the population that was working was doing so outside the formal economy as home-based workers, street vendors, or temporary agricultural workers. When it came to net job creation, fewer than 1 in 10 people were entering into formal employment, and many people in rural areas were barely subsisting. In fact, the economy appeared to be on the verge of collapse.[18]

The apartheid economy had performed well until the 1970s. The country's growth rate in the 1960s was among the highest in the world, matching that of Japan, South Korea, and Brazil. Job creation, savings, and investments were all at levels that allowed the country to prosper and provide a good standard of living, albeit for a minority of its people.

The foundation of the economy at that time was the strength of the price of gold and the country's manufacturing capabilities, primarily in mining and energy. Up until 1971, the price of gold was fixed to the US dollar, so the only factor affecting profits was the cost of inputs, including labor costs. That gave South Africa an advantage, as its labor pool was stable and wages were low. As for manufacturing, unlike the gold sector, it was only competitive regionally, contributing little to exports. For example, 90 percent of locally manufactured clothes were domestically consumed, while only 10 percent were exported.[19]

In the early 1970s, South Africa's economy began to decline as a result of a number of factors, including: (1) the end of the gold standard, which allowed the price of gold to fluctuate, (2) the oil crises of 1973 and 1979, which doubled the cost of oil for oil-importing countries, and (3) the global economic recession, which affected much of the developed world and resulted in a worldwide debt crisis. Then, in the early 1980s, the liberalization of international capital markets and the elimination of trade barriers, along with the introduction of new technologies, created competition in gold production from the United States, Canada, Australia, and Russia. Not only did South Africa see its share of world gold sales shrink but prices dropped as well when the International Monetary Fund and then the European central banks began selling off their gold. That was also the time when economic sanctions against South Africa were tightening. In response, the government began pumping resources into the economy through infrastructure projects such as roads and dams.[20]

The Economy at the Time of Transition

The Population Registration Act of 1950 divided the South African population into four main racial groups: whites, Natives (Africans or Blacks), colored people (people of mixed race), and Indians. And during the final two decades of apartheid under the leadership of the National Party, the economic climate was difficult for many South Africans, particularly for blacks, coloreds, and Indians who were living in poverty and underdeveloped communities. The apartheid system institutionalized throughout the country racial discrimination, oppression, and the repression of civil rights, as well as, to a lesser extent, economic rights. The economy was built on exploitation through segregation and a controlled migrant labor system, whereby Africans were required to work in urban areas yet prohibited to live there.

That affected both men and women, although they experienced such difficulties differently. For example, the government restricted rural women from entering urban areas and, as such, confined them to agricultural work and informal earnings—leaving many vulnerable to attack and theft while the men were off working in the cities. Unprotected by inheritance or property rights, they were especially vulnerable to poverty and violence, as the death of a husband or another income-generating member of the family often meant a total loss of their property.

Most of South Africa's national income went to whites, who had per capital personal incomes of more than nine times those of blacks, almost five times those of Coloreds, and three times those of Asians. Because black South Africans, who represented the majority of the population, were not the beneficiaries of economic development programs and policies, the country had one of the most unequal distributions of income in the world. The disparity between rich and poor was staggering, with 65 percent of all income held by just 20 percent of the richest South Africans. Moreover, by 1994, the country's health status relative to income was one of the worst in the world.[21]

By the time the National Party government announced the dismantling of apartheid, the economic system was no longer viable and was instead hampering the country's ability to compete globally. Economic growth was stagnant, with an average growth rate of 1.7 percent. Per capita income had declined to an average of –0.7 percent annually and unemployment had increased. The national debt had gone from less than 3 percent of GDP in 1989 to more than 9 percent in 1994. And by 1993, one year before the end of apartheid, 60 percent of the population lived in absolute poverty.

Economic Foundations and the Future

The combination of economic sanctions, the lack of growth, and the increased cost to maintain the apartheid system left the post-apartheid government with a struggling and broken economy. Yet some strong economic foundations remained. The country had a solid infrastructure that, although racially skewed, included roads, electricity, railways, harbors, bridges, and a water system; a relatively robust financial system, by international standards; human resources; technological capabilities; a vibrant business community; and an annual per capita income that put the South Africa in the upper-middle-income bracket for developing countries.[22] The new government's challenge was to leverage those assets, minimize the liabilities, and steer a new economic direction that would benefit all South Africans.

The Higher Education Landscape

The new government also inherited a country with significant educational challenges as a result of the apartheid system. While segregation in education existed before the establishment of the National Party's 1948 apartheid policies, the division along racial and ethical lines became formalized, institutionalized, and legalized under apartheid. Due to that divide, 14 different education systems were operating in the country by the early 1990s, administered by a large bureaucracy with centralized control.

The apartheid policies had a direct influence on higher education as universities established under the system became exclusively white or in some cases exclusively black, as in the case of the University of Fort Hare. In addition, new non-white universities were created to further segregate students based on ethnicity and later strictly by race. In this system, a disparity in funding, curriculum, and student/teacher ratios contributed to lower literacy rates, enrollment rates, graduation rates, and employment opportunities for non-whites.[23]

By the late 1980s, the state was spending seven times more per capita on the education of white South Africans than it was on black South Africans. Although whites accounted for only 20 percent of the nation's population, they consumed approximately 45 percent of the education budget and 70 percent of the higher education budget.

Key Education Legislation Under Apartheid

The major legislative policies enacted during apartheid concerning education were:

- the 1953 Bantu Education Act, which transferred and centralized all responsibility for the education of Africans from local governments and missionaries to the state under the Native Affairs Department;
- the 1959 Extension of the University Act, which created separate higher education facilities for blacks, coloreds, and Indians and forbade those groups from attending predominately white universities without approval from the state;
- the 1959 University of Fort Hare Transfer Act, which established that institution for Xhosa students; and
- the 1983 Universities Amendment Act, which provided the legal framework for the establishment of higher education institutions as part of the Bantu (black) self-government policy.

As a result of this legislation, 11 universities were operating in what were called the self-governing territories in 1988.[24] Back in the 1950s, the government had designated such self-governing territories as national homelands for black Africans (classified by the government as Bantu). A major administrative device for the exclusion of blacks from the political system and other parts of life, Bantustans were organized on the basis of ethnic and linguistic groupings. For example, KwaZulu was the designated homeland of the Zulu people, and Transkei and Ciskei were designated for the Xhosa people; North Sotho, South Sotho, Venda, Tsonga, and Swazi were each designated for their people as well. Despite the efforts of the government to promote the Bantustans as independent states, no foreign government ever recognized the Bantustans. The Bantustans were renamed "homelands" in 1959 with the Promotion of Bantu Self-Government Act. Later in 1970, the Bantu Homelands Citizenship Act defined blacks as legal citizens of the homelands designated for their particular ethnic groups, in essence stripping them of their South African citizenship and the few civil and political rights they still had.[25]

A statement by the Minister of Bantu Affairs in 1953 explained the rationale for a separate higher education system for blacks:

> More institutions for advanced education in urban areas (white areas) are not desired. Deliberate attempts will be made to keep institutions for advanced education away from the urban environment and to establish them as far as possible in the Native reserves. There is no place for the Native in the European community above certain forms of labor. Within his own community, however, all doors are open. For that reason it is of no avail

> for him to receive training which has as its aim absorption into the European community, where he cannot be absorbed. Until now he has been subjected to a school system which drew him away from his own community and misled him by showing him the green pastures of European society in which he is not allowed to graze. This led to the much discussed frustration of educated natives who can find no employment which is acceptable to them . . . it must be replaced by planned Bantu education . . . with its roots entirely in the Native areas, and in the Native environment and community.[26]

The Extension of the University Act of 1959 essentially was legislation to enforce apartheid in higher education. It reconfigured higher education by steering black students away from the established white universities and creating black universities, which offered a completely different quality of education and curriculum. The government specified that from December 1960 forward, no black students would be allowed to study at an "open university."

Before the Extension Act, two white universities, Wits and University of Cape Town (UCT), admitted blacks, although there were segregated living spaces and sporting facilities. In addition, black students could not enroll in the following disciplines at the open universities: physics, zoology, botany, mathematics, applied mathematics, geography, psychology, agriculture, Afrikaans, English, history, economics, commerce, sociology, social work, anthropology, native administration, Bantu languages, classical languages, philosophy, political science, law or divinity, or in the faculty of education.[27] The year after the act was passed, 190 black students applied to white universities, four were given approval, and two were admitted, one to Wits and the other to UCT. That meant that, by 1960, only two black students in the entire country were attending a non-black university.[28]

Admittedly, few black students were enrolled in white universities prior to the 1959 act, but the decline in enrollment the following years demonstrates the effectiveness of the government's effort to segregate and control education along racial divisions. The numbers are revealing. In 1960, 14.8 percent of all students in the higher education system were attending a segregated black university; by 1976, 46.9 percent were attending one.

The establishment of black universities in black areas created what the government intended: the education of different racial and ethnic groups in their own culture, and learning in subjects that would reinforce and support the apartheid system. Of course, a consequence of the 1959 legislation was a period of growth within such universities: Between 1960 and 1968, black student enrollment increased 83 percent at the University of the North Zululand and University of Western Cape.[29] But despite the fact that the student body was black and the universities were located in black areas, Afrikaners made up the administration, staff, faculty, and governing bodies of the institutions. This created two cultures within the institutions, resulting in tension and conflict—and creating a climate ripe for protest.

The 1983 Universities Amendment Act coincided with the adoption of a new constitution in South Africa. The legislation established education as part of the "own affairs" structure in the new constitution. The constitution called for the establishment of separate Houses of Assembly (for whites), Representatives (for coloreds), and Delegates (for Indians), allowing each group to direct its "own affairs."[30] As the new framework provided no representative body for them, nothing changed for black South Africans. Their education was to remain separate, with a white minister in charge.

From 1983 onward, there were three sub-sectors of higher education, each with separate responsibilities for all higher education institutions within its racial classification. A department of education and training was responsible for a few higher education institutions for Africans. The self-governing territories[31] had six departments of education responsible for some technikons and colleges. And, there were four departments of education responsible for universities, technikons, and colleges of education in the "independent states" of Transkei, Bophuthatswana, Venda, and Ciskei.[32] As for the national Department of Education, it no longer had other education departments or higher education institutions reporting to it. Its role was to monitor and set financial and academic norms and standards for higher education. That fragmented, inefficient and discriminatory higher education system, operating under different governance model, remained in place until the end of apartheid.

Unintended Consequences

Officials of the national government brought higher education into the apartheid system to limit the number of black South Africans who could obtain positions of leadership or authority in politics, government, business, or the sciences. What they didn't realize was they were creating a strong foundation and platform for black resistance and protest. A black student organization called the South African Student Organization (SASO) was formed in 1968 based on the black consciousness philosophy. The black consciousness movement was a grassroots, antiapartheid activist movement that emerged in South Africa in the mid-1960s. It arose out of the political vacuum created by the jailing and banning of the leadership of the ANC and the Pan-Africanist Congress after the Sharpeville Massacre in 1960, when police killed 69 people who were protesting the pass laws that required black South Africans to carry pass books outside their homelands or designated areas. The objectives of SASO were to promote contact and coordination among students and to represent non-white students nationally.[33] SASO played a key role in the early 1970s on the campuses of black universities and in the antiapartheid movement.

By 1976 a perfect storm was brewing with the Soweto uprising (a series of protests against the compulsory use of Afrikaans in schools), the increased number of students enrolled in higher education, the visibly repressive environment of apartheid on campuses, the obvious material differences between the conditions of black and white students, and black student mobilization. Those elements all came together to begin a period of ongoing protest and resistance by black university students against the apartheid government. From the mid-1980s until the early 1990s, universities became key sites for antiapartheid activities, with weekly protests and other disturbances.[34]

In addition to the protests, the mobilization of black students on campuses led to the creation of different liberation slogans that would become rallying calls for the antiapartheid movement. The first slogan, "Liberation Now and Education Later" emerged in the mid-1980s in opposition to apartheid education. This slogan was not well received by the ANC, which saw education as a vital tool in the struggle for freedom. It viewed the campuses as important sites for protest and believed the university provided structure for young people and engaged them in the fight against apartheid in a constructive way.

Thus, the ANC proposed as an alternative slogan, "People's Education for People's Power," which shifted the focus of protest against apartheid education to the development of alternative education in the schools.[35] That shift allowed the ANC and those in the higher education system to begin thinking about the new strategies, policies, and structures that would be needed in the future—in a new democratic South Africa.

And much thought would be required. By the time the ANC government came into power in 1994, almost 12 million students attended more than 27,000 schools, including 350,000 students at 21 universities and another 135,000 students in technikons. These students were being taught by 375,000 educators with approximately 100,000 staff. The government was spending 23 percent of the budget and nearly 7 percent of GDP on education.[36] Yet despite that significant government investment, the ANC ultimately inherited a racist, fragmented, broken, and inefficient educational system.

The Women Insist: Having a Voice in the Formation of a New South Africa

Black South African women played a pivotal role in the fight against apartheid, as they as well as men faced discrimination and sought freedom for themselves and democracy for their country. However, women were often overlooked and overshadowed by the men, their contributions not fully recognized or acknowledged. Moreover, while all women were oppressed in apartheid South Africa, they were not oppressed equally. Black women, especially rural women, bore the burden of extreme poverty and disadvantage when it came to their rights, education, and employment. And as women resisted and fought, both at home and abroad, alongside and independently of men, the apartheid government increasingly forced them into controlled townships or rural areas as a means of containing their efforts and influence.

In 1991, with the end of apartheid fast approaching, the National Women's Coalition (NWC) was launched to advise CODESA on gender issues and to advocate for a voice for women at the negotiating table. Several women's organizations, such as the National Executive Committee of the ANC on the Emancipation of Women, which were also pushing for women's rights, described women's suffering as the "triple yoke of oppression" whereby they were oppressed on the basis of sex, class, and race.[37]

But, at the same time, there were deep divisions within the South African women's movement that became hostile at times. Those hostilities and the divisions came to a head in 1991 during a conference at Natal University when, during the first session, scholars introduced two papers criticizing the women's movement in general and its failure to effectively fight for women's rights. Many of women activists took offense at the content of the papers and allowed their antiacademic views to surface. Although it was difficult, the conference did allow women to openly discuss the issues and concerns they had and to reaffirm their commitment to the movement, recognizing that their divisions and differences would continue to challenge them.[38] Many of those divisions and differences had their roots in the apartheid system as well as in other cultural trends that had influenced women's lives and opportunities in South Africa—and not just for decades but also for centuries.

An Entrenched Patriarchal Culture

South Africa is a patriarchal society. It is deeply entrenched in the country's long-time pastoral economy and way of life. Reaching back over millennia, the men in the tribal culture controlled the weapons and livestock, while the women were primarily responsible for crops and taking care of the children and elderly. Men ran their households in an authoritarian manner, and clan-based councils or chiefs controlled important decisions like land-use allocation. Women often had little to no say in their personal, economic, and political lives. In fact, up until 1998, African women were regarded as minors in Customary Law. (See Box, "Customary Law in South Africa.")

The European settlers who arrived in the 1600s were more individualistic and allowed more personal control over property ownership and other financial matters. However, theirs was still a very patriarchal culture, as well, in that men typically controlled capital and land while women were responsible for children and the home. Under Dutch-Roman law, it was very difficult for married women to independently own property or enter into contractual agreements. Those laws reinforced a culture in which women were quite limited in their ability to participate in the formal economy.[39]

The division of labor established under apartheid in the late 1940s greatly influenced women's lives. The Europeans recruited black South African men to work in the fields and later the mines. African women in turn were brought into Europeans' homes to supplement or relieve European women of their household and child-rearing responsibilities. While both genders were pulled from their local communities, men were needed in greater numbers than women.

At the same time, the Europeans were reluctant to have "too many" black South Africans in their mining or farming communities. As a result, the government established a policy that essentially kept most African women in rural areas and moved the working-age men back and forth as migrant workers.[40] With the introduction of pass laws in 1959, which required black South Africans to carry pass books outside their homelands or designated areas, the apartheid system successfully discouraged and then banned rural African women from coming into towns. That significantly reduced the options that rural women had to earn a living. The only possibilities they had were to perform basic agricultural work, work in the informal sector—which meant low wages and little to no job security—or rely on remittances and transfers from their male partners with jobs in urban areas.[41]

By the mid-1990s, the rural population accounted for 71 percent of poor households in South Africa. Black South Africans at the time were carrying 95 percent of burden of poverty with the rural population carrying 75 percent of that burden.[42] And women made up the majority of the poor in rural and less-urbanized provinces.

The women in rural areas who relied heavily on remittances from absent male partners were especially vulnerable. The men were often were not reliable, and when a woman lost her source of income for whatever reason, she risked of loss of her property—especially given women's lack of inheritance and property rights or the ability to enforce those rights in areas where African customary law prevailed. Female-headed households, especially black households, were significantly poorer than average households, and female-headed families in rural areas were "at the bottom of the economic pyramid." [43] By 1995, 49 percent of female-headed households and 65 percent of black female-headed households were classified as poor, compared to 31 percent of male-headed households.[44]

Moreover, single women headed a much greater percentage of black and colored households than white households. The percentage of single-parent families headed by women reported in 1989 varied between 4.7 for whites, 5.8 for Asians, 9.3 for blacks and 9.6 for coloreds. Multigenerational families had a significantly higher number of female-headed households: 6.2 for whites, 11.4 for Asians, 21.4 for coloreds and 25.5 for blacks.[45]

The government's restriction on the movement of women contributed to their lack of participation in the formal economy and blocked their upward mobility. And, as will be discussed later, women's protests against that restriction became a defining moment in the future role they would play and contributions they would make in the antiapartheid resistance movement.

Customary Law in South Africa

Customary Law in South Africa was in existence prior to colonization in 1652. It was an authoritative form of justice with legitimacy from the notion that it had been around since anyone could remember and it was evident in the day-to-day practices and traditions of a given community.

With the arrival of the Dutch colonist, Roman-Dutch laws prevailed, with no recognition of Customary Law. It wasn't until the British took control and established the Natal Code of 1878 that customary law was recognized. The Code made an attempt to codify Customary Law around three principles from which all the other laws were derived—the subjugation of women to men, subjugation of children to their father or head of the family, and the rule of inheritance based on birth order and gender. As a result, Customary Law lost its dynamic nature and was recognized in a rigid way based on the colonists understanding and views.[46]

Customary Law is recognized, not because it is backed by the power of some strong individual or institution, but because each individual recognizes the benefits of behaving in accordance with other individuals' expectations, given that others also behave as expected. Typically, if a law is imposed from above (government), then that law will require much more force to maintain social order. In contrast, reciprocities are the basic source both of the recognition of duty to obey law and of law enforcement in a customary law system. That is, individuals must "exchange" recognition of certain behavioral rules for their mutual benefit. [47] Customary Law in South Africa also significantly limited women's property rights.

The end of apartheid brought formal recognition, through the constitution, of Customary Law within the country's legal system.

Education, Health, and Safety Issues

Apartheid policies also created a lack of urgency among government authorities for the training and education of African women. Since African women weren't key drivers in the formal economy, and their unemployment rates were higher than male rates in all provinces, it was easier to ignore their education.

While 35 percent of the overall population of South Africa had an incomplete education or none at all, 53 percent of the rural poor had little or no education. And for women in the age group 25 years and above, the percentage that lacked education was higher (18 percent overall and 23 percent for blacks) than for men (12 percent overall and 16 percent for blacks).

Persistence was a problem as well: in 1993, girls accounted for 57 percent of matriculation candidates but represented only 45 percent of those who graduated from high school. Several reasons were identified for this problem, including sexual harassment and abuse, pregnancy, the inability to go to school at night due to concerns about violence, and the burden of domestic responsibilities.[48]

Women were the primary caregivers for the family and were responsible for tending the home. A 1993 assessment of living conditions for the poorest 40 percent of households in the country showed 35 percent living in shacks, 79 percent without access to electricity, and 72 percent without piped water in the home. Only 18 percent had a flush toilet, and as many as 47 percent relied on wood as the main fuel source for cooking.[49] The lack of access to basic services meant that women and young children, most often girls, spent a considerable amount of time collecting water and firewood, and performing other tasks related to the care of the family and home.

Other issues of concern to women included the incidence of violence, rape, and HIV/AIDS. The lack of economic options for women, especially among the poor, made women especially vulnerable to these problems, as did the prevalence of patriarchal attitudes and norms. From 1990 to 1996, the rate of HIV infection increased at a higher rate for women than men. The prevalence of infection was 25 percent for a 20-year-old female versus an 8 percent infection rate for a 20-year-old male[50]

As the end of apartheid approached, the government passed several laws that gave married women more rights and power. Before 1993, men had legal power and control over their wives and family, except in cases where an antenuptial contract (one that governs that status of assets and liabilities on death or divorce), had been signed. However, even with an antenuptial, the husband remained the legal guardian of the children unless a court order allowed for other arrangements. The Domicile Act of 1992 gave women for the first time the right to determine the jurisdiction of the court during divorce proceedings. That was followed by The General Law Fourth Amendment Act 132 of 1993, which abolished "all exclusively male marital power, although consent by both parties for important transactions was required."[51] Women also were entitled at the end of a marriage, whether due to divorce or death, to half of any assets they accrued during the marriage.

Unfortunately, however, despite these legislative advances, many black married women were still largely subject to the traditional authority of their husband's family, the clan, and chiefs.[52]

The Women Organize

The women who came to the negotiating table during the 1994 meeting of CODESA stood on the shoulders of many women activists who came before them. In the early 1950s, the ANC Women's League began to establish a branch structure in townships and to participate actively in ANC campaigns. The Federation of South African Women (FEDSAW) was also launched at a conference on April 17, 1954, with the intent of promoting women's rights. Its members included women from all races across the country, and it created a Women's Charter, setting out basic demands: equal opportunities for women, equal pay, maternity rights and benefits, and the removal of control and racial discrimination.[53]

On August 9, 1956, as many as 20,000 African, Indian, colored, and white women marched and then demonstrated at the Union Buildings in Pretoria in protest against the extension of the pass laws to African women. It was at this demonstration where they chanted the words: "wathint' abafazi, wathint' imbolodo uzokufa" ("you have touched the women, you have struck a rock") to mock then Prime Minister J.G. Strijdom.[54] Yet despite opposition and protest by the league and FEDSAW, the pass laws, which had been applied only to men, were extended to women in 1959.[55]

Throughout that period, the apartheid government took the women's groups and their role in the resistance movement seriously and attempted to eradicate them. From the late 1950s into the 1960s, it continued to detain, ban, imprison, put under house arrest, and force their members into exile.[56] As a result, the federation became largely inactive, although it never formally dissolved.

Finally in the mid-1980s, two attempts were made to re-launch FEDSAW. And in November 1989, a FEDSAW Newsletter called on women to unite despite their differences, saying: "The nature of women's oppression might well differ for different groups of women, but the underlying causes are the same."[57] Unfortunately, however, both attempts failed, and it is still unclear why.

Two theories, however, have emerged. The first is that powerful men in the resistance movement wanted it blocked because they felt threatened by the presence of a strong and independent women's organization. The second is that it was thwarted because of concerns that it would allow Winnie Mandela, the wife of Nelson Mandela until their divorce in March 1996,[58] to build her personal power base at a time when the Stompie Seipei incident was gaining press.[59] Winnie was an activist and politician who held several government positions and headed the ANC Women's League. In 1991, she was tried for the murder of a 14-year-old activist Stompie Seipei, having been accused of ordering his kidnapping and torture. She was convicted of kidnapping and fraud. The failure to reestablish FEDSAW left many women feeling disillusioned and confused.[60]

The 1980s were also the time when women began debating whether women's organizations like the ANC Women's League should be autonomous or remain subsets of organizations under male leadership and control. It was common for many of the women's organizations to be seen as an extension of, or to strongly affiliated, with other organizations that were led and managed by men. For example, the Natal Organization of Women (NOW) was strongly affiliated with the United Democratic Front (UDF), responsible for massive antiapartheid protest.

Meanwhile, the leadership of ANC did recognize women's efforts and the specific challenges they faced within the resistance movement. ANC president Oliver Tambo said to an ANC women's conference in exile in 1981:

> The struggle to conquer oppression in our country is the weaker for the traditionalist, conservative and primitive restraints imposed on women by man-dominated structures within our movement, and also because of equally traditionalist attitudes of surrender and submission on the part of women.[61]

The argument for keeping male control was that, by becoming autonomous, women could potentially be weakening the national struggle against apartheid rule. Those debates, along with women's active engagement in the resistance movement throughout the 1970s and 1980s, stimulated the emergence of a strong women's leadership that carried women's interests in the 1990s.[62]

As they entered the industrial workforce in greater numbers in the 1980s, South African women also became increasingly involved with trade unions and the labor movement. They were concerned about poor wages, working conditions, sexual harassment, maternity benefits, and the use of strip-searching as a means of controlling theft.[63] Yet although women made up the majority of workers in many industries, it was rare for unions to elect women to leadership positions.

In 1988, at the COSATU conference, a divisive debate broke out among women from the different unions about whether they should organize within the COSATU structure or create a new national women's organization. Ultimately, they drafted a resolution and decided to develop structures both within COSATU to address women's specific concerns in the workplace, as well as outside of COSATU to unite women in the community.[64]

Yet, as was the case in political organizations, patriarchal attitudes continued to dominate how and what women did within their unions. The expectation was that, while men would go about changing the world, women would follow traditional gender roles and tend to the children and family—although at times, assisting the men in their quest for change. As a result, many women's organizations were formed not only to fight the injustices of apartheid but also to give voice to women's issues and the women's movement. Such women's organizations challenged the limitations that men in the movement imposed on them as well as the patriarchal values that ruled their personal lives.[65]

The Women's Charter Campaign

In 1990, after the national government allowed the emergence of previously banned political parties, the ANC's Women's League began to operate again in South Africa, while other organizations like NOW began to disband. The ANC women who had lived in exile began to return to the country, bringing with them the ideas and strategies related to women's roles and rights that they had advocated for within the ANC. These women were pushing the envelope, as the ANC was still a patriarchal organization—despite its recognition of the important role women played in the resistance movement both within the country and in exile.

Once again, at the national conference of the ANC Women's League in April 1991, ANC president Oliver Tambo acknowledged the important role women played in the fight against apartheid, the importance of women's issues, and the difficulty women were facing within the ANC:

> Comrades and Friends, women constitute the overwhelming majority of our population. This majority, especially black women, suffer the worse form of oppression under apartheid rule. This much is accepted by the ANC and indeed the entire democratic movement in the country. Accordingly, many of us have accepted the reality that any liberation which does not result in the emancipation of women will be just a shadow of what would otherwise have been a true liberation. This correct principled view is enshrined in the many resolutions the ANC has passed over the years. However, we all share in the guilt of failing to systematically implement programmes which must result in the liberation of women within our ranks let alone our society in general.[66]

During the CODESA negotiations that produced the framework for the final constitution, women's organizations lobbied heavily for the inclusion of women in the process. In the words of Frene Ginwala, who was a key player in the formation of the coalition and an elected convener:

> Our experience has been that the more powerful the committee, the fewer the women. The exclusion of women in the CODESA process is both a symbol of our present society and a grim warning of the future. They will talk of non-sexism, they will not practice it. The air around us is thick with talk of change, of the end of racism and apartheid, of a new era of democracy. Is the change we are talking about going to mean simply adding some black men where white men sat before?[67]

Shortly after the National Women's Conference was formed in 1991 to advise CODESA, Pregs Govender was appointed to head the NWC Women's Charter campaign. The objective of the campaign was to take up the work of the Women's Charter of 1954 and to mobilize women across the country to take participate in a research campaign to ensure women's voices were heard during CODESA's negotiation sessions. The NWC was concerned that women would be excluded from the decision-making process if they did not have the strong support of their comrades throughout the country—support which would be demonstrated by the success of the research campaign and the Women's Charter. To achieve that, the campaign needed to bring women's issues to the attention of political parties, trade unions, academe, the news media, and the nation's legal institutions.

The Women's Charter campaign was introduced and launched on International Women's Day on March 8, 1993. The event generated extensive publicity and, given that half the voters in the country were women, the news media positioned it as an indication of their intent to leverage their numbers in the upcoming election. In April, during CODESA negotiations, NWC was able to get each political group and organization in attendance to agree to appoint an extra woman to their delegation. Then, in June, a national workshop was held with women from all the regional coalition groups participating. The primary purpose of the workshop was to lay out a set of five issues that had emerged as most crucial to women: legal status, land, violence, health, and work. With the focus on those issues, the regional coalitions went forward and rolled out the campaign in their respective regions.[68]

Women and the Creation of a New Constitution

The women of South Africa, especially rural women, were facing significant economic, social, legal, and political challenges when the NWC was negotiating to have women's rights incorporated into the Interim Constitution. Their efforts materialized in November 1993, when the Interim Constitution did include women's rights provisions, and the Women's Charter was finalized in February 1994.

To CODESA's credit, the women were formally included without too much resistance, in part due to the role women's organizations played during the antiapartheid movement, particularly in the ANC. Many of the men responsible for driving the formation of a new government were now open to the issues and challenges facing women in the country and worked with them to negotiate gender into the constitution. An outcome of the negotiation process was ANC's commitment to list women—at least 30 percent of the total number of candidates—on their ticket for national elections.[69]

The Women's Charter was presented to the Constitutional Assembly in August 1994, the preamble of which states, "South Africa is poorer politically, economically, and socially having prevented more than half of its people from fully contributing to its development. Women's subordination and oppression has taken many forms under patriarchy, custom and tradition, colonialism, racism and apartheid."[70] The charter sets out 12 articles covering all aspects of women's private and public life: equality; law and the administration of justice; economy; education and training;

development, infrastructure, and the environment; social services; political and social life; family life and partnerships; custom, culture and religion; violence against women; health, and media.[71]

But while it reflected the ideas of gender equality, the charter came too late to have a major influence on the final constitution adopted in 1996 or to become part of the Bill of Rights. And the NWC fell apart after the adoption of the South African constitution, partly due to women's shift in interest to party politics. Meanwhile, the December 1994 report of the ANC Commission on the Emancipation of Women did not paint a favorable picture of the ANC's attitude about and commitment to gender equality among its members. It reported that many women were still filling the role of secretary in ANC departments and that little was being done to empower them or integrate them into the mainstream of the organization's policy-making or decision-making activities.[72]

South Africa changed many laws, acts, and policies after the end of apartheid rule and the 1994 elections. For example, as will be discussed in more depth in later chapters, by eliminating many of the discriminatory elements of Customary Law in 1998, including the restrictions on property rights, women's position in their households shifted significantly.[73] Such efforts, along with the creation of the new constitution, reflected the desire to establish a society based on women's empowerment and equality.

But old patriarchal attitudes, practices, and traditions continued to have a very strong hold on South African society and culture. Even though women's empowerment and equality was considered important to the development of the country and reflected the spirit of the country's democracy, the idea did not permeate individual households. For many men, "democracy is for the government of the country, not the family home."[74]

The persistence of patriarchal traditions posed challenges for men and women during the constitutional negotiation process. While the men were supportive of gender empowerment and equality, they felt the need to respect and maintain traditional African customary law and cultural practices. The end result was a constitution that supported both interests, thereby creating a "power struggle between patriarchal traditionalists and feminists over the social and economic content of South African democracy," in the words of Michael H. Allen in his book, *Globalization, Negotiation, and the Failure of Transformation in South Africa: Revolution at a Bargain?* [75] This power struggle persists to this day. Women have grown and benefitted from post-apartheid laws, policies, and initiatives. But, as will be discussed at length in later chapters, they have continued to pay a price for their advancement.

Profiles of South African Women

The following women helped shape South Africa's history and future. Their commitment and efforts illustrate the important and key role women played in the struggle and fight against apartheid rule. They gave their all, and some their lives, to inspire and rally others to resist and fight and to contribute to the cause.

Annie Silinga

Annie Silinga completed only a few years of primary school and was basically illiterate. Yet she was to become one of the most important and forceful leaders of the women's antipass campaign, which fought to eliminate the government's requirement that women carry passbooks whenever they traveled throughout the country, limiting their mobility. She was also among the first to serve on the executive committee of the FEDSAW when it was established in 1954 and as president of the Cape Town ANC Women's League.

Silinga joined the African National Conference in 1952 during the Defiance Campaign, the largest non-violent call to resistance and the first time racial groups came together in protest under the leadership of the ANC and South African Indian Congress. It was also during that period that Silinga was first imprisoned for civil disobedience, although it wouldn't be the last time. She was arrested again in 1955 for refusing to obey the pass regulations, which led to her banishment to the Transkei. When women were required to start carrying passes, she refused and never wavered, and did not carry a pass until the day she died. She later returned illegally to Cape Town to be with her three children and husband.

In 1956, Silinga was arrested yet again and imprisoned in the Fort Prison in Johannesburg for participating in the Congress of the People conference held in 1955. She was one of 156 leaders of the organization put on trial for high treason, and the only African woman from the area to be arrested. The charges against her were later dropped and she returned to Cape Town. It was after the trial for treason that she was elected president of the Cape Town ANC Women's League, only to be jailed and released again without charges, in 1960 after the Sharpeville and Langa massacres, in which many people were killed for protesting apartheid.

Silinga died in 1984 and was buried in an unmarked pauper's grave.

Sources:

Encyclopedia.com website Women in the World History: A Biographical Encyclopedia, 2002, Gale Research Inc., http://www.encyclopedia.com/article-1G2-2591308523/silinga-annie-19101983.html (accessed July 1, 16)

South African History Online, Annie Silinga, October 24, 2012, http://www.sahistory.org.za/people/annie-silinga (accessed July 1, 16).

Ruth First

Ruth First was the first white woman that the apartheid government arrested in 1960 and again in 1963 under the 90-day detention law. During the latter arrest, she was held in solitary confinement during the duration of her imprisonment.

First's parents were Jewish immigrants from Latvia who went on to become founding members of the Communist Party of South Africa. Ruth herself joined the party and the ANC, becoming an activist against apartheid rule with the aim of overthrowing of the government. During her time at the University of Witwatersrand, she became acquainted with Nelson Mandela and other antiapartheid activists who were involved in the Federation of Progressive Students, an organization she helped found. Upon graduation she began a career in journalism and became editor-in-chief of *The Guardian*, a radical newspaper later banned by the government. It was during this period in the 1950s that she was involved in riots erupting throughout the country.

Forced into exile in 1964, First went to London where she became active in the antiapartheid movement there. From 1972 to 1978, she held various posts at several universities, including the University of Manchester and the University of Durham, after which she secured a position as director of a research training program at the Universidade Eduardo Mondlane in Mozambique—all the while continuing her antiapartheid work. It was there on August 17, 1982, that at the age of 57, First opened a letter bomb that had been delivered to the university by order of Craig Williamson, a major in the South Africa police force. She had been assassinated.

Source:
South Africa History Archive, Women Hold Up Half the Sky: Commemorating Women in the Struggle, http://www.saha.org.za/women/leading_women.htm (accessed June 30, 2016)

Dr. Frene Ginwala

In 1960, Frene Ginwala played a key role in the establishment of an underground escape route into Tanzania for ANC leaders in the wake of the Sharpeville massacre, which involved the killing of many black South Africans who were protesting apartheid, and the apartheid government's declared State of Emergency. She specifically organized the escape of Oliver Tambo, deputy-president of the ANC, and Yusuf Dadoo, a leader in the liberation movement. In addition, she helped establish safe houses for those unable to escape and raised money from all over the country to provide support to those families who had lost their primary source of income when a family member was forced into exile or went underground.

By late 1960, Ginwala herself was forced to flee, going into exile in Tanzania where she joined Tambo and Dadoo. With them, she formed an ANC office from which they continued their antiapartheid work. She also hid Nelson Mandela for two days when he passed through Tanzania on his way to Ethiopia for the conference of the Pan-African Freedom Movement of East, Central and Southern Africa before moving on to Algeria and London. During her 30 years in exile, Ginwala established the ANC's publicity and information department, and she became a journalist, lecturer, and researcher who traveled the world to speak about the injustice and brutality of apartheid.

In 1991, she returned from exile and, in the country's first democratic election, was elected to Parliament in 1994. She served as the first female Speaker of the House until 2004. In 2005, she was elected vice-chancellor of the University of KwaZulu-Natal.

She holds a doctorate in philosophy from the University of Oxford and is the recipient of many honors and awards.

Sources:
South Africa History Archive, Women Hold Up Half the Sky: Commemorating Women in the Struggle, http://www.saha.org.za/women/leading_women.htm (accessed June 30. 2016)

Tara Turkington, *In Conversation with Dr. Frene Ginwala*, Nelson Mandela Foundation, June 14, 2008, https://www.nelsonmandela.org/news/entry/in-conversation-with-dr-frene-ginwala (accessed July 1, 2016).

Notes

1. Bill Freund and Vishnu Padayachee, "Post-apartheid South Africa: The Key Patterns Emerge," *Economic and Political Weekly* 33, No. 20 (May 16–22, 1998), 1173–1180.
2. Ibid., 1173–1180.
3. Julian Kunnie, *A Comprehensive History of South Africa's Struggle* (Oxford, UK: Westview Press, 2000), 61.
4. Nigel Worden, *The Making of Modern South Africa* (Oxford, UK: Blackwell Publishers, 1994), 137.
5. Nelson Mandela, *Long Walk to Freedom* (Boston, New York, London: Little, Brown and Company, 1994), 556.
6. Worden, 154–155.
7. Freund and Padayachee, 1173–1180.
8. Herman Giliomee, *The Afrikaners: Biography of a People* (Charlottesville, Virginia: University of Virginia Press, 2003), 633.
9. Ibid.
10. Erik Melander, "The Limits of Manipulation Theory: The Apartheid Third Force and the ANC-Inkatha Conflict in South Africa," *Peace Economics, Peace Science and Public Policy* 8, no. 4 (2002).
11. Giliomee, 634.
12. Mandela, 602.
13. Freund and Padayachee, 1173.
14. Constitution of the Republic of South Africa, South African Government Information. http://www.info.gov.za/documents/constitution/index.htm (accessed November 27, 2009).
15. Worden, 155.
16. The Official Site of the Nobel Prize, https://www.nobelprize.org/nobel_prizes/peace/laureates/1993/ (accessed June 27, 2016).
17. Hirsch, 23, and Freund and Padayachee, 1173–1180.
18. Freund and Padayachee, 1173–1180 and Adam Habib and Vishnu Padayachee, "Economic Policy and Power Relations in South Africa's Transition to Democracy," *World Development* 28, no. 2 (2000), 245–263, and World Bank Southern African Department, 6.
19. Alan Hirsch, *Season of Hope: Economic Reform under Mandela and Mbeki*, (Scottsville, South Africa: University of KwaZulu-Natal Press, 2005), 20,

and P. Mohr and C. Rogers, *Macroeconomics* (Johannesburg: Lexicon Publishers, 1996), 40.

20. Hirsch, 23, and Freund and Padayachee, 1173–1180.
21. The World Bank Southern African Department, *South Africa Economic Performances and Policies Overview* (Washington, DC: The World Bank, 1994), 6.
22. Habib and Padayachee, 245–263, and World Bank Southern African Department, 3.
23. Punday Pillay, "The Political Economy of Higher Education in South Africa," *International Journal Educational Development* 10, no. 2/3 (1990), 211–215.
24. Y. G. M. Lulat, *A History of Higher Education from Antiquity to the Present: A Critical Synthesis* (Westport, CT: Prager, 2005), 286, and Organization of Economic Co-Operation and Development (OECD), *Reviews of National Policies for Education: South Africa* (Paris, France: OECD, 2008), 38.
25. Thiven Reddy, *Higher Education and Social Transformation: South Africa Case Study* (Pretoria, South Africa: Council on Higher Education, 2004), 13.
26. Cited in Hirsch, 18, and Lulat, 288.
27. Reddy, 13.
28. Ibid., 13.
29. Ibid., 16.
30. Trevor C. Sehoole, *Democratizing Higher Education Policy: Constraints of Reform in Post-apartheid South Africa* (New York: Routledge, 2005), 20.
31. Encyclopedia Britannica, www.britannia.com/EBchecked/topic/683115/Bantusan, (accessed December 24, 2009).
32. Sehoole, 21.
33. Ibid., 30.
34. Ibid., 34.
35. Ibid., 38, and Reddy, 26.
36. OECD, 326.
37. Ray Simons, *Women in Urban and Rural Areas*, Lusaka, Zambia, February 1989, AL2517, 1, The Original South Africa History Archives Collection, South Africa History Archives, Wits University, Pretoria, South Africa.
38. Pregs Govender, *Love and Courage: A Story of Insubordination* (Auckland Park, South Africa: Jacana Media Ltd, 2007), 125.
39. Michael H. Allen, *Globalization, Negotiation, and the Failure of Transformation in South Africa: Revolution at a Bargain?* (New York: Palgrave Macmillan, 2006), 32.
40. Allen, 33.
41. Francis Wilson and Mamphela Ramphele, *Uprooting Poverty: The South African Challenge*, Report for the Second Carnegie Inquiry into Poverty

and Development in Southern Africa (Cape Town and Johannesburg: David Phillip, 1989), 212.
42. Reconstruction and Development Programme, *Key Indicators of Poverty in South Africa* (Pretoria: Ministry in the Office of the President, 1995), 15.
43. Wilson and Ramphele, 179.
44. Allen, 41.
45. Janet M. Billson and Carolyn Fluehr-Lobban, *Female Well-being: Toward a Global Theory of Social Change* (New York: Zed Books, C, 2005), 7.
46. Devon Wall, South African History Online, *Customary Law in South Africa: Historical Development as a Legal System and its Relation to Women's Rights*, http://www.sahistory.org.za/article/customary-law-south-africa-histori cal-development-legal-system-and-its-relation-women%E2%80%99s-righ accessed November 22, 2016.
47. Bruce Benson. 1990. The Enterprise of Law: Justice Without the State. Pacific Institute for Public Policy Research, San Francisco, CA. pp. 12–15. http://www.ncjrs.gov/App/Publications/abstract.aspx?ID=131192
48. Ibid., 43.
49. Reconstruction and Development Programme, 17.
50. Shisana O, Rehle T, Simbayi L, Parker W, Zuma K, Bhana A, et al, eds. *South African National HIV Prevalence, HIV Incidence, Behaviour and Communication Survey* (Cape Town: HSRC Press, 2005), xvii.
51. Viviene Taylor and Ina Conradie, *We Have Been Taught by Life Itself: Empowering Women as Leaders-The Role of Development Education* (Pretoria: HSRC, 1997), 93.
52. Taylor and Conradie, 57.
53. History of the Federation of South African Women, AL2457, 1, The Original South Africa History Archives Collection, South Africa History Archives, Wits University, Pretoria, South Africa.
54. History of the Federation of South African Women, AL2457, 2, The Original South Africa History Archives Collection.
55. Sally Biden, Shireen Hasim, and Shelia Meintjes Studies, *Country Gender Profile: South Africa* (University of Sussex, Brighton, UK: BRIDGE Institute of Development, July 1998), 7.
56. Chronology of Resistance of Women in South Africa, The Original South Africa History Archives Collection, AL2457, 1, South Africa History Archives, Wits University, Pretoria, South Africa.
57. FEDSAW Unity in Action, November 1989 Newsletter, AL 2491, 1 (South Africa History Archives, WITS University, Pretoria, South Africa, accessed September 21, 2009).
58. John Thynne, "Can Winnie Mandela's Heroism Outshine Her Crimes?"1/25/10. *BBC News*, January 25, 2010, http://news.bbc.co.uk/2/hi/africa/8474580.stm (accessed February 10, 2010).

59. R. W. Johnson. 2009, *South Africa's Brave New World: The Beloved Country Since the End of Apartheid* (New York: Penguin Group, 2009), 127.
60. Govender, 135.
61. Statement of the National Executive Committee on the African National Congress on the Emancipation of Women in South Africa, May 2, 1994, AL2517, 2, South Africa History Archives, The original SAHA Collection, Wits University, Pretoria, South Africa, accessed September 21, 2009).
62. Biden, Hasim, and Meintjes, 8 and Geisler, 72.
63. Georgina Jaffee and Collette Caine, "The Incorporation of Women into the Industrial Workforce: Its Implications for the Women's Question in South Africa, (conference paper presented at the University of York Centre for Southern African Studies, Social Dynamics Q1, no. 10, September 29–October 2, 1986).
64. Govender, 138, and Biden, Hasim, and Meintjes, 7.
65. Govender, 2007, 138, and Geisler, 72. BRIDGE Institute of Development.
66. Statement of the President of the African National Congress, Comrade Oliver R. Tambo to the National Conference on the ANC Women's League, Kimberley, April 1991, AL 2517, South Africa History Archives Original Collection, South Africa History Archives, Wits University, Pretoria, South Africa.
67. Govender, 126.
68. Govender, 129, Geisler, 81, and Frene Ginwala, Maureen Mackintosh, and Doreen Massey, "Gender and Economic Policy in a Democratic South Africa," (Ann Marie Wolpe Papers, A 14, 9, 1991, University of Cape Town Library Archives, University of Cape Town, Cape Town, South Africa September 28, 2009), 1–24.
69. Allen, 5.
70. The Women's Charter for Effective Equality Adopted at the National Convention Convened by the Women's National Coalition, AL2457, 2, February, 1994, The Original South Africa History Archives Collection, South Africa History Archives, Wits University, Pretoria, South Africa, 25–27.
71. Ibid.
72. Geisler, 84.
73. Commission on Gender Equality, *Strategic Plan 2008-2013* (Pretoria, South Africa 2008), 10.
74. Allen, 137.
75. Ibid., 6.

CHAPTER 4

Building the Rainbow Nation

Before 1994, the apartheid government's election laws restricted the voting rights of the majority of South Africans. Only registered voters were permitted to participate in elections, and to be registered, you had to be more than 18 years old and belong to one of the three racially based houses of Parliament—white, colored, and Indian—as stipulated in the 1983 constitution.

But in 1994, all South Africans were invited and encouraged to participate in the national and provincial elections, from April 26 to 29. Approximately 16 million of the estimated 22.7 million registered voters had the opportunity to vote for the first time in their lives. And vote they did, with 19.5 million people casting their ballots during the three-day election.

What were they voting for? Not for individual candidates but for a political party, at the both the national and provincial level. Voters received two ballots, one to select a party to represent them in the National Assembly, and the other to select a party to represent them in the provincial legislature. In total, 19 political parties appeared on the ballots. A political party would be granted a number of seats in each body according to the number of votes it received.

The result: of the 19 political parties, seven won seats in the National Assembly. Those parties were:

© The Author(s) 2017

D.E. Eynon, *Women, Economic Development, and Higher Education*,
DOI 10.1007/978-3-319-53144-1_4

- the ANC, which won 252 of the 400 seats with 62.6 percent of the vote;
- the National Party (NP),which won 82 seats with 20.4 percent of the vote;
- the IFP, which won 43 seats with 10.5 percent of the vote;
- the Freedom Front (FF), which won nine seats with 2.2 percent of the vote;
- the Democratic Party (DP), which won seven seats with 1.7 percent of the vote;
- the Pan African Congress of Azania (PACA), which won five seats with 1.2 percent of the vote; and
- the African Coalition Democratic Party (ACDP), which won two seats with 0.05 percent of the vote.

On the provincial level, the ANC won a majority in seven of the nine provincial legislatures with the NP and Inkatha Freedom each winning a province.[1]

The Building Blocks: The Constitution and Bill of Rights

The ANC, the NP, and the IFP formed the Government of National Unity (GNU) after the election. Working as the Constitutional Assembly (CA), their task was to create a new path forward for the nation by writing the final constitution that would take the country into the future.[2] While the ANC was the leading group in the constitutional negotiations process, working with the NP and the IFP, other organizations—such as the South African Communist Party (SACP), the Congress of South African Trade Unions (COSATU), and the ANC Women's League—had a strong influence on the negotiations. They collaborated with the ANC to ensure that their respective concerns and visions for the country were reflected in the new constitution.

The ANC, as the major party, had a significant task at hand: to set the course and direction of the country. The challenge was to create a constitution that would reflect the new South Africa and embrace its entire people, as complex and diverse a nation as it was. For the ANC in particular, it was the final stage of its transition from a resistance and protest organization to a governing body, requiring a different set of skills, resources, and knowledge. The burden was clearly on the ANC leadership and its supporters to ensure that what they created would begin the healing and recovery process, address the multiple and complicated challenges facing the country, and set the course for South Africa's future.

To fully appreciate the magnitude of the task facing the ANC and the GNU in creating a new constitution, it is important to keep in mind what they had to dismantle. The apartheid government had formalized, institutionalized, and legalized racial discrimination against and segregation of the majority of its citizens. When the ANC and Nelson Mandela came into power in South Africa in 1994, they inherited the economic and social legacies of that system. The country was struggling with a large pool of unskilled and unemployed labor, widespread and deep poverty, and limited access to education, health care, and other basic public services for a majority of its population. The economic sanctions and political isolation that other nations had imposed on the country to protest the apartheid government were still in place. In essence, South Africa was cut off from the rest of the world when the ANC came into power.[3]

The promise of the new South African government was also constrained by the power-sharing pact negotiated with the apartheid government and from pressures imposed by the external global environment. These two factors, which will be discussed at length later in the book, had a great influence on the construction of the new government, which had to develop policies that were globally relevant at the same time it pursued a profound transformation of the country's political and economic systems to those based on social justice, democracy, and equity.[4]

The end of apartheid in 1994 allowed South Africa to shift from a one-party bureaucracy to a democratic system. In order to make that change, the new government had to dismantle the framework that had created apartheid and establish and integrate new democratic structures. And it had to develop an economic model that would allow the country to move from a state-led to a market-led economy.

A first step was the creation and acceptance of a new constitution two years later. Understanding the constitutional framework around the key issues then confronting the nation can help provide perspective on the advances that South Africa has made—and hasn't made—since the end of apartheid and the beginning of the new Rainbow nation. And it will demonstrate how those key issues, while interconnected, often times contradict one another—leading, at best, to mixed results and limited progress.

Introducing the New Constitutional Framework

Just two years after the election of 1994, on May 8, 1996, the Constitutional Assembly adopted the final constitution as put forth by the GNU. In that final constitution, a new government that recognized majority rule replaced the GNU. That meant that the majority party, the ANC, did not have to share executive power and could appoint cabinet members without consulting the minority parties in the National Assembly.[5]

After approval by the constitutional court in September 1996, the Constitution of the Republic of South Africa was formally proclaimed on December 18, 1996, and become effective on February, 4, 1997.[6] From the very beginning, in the preamble to the constitution, South Africans were asked to recognize their past, to embrace their diversity, and to believe in the promise of a united South Africa:

> We, the people of South Africa,
> Recognise the injustices of our past;
> Honour those who suffered for justice and freedom in our land;
> Respect those who have worked to build and develop our country; and
> Believe that South Africa belongs to all who live in it, united in our diversity.[7]

Chapter one of the constitution, "Founding Provisions," describes South Africa as a democratic state founded on the following values: (a) human dignity, the achievement of equality and the advancement of human rights and freedoms; (b) non-racialism [8]and non-sexism; (c) supremacy of the constitution and the rule of law; and (d) universal adult suffrage, a national common voters roll, regular elections and a multiparty system of democratic government, to ensure accountability, responsiveness and openness.[9] Those provisions are followed by the Bill of Rights, described in the constitution as "the cornerstone of democracy in South Africa." That section guarantees more than 27 rights of all South Africans and recognizes the values of "human dignity, equality, and freedom."

The Bill of Rights states that the government may not discriminate against anyone directly or indirectly on the grounds of race, gender, sex, pregnancy, marital status, ethnic or social origin, color, sexual orientation, age, disability, religion, conscience, belief, culture, language, and birth. Other rights include the freedom of trade, occupation, and profession; the right of workers and employers to fair labor relations; the right of everyone to have an environment that is not harmful to their health or well-being; the right to access adequate housing; and the right to access health care, food, water and social security.[10]

The constitution also addressed four issues that are of particular relevance to this book: gender equality; the recognition of cultural, religious and linguistic communities; education; and language and culture.

The constitutional framework specifically related to gender equality can be found in both the Bill of Rights and in Section 9, "State Institutions Supporting Constitutional Democracy." Although not explicitly stated, the Bill of Rights protected women's rights by prohibiting discrimination based on gender, sex, marital status, and pregnancy. Section 9 established the Commission for Gender Equality (CGE). The purpose of the commission was to "promote respect for gender equality and the protection, development and attainment of gender equality. It had the power to monitor, investigate, research, educate, lobby and advise and report on issues related to gender equality."[11]

Other rights included in the Bill of Rights were:

- *Cultural, religious, or linguistic rights.* Individuals could not be denied the right to practice their religion, enjoy their culture, or use their language, and they could form, join, and maintain those associations. However, those rights had to be consistent with the other provisions in the Bill of Rights. A Commission for the Promotion and Protection of the Rights of Cultural, Religious, and Linguistic Communities was established with the primary purpose of promoting respect for the rights of those communities—with the power to "monitor, investigate, research, educate, lobby, and report on issues of concern to cultural, religious, and linguistic communities." [12]
- *Educational rights.* Section 29 of the Bill of Rights gave everyone the right to basic education and adult basic education.
- *Language rights.* The constitution established 11 official languages of the country: Sepedi, Sesotho, Setswana, siSwati, Tshivenda, Xitsonga, Afrikaans, English, isiNdebele, isiXhosa, and isiZulu. [13] It set forth that individuals had the right to their education in one of the official language or languages of their choice in public educational institutions, stating that everyone had the right to use their language of choice and to participate in a cultural life of their choosing.[14]

Intersecting Rights and Conflicts

Gender equality rights; cultural, religious, and linguistic rights; educational rights; and the right to speak in any language were important as they all sought to redress many inequalities that existed under apartheid. In and of themselves, such rights served a good purpose. However, when several of those rights intersected, one could become diluted or, in some cases, conflict with another.

An example, which is still playing out in various forms in South Africa today, is the conflict between gender equality and the recognition of traditional and tribal customs as provided under the right to cultural, religious, and linguistic communities. As will be explored in detail in the next chapters, black South African women, particularly those in rural areas, are still living under the Customary Law and tribal rules of their communities. Those customs and norms at times run counter to the rights that the Bill of Rights provided women. Although the legitimacy of Customary Law and practices are secondary to the rights granted in the constitution, according to the late Elaine Salo, former professor and the director of gender studies at the University of Pretoria,[15] many South Africans abide by and identify themselves through them. And, the reality is that the South African government continues to support those laws and practices.

For example, the Recognition of Customary Marriage Act of 1998, enacted in Section 15 (3) of the constitution,[16] recognizes polygamous marriages, the practice of *ukuthwala* (the abduction of a girl to another family household in order to force the girl's family to give permission for the marriage), and *lobolo* (negotiation of marriage based on the price of the bride).[17] Those practices, acknowledged in the constitution, have been seen by some people as contradictory to the rights of women as guaranteed in the Bill of Rights.

Part of the debate related to the recognition of Customary Law is that, while the Bill of Rights recognizes individual rights, Customary Law reflects the rights of a community or collective. That debate intensified when the cabinet of Jacob Zuma, who was elected president in 2009, approved the establishment of the ministry of traditional affairs, the role of which was to give traditional leaders a more structured way to engage with the government. Many observers viewed the acceptance of a ministry of traditional affairs as a political move to satisfy traditional leaders, who hold sway over many voters.[18]

Another example of when two individual rights intersect and the exercise of one right dilutes the other is when the right to education and the right to speak in any language creates an unintentional consequence for students who enter the higher education system. That happens when the language of the university they attend is not the language they have chosen to learn or use. By exercising their right to choose any official language, they may have diluted their right to education because they must then struggle to learn in a different language. Although there are 11 official languages, most universities use one of only two languages, English or Afrikaners.

A 2009 report produced for the vice chancellors association Higher Education South Africa (HESA) by the National Benchmark Tests Project found that many students had difficulty performing at a level necessary to be successful in their classes. According to the report, 47 percent of the students who took the test were proficient in English, the dominant language in higher education, while 46 percent were intermediate, and 7 percent had only basic academic literacy. Half the students in the higher education system were African first-language speaking, 42 percent English speaking, and 8 percent Afrikaans speaking.[19] That means that many students have effectively been learning in a language for which they have limited proficiency—which ultimately has had an impact on their retention and graduation rates.

The problem is a difficult and complex one. The challenge is to create a solution that minimizes the language barrier for students entering into the higher education without also limiting people's right to their choice of language. These issues will be explored in detail in Chapter 7.

Expectations Outpacing Reality

The Constitution of South Africa is one of the most progressive of any country in the world—which, of course, helps to explain why South Africans and other people around the world had high hopes and expectations for the country and the new government. Yet today, 23 years after the end of apartheid, the promise and hope that South Africans had for themselves and the country is being challenged. Unemployment, poverty, violence, and housing shortages continue to increase, and the incidence of HIV/AIDS is one of the highest in the world.[20]

South Africans are disenchanted, disappointed, and frustrated with the country's current state of affairs. After the nation's transition to democracy, only 42 percent of those surveyed thought their lives were better, while 17 percent thought they were worse, and 14 percent thought they were much worse.[21] And according to the most recent poll (2015), South Africans are still disillusioned, with 54 percent of citizens rating the economic situation as "fairly bad" or "very bad" (a 4 percent increase since the last poll in 2011) and 64 percent saying they believe the country is headed in the wrong direction (an 18 percent increase since the last poll in 2011). [22]

The constitution and Bill of Rights were indeed very powerful and went beyond the narrow definition of rights given by many other constitutions. They provided the basis and foundation of the new South Africa, a country based on human dignity, equality, and the advancement of human rights and freedoms. Yet the fact is that these documents created the high expectations that may have heightened the sense of disappointment that some of the survey respondents have felt.

It should be acknowledged, however, that it has only been a little more than two decades since the end of apartheid and the beginning of democratic rule. The constitution is a statement that tells its citizens and the world what kind of country that South Africa hopes and strives to be—not what it is. To help put that in perspective, the US constitution is 226 years old, yet American continues to struggle to live up to its full promise. South Africa's journey has, in many ways, just begun.

Discussing the disconnect between the reality of gender equality in South Africa and what is guaranteed in the constitution, former Minister of Education for the Western Cape Cameron Dugmore, former provincial minister of education and now minister of cultural affairs and sport at West Cape, stated:

> It's not as though the consciousness of the society has been totally changed in that we have a kind of gender sensitive and non-patriarchal society, no way. But the fact that those policies are in place, and that the legislation is in place has opened up opportunities, and attitudes have also begun to change. [23]

The challenge is for the government and the people of South Africa to continue to work together to lift more South Africans out of poverty, violence, unemployment, and the ravages of HIV/AIDS so they may realize the full promise of their rights under the constitution.

Restructuring the Economy

The South African economy in 1994 was confronted with the challenge of integrating itself into the competitive landscape of international production and finance at the same time it had to reconstruct domestic, social, cultural, and political structures to redress the inequalities of apartheid. That created difficult political and social choices for the new government and raised the issue of trade-offs between the various principles, goals, and the strategies it could pursue.

As discussed in the previous chapter, South Africa's major economic indicators showed significant decline during the final two decades of apartheid rule. By 1993, one year before the end of apartheid, 70 percent of black South Africans had no electricity, 65 percent of the population was illiterate, and 60 percent lived in absolute poverty. As many as 12 million lacked access to clean water, 21 million did not have adequate sanitation, and millions were without health care.[24] The country was also one of the most unequal in the world in terms of the distribution of wealth: the economy benefited a small minority while about 17 million people, including 11 million in the rural areas, lived below the poverty line.

The economic problems facing South Africa when the ANC came into power included the need to (1) accelerate the rate of economic growth, (2) increase the rate of investment to stimulate growth and modernize production, and (3) pursue those goals in a way that would increase employment and wages, as well as promote a more even distribution of wealth.[25]

Before the elections, the ANC had begun working on a plan to improve South Africa's economic situation. Its first comprehensive economic statement was the 1994 pre-election draft of what was called the Reconstruction and Development Programme (RDP). The RDP was the result of months of discussions, consultation, and negotiation between the ANC and its alliance partners, COSATU and SACP, as well as other organizations. It drew heavily from the 1993 economic policy of the ANC's Macro Economic Research Group (MERG), which the COSATU supported. MERG focused primarily on identifying the social and economic inequalities that the new government had to address. MERG made the argument that the economy could be restructured through improved training and higher wages.[26]

The plan that the RDP put forth was designed to address the social and economic problems facing the country, notably violence, a housing shortage, too few jobs, inadequate education and health care, the lack of democracy, and a failing economy. The authors of the RDP recognized that those issues and problems were connected, and as such, the government could not build a successful economy if millions of people did not have homes or jobs, among other basic needs. Essentially, they designed the RDP to allow the government to create, steer, and fund economic policies that would improve the quality of life for the poor and reduce inequalities through a redistributive process. At the same time, another key goal was to spur economic growth through opening up the domestic market and increasing the efficiency of the economy.[27]

Once the ANC came to power in 1994, it had to turn the RDP's promises into action. Government leaders reviewed, debated, and discussed how best to implement its proposals. From that process, the ANC wrote and released a white paper in September 1994 that stressed two goals: (1) the creation and stimulation of employment and (2) the alleviation of poverty and wage and wealth disparities in order to ensure that every South African had economic security and a decent standard of living. The white paper emphasized the need for the government to bring about a more equal distribution of income, yet unlike the original document, it recognized that neither redistribution nor economic growth alone would resolve the challenges facing the country. It stated that government policies would now focus not only on an equitable distribution of assets but also on an equitable pattern of growth and ensuring macroeconomic stability.[28]

When the RDP white paper was presented by the GNU to the South African Parliament in September 1994, supporters heralded it as a completely new macro- and socioeconomic framework—one that acknowledged the need to create an achievable and sustainable strategy to meet the objectives of freedom and democracy, improve the standard of living and quality of life for all South Africans, and provide a peaceful and stable society characterized by equitable economic growth. [29] It outlined five sub-programs to meet those objectives, each with a specific aim:

1. The *basic needs program* was aimed at creating jobs and improving working conditions; improving access to services such as water, health, and education; and creating a social security system for the poor and aged.
2. The *human resources program* focused on overcoming the legacy of apartheid by (a) lifting the level of education of the whole nation

and restoring access to education to those who had been excluded from it, (b) opening access in the arts, sports, recreation, and (c) regaining a balanced representation of the country's diverse cultures.

3. The *macroeconomic program* emphasized the need to address the issues of economic stagnation, inequalities among people and regions, productive inefficiencies related to human resource capacities, and the re-entry of South Africa into the world economy. Growth was to be linked to development.
4. The *democratization program* attempted to redefine the balance of political power by providing all citizens access to a democratic state. It advocated for the empowerment of those citizen to determine the shape and direction of the government through measures that improved access to, accountability by, and responsiveness from government.
5. The *nation-building program* was responsible for identifying the processes and institutions needed to carry out and implement the first four programs.[30] It was specifically designed to fight poverty and address the shortfalls in social services across the country.

The National and International Economic Context

The creation of the RDP and its aftermath should be considered in the broader economic context. From the 1940's to the late 1960s, many ideas, theories, and concepts for economic and social development came out of the United Nations (UN) system. In general, the UN focused on employment and basic-needs-oriented development strategies.

By the 1970s, however, two opposing trends in development thinking had emerged. One group of economists advocated for widening national development strategies by including social considerations such as education, health, nutrition, employment, income distribution, basic needs, poverty reduction, environmental considerations, gender, and other issues. Another group of economists called for a return to classical economic thinking, relying more on market forces than government intervention.

In the RDP, the alleviation of poverty and building of the economy were seen as interrelated and mutually supportive objectives: development without growth wouldlead to financial instability, while growth without development would fail to bring about the structural transformational change needed to bring equity and prosperity to all South Africans. The RDP clearly set the tone and direction for post-apartheid South Africa where growth, development, reconstruction, and redistribution were all key components of the country's macroeconomic framework. It sought both redistribution and growth, with the government taking a lead role in directing the economy through reconstruction and development.[31]

Yet within the ANC, people held different philosophies that conflicted with one another when it came to how to address the problems facing South Africa. Some party leaders were inclined toward redistributive policies as outlined in the 1994 RDP. That thinking and approach, however, ultimately gave way to a neo-liberal model based on the following tenets: (1) minimum state involvement or intervention is best, (2) the market is not only a substitute for the state but also preferred because it performs better, (3) resource allocation and utilization should be based on market prices, and (4) national political objectives and domestic economic concerns should not act as constraints on economic policy.

The foundations of globalization are based on the neo-liberal model. Globalization is perceived as a means of ensuring not only efficiency and equity but also growth and development in the world economy.[32] The policy makers who support this model believe globalization promises economic prosperity for countries that engage in it and economic deprivation for countries that do not.

Since the 1970s, Western countries and international organizations have been moving toward a neo-liberal approach to economic growth and development. That approach was reinforced when, in the 1980s and first half of the 1990s, reliance on government actions to promote industrial growth came under heavy criticism in the wake of a crisis in Asia. As the nations of East Asia became newly industrialized countries, they were experiencing rapid economic growth and development. Their governments were following economic paths that were market-oriented but with a high degree of government intervention. The inflow of capital into East Asia showed confidence in the region's ability to continue on this path of growth, and other developing countries began to look to East Asia as a model. Economists began studying those countries' economic policies, but they were unable to provide an explanation for the rate of growth and development that was occurring in the region.

And then, quite unexpectedly, in late 1997 and into 1998, East Asia experienced an economic reversal that created a financial crisis in the region. It was the first time that such a crisis in the South had a significant impact on capital markets in the North. Critics believed East Asian growth may have been even stronger had there been less government intervention. And the prevailing thought was that, even if government involvement did contribute to East Asia's growth rates, it wouldn't work in the Third World countries because, unlike those in East Asia, they lacked a strong state.[33]

All the countries in the Organisation for Economic Co-Operation and Development (OECD) [34] soon adopted neoliberalism, and it increasingly became the conventional approach of the industrialized world. That meant growth was emphasized more than income distribution and social objectives. In such an era of globalization, governments across the world became focused on the need to attract foreign investment and to deregulate and liberalize national economies so they could integrate into the global economy.

While the Western nations adopted this approach at first, the World Bank and International Monetary Fund soon adopted it, as well. It was not long before the entire globe, with the exception of a few East Asian countries, was operating under these principles—although not always voluntarily, as not doing so jeopardized a country's ability to seek and gain monetary support from the IMF.[35]

The Creation of GEAR

That was the global economic environment South Africa faced after two decades of economic isolation under the apartheid government. Nelson Mandela and the ANC leadership believed the country had to move in this globalized neo-liberal direction to meet its economic growth and development objectives. As stated in an ANC discussion document, "South Africa must resist the illusion that it can elaborate solutions that are in discord with the rest of the world."[36] The document goes on to say that South Africa should abandon "command economics and take on board the globalization of trade and financial markets".[37]

It was that conceptual framework that informed the government's macroeconomic policy—Growth, Employment and Redistribution (GEAR)—which became the macroeconomic plan of the South African government in 1996 and represented a significant shift from the RDP.

This change to lower government expenditures, smaller deficits, deregulation, privatization, and minimum state intervention was seen as a clear move toward more neo liberal economic policies with an emphasis on a market-based economy with little government intervention.[38]

Unlike the RDP and other previous documents, GEAR did not mention reducing inequality as a policy goal. Its focus was on cutting back government expenditures, maintaining private and public sector wages, implementing tariff reform, and increasing the country's economic growth rate by an average of 4.2 percent between 1996 and 2000.[39] The shift to a neo-liberal approach led to the creation of a new Department of Finance and the formation of policies that tended more toward fiscal austerity and less toward the redistribution policies originally stated in the RDP. Those fiscal austerity policies were accomplished through deficit reduction, expenditure restraint, and tight monetary policies, along with trade liberalization. The transition from RDP to GEAR took approximately two years.[40]

Why did the government move from a redistribution and equity approach, as found in the RDP, to the neo-liberal economic approach? Once in power, the ANC had to move from the policies of a resistance movement to those of a government. That required an open dialogue with other interest groups within and outside the county, including international organizations and the governments of major industrialized nations. Those groups often pressed the new government to acknowledge that the world was operating in a global economy and that South Africa needed economic policies that would appeal to international capital markets.

The government positioned GEAR with policy makers and the public as an integrated strategy for building and restructuring the economy that was ultimately in keeping with the goals set in the RDP. Its main assumption for that integrated strategy was the belief that sustainable growth at a higher level required the country to pursue a competitive outward-oriented economy. In order to accomplish that, the administrators of GEAR proposed an accelerated program of privatization, deregulation, and fiscal restraint to help to attract foreign investors.

Members of the governing party's alliance partners—COSATU, SACP, and others—criticized the South African government for moving from the original RDP to GEAR, arguing that it was essentially caving in to neo liberal policies at the expense of equity goals. They viewed GEAR an inappropriate policy tool for addressing the country's socioeconomic and political problems. To such critics, GEAR was a neo-liberal strategy associated with the Washington Consensus—a set of informal rules for instituting structural economic reforms that the International Monetary Fund often uses in developing countries, which, in the critics' view, limited economic transformation. They advocated for the reversal of GEAR's restrictive policies and proposed that legislation be passed allowing Parliament to amend the budget to meet the socioeconomic needs of the South African people.[41]

But, in spite of the strong opposition, the leaders of the new government stood firm in implementing the measures outlined in GEAR. They were able to continue on the neo-liberal path despite such opposition in part because they had insulated the National Treasury from political pressure. In fact, former Minister of Finance Trevor Manuel was a strong advocate of GEAR and former President Thabo Mbeki one of its main architects. Nelson Mandela also offered his continuing support for GEAR.[42]

By sticking to the fundamentals of GEAR, the South African government was able to bring macroeconomic stability to the country, unlike many of its neighbors on the continent that have struggled in their postcolonial existence. South Africa has avoided some of the pitfalls of some developing countries like Zimbabwe, where an unbalanced spending cycle led to financial collapse. That government's vastly increased spending on social services in the 1990s created a ballooning budget deficit, which it financed primarily through monetary expansion. The massive inflation that ensued left many Zimbabweans unable to pay for basic goods. In the end, the very people whom the government was trying to help through redistribution policies were hurt.[43] In contrast, the South African government has consistently emphasized that sustained economic growth was a necessary and vital condition for its transformation.

Creating a New Higher Education System

As described in the previous chapter, the ANC inherited a higher education system that was racially and socially fragmented, discriminatory, inefficient, and massive—with millions of students scattered across 20,000 different schools and the government spending as much as 7 percent of GDP just to maintain it.[44] The South African government oversaw all those students and schools through four education departments, one for each recognized race—black, colored, Indian, and white. Each department had its own philosophy, curriculum, governance system, and resources. As a result, not surprisingly, the infrastructure, curriculum, quality of educators, and resource allocations differed tremendously across many institutions. [45] The country had a few good universities, but the rest were mediocre or extremely poor. No other country in the world has had such a discriminatory and, frankly, odd educational system.

Likewise, no other country has ever embarked on such a complete restructuring of its higher education system, with the possible exception of Eastern European countries. The ANC saw education reform as a priority and a way to redress many of the injustices of apartheid. The challenge before the leaders of the new government was to create a uniform system across the country and to eliminate the inequalities that existed under apartheid. They focused on the establishment of such a single unified national system, as well as on improving access, adopting funding policies for the poor, decentralizing school governance, revamping the curriculum, and improving the quality of higher education.

The result? Since South Africa became a democracy, significant changes have clearly occurred. The apartheid government's higher education structure has been dismantled through a number of important structural and policy reforms. The 1995, 1997, and 2004 White Papers on higher education policy—which addressed the issues of access, equity, and quality of higher education—formed the framework for those efforts. The following sections will describe them in further detail.

New Policies and Reforms

In 1994, the new government of the ANC formed the National Commission on Higher Education (NCHE). That commission was the beginning of a formal process designed to provide a space to debate, negotiate, and build consensus on a higher education policies for the country. In 1995, it produced the first White Paper on education and training, which called for increased access to higher education, the development of a single coordinated higher education system, and the expansion of the role of distance education.

Then, in 1995, the government established the South African Qualification Authority and charged it with producing three main deliverables: (1) a system to create qualifications and standards, (2) a quality assurance system, and (3) an information system, which became known as the National Learner's Records Database. South Africa Qualifications Authority (SAQA) provided the structure for the education and training system in the country and established the National Qualifications Framework (NQF), which defined and monitored the qualifications for each of the eight levels of the education system—with higher education and training occupying levels 5–8. It developed an outcomes-based system where skills and knowledge could be measured at the end of each level. In essence, the NQF brought together schooling, higher education, and training under a single qualifications framework.[46]

That was followed in 1996 by "The Green Paper on Higher Education," published by the South African Ministry of Education. This paper made a commitment to the principles of equality, redress, justice, and redistribution, recommending mergers as a way to restructure the higher education system. Also in 1996, the Constitution of South Africa identified higher education as a national government responsibility with administrative duties falling under the national Department of Education.

The Higher Education Act of 1997 provided the legal foundation and framework for the administration of higher education. That same year, the ANC-led government published a second White Paper on higher education." That paper abandoned equity goals and instead emphasized managerial efficiency. It was seen as a major shift to align with the objectives of GEAR, moving from redressing conditions that led to inequality in higher education to addressing the problems in higher education and its inefficiency.

The government appointed a National Working Group to provide advice to the Minister of Education on how to reconfigure and restructure the higher education system.[47] In addition, it established the Council of Higher Education to monitor and oversee the quality of higher education and its outputs. Based on advice provided by that council on the restructuring of the higher education system, Kader Asmal, then the education minister, introduced the National Plan for Higher Education (NPHE) in June 2001. The National Plan established the targets for the size and shape of the higher education system, including overall growth and participation rates, institutional and program mixes, and equity and efficiency goals. It also provided the framework and outlined the processes and mechanisms for restructuring the system. The National Plan set a target participation rate in higher education of 20 percent over a 10 to 15-year period.[48]

Following up on that plan in 2002, the National Working Group presented a report with recommendations to restructure the higher education system to make it more equitable in the distribution of resources and to provide more opportunities for all South Africans. Based on the work of that group, a third White Paper on higher education, published in 2004, recommended the reorganization and merger of a number of institutions within the higher education system. Minister of Education Asmal called for the dismantling of the old structure with the intent to create a new system that strengthened central control over South African higher education.

As a result, the number of higher education institutions was reduced from 36 to 23, creating universities of technology and comprehensive universities in addition to traditional research universities.[49] It was a huge undertaking involving the merger of students, faculty, facilities, and campuses. The result, as will be described in more detail in Chapter 7, was similar to a corporate merger, causing some confusion, disruption, stress, anxiety, and uncertainty that lasted for years.

That said, the reforms also created clear benefits. The Higher Education Act of 1997, which brought higher education under one centralized system, and the 2004 White Paper, calling for the reorganization and merger of higher education institutions, were attempts to put all the institutions in one basket as a way to create equal education for all. They resulted in the desegregation of higher education institutions, higher enrollment rates for a wide segment of the population, and greater efficiency through the consolidation of administrations and institutions. In many ways, those reforms also helped institutions that historically were attended by predominately colored and black students. Placed under the same quality umbrella set up by the Council on Higher Education (CHE) as other institutions, they were able to improve their offerings and expand programming.

Yet while much progress has been made, the intended outcomes have not fully materialized. While there was clearly a need for these initiatives, a number of concerns remain to this day. The reorganization of the higher education system and both its positive and negative ramifications will be examined in more depth in Chapter 7.

Establishing a National Gender Machinery

What about the women of South Africa? What changes did the new Rainbow Nation usher in for them? What impact, if any, did the political and economic policies and reforms outlined in previous sections have on women?

After the general elections in 1994, the South African government passed legally binding initiatives to promote gender equality and established a National Gender Machinery (NGM) to implement and monitor those initiatives. The emphasis was on increasing the representation of women across sectors and institutions and on creating an environment where women's voices could be heard.

As a result of those governmental efforts, women's access to political power, decision-making, and influence has improved a good deal in the little over two decades since that time. For example, by 2000, women constituted almost 30 percent of the ministers and 62 percent of the deputy ministers in the national government, 30 percent of the members of Parliament, and 24 percent of members of provincial legislatures. And by 2015, women represented 43 percent of the ministers and 46 percent of the deputy ministers in the national government and 39.5 percent of the members of Parliament, as well as 47 percent of the members of provincial legislatures.[50] To date, although a woman has not held the country's highest political position, South Africa ranks seventh in the world for women's representation in Parliament.[51]

Moreover, the government continues to support gender parity in government and industry. In March 2014, just before the most recent elections, the national assembly passed the Women Empowerment and Gender Equality Bill, which obligates both public and private sector to ensure at least 50 percent representation of women in decision-making structures.[52]

Yet although such laws and structures were important first steps, they alone cannot guarantee equality. In fact, despite all the laws, policies, initiatives, and a strong national economy, a majority of South African women continue to be at the bottom of the pyramid socially, culturally, physically, and economically. Why?

Part of the answer lies in the patriarchal mindset held by both men and women and their continued support of traditional practices. To illustrate, a 1999 study based on a survey administered in the Eastern Cape, Northern Province, and Mpumalanga found that 82 percent of women believed that wives should obey their husbands. In addition, about 60 percent felt that women do not have the right to refuse sex with their partners, 50 percent thought that a husband has the right to punish his wife, and 10 percent said that hitting by husbands is sometimes or always acceptable. [53] Therein lays the fundamental problem for women in South Africa, as will be seen throughout this book and described in more detail in coming chapters. The attitudes, norms, perceptions, and cultural practices regarding women must change along with the laws and institutions.

The problem can also be linked to a lack of implementation of government policies, laws, and initiatives related to women's empowerment and gender equality. The following section will explore those policies, laws, and initiatives, which provide a framework for considering women's progress, or lack thereof, since the beginning of the Rainbow Nation.

Legislative Reforms

At the outset of the new democratic government that was formed at the end of apartheid, numerous legislative measures addressing the status of women were passed:

- In 1993, the Joint Standing Committee on Justice met to consider legislation promoting equality between men and women and the prevention of family violence.
- The 1996 Constitution of the Republic of South Africa recognized and protected the right to equality, including gender equality.
- In January 1996, the government ratified the United Nations Convention on the Elimination of All Forms of Discrimination Against Women (CEDAW). This legally bound Parliament and the Executive Office to work actively toward the abolition of gender discrimination in the governance of the country.
- In September 1997, the heads of state of the governments of the Southern African Development Community (SADC), including South Africa, signed a declaration committing their governments and countries to ensuring the equal representation of women and men at all levels of their decision- making structures, as well as in SADC structures; to promoting women's full access to and control over productive resources; to the repealing and reforming of all laws and the changing of social practices that subject women to discrimination; to enhancing access to quality education by both women and men and removing gender stereotypes from the curriculum, career choices, and professions; and to taking urgent measures to prevent and deal with the increasing levels of violence against women.[54]

The South African government also established, as mandated in the constitution and the Commission on Gender Equality Act of 1996, (1) the

Commission for Gender Equality (CGE), (2) the National Gender Forum, and, in 1997, (3) the Office on the Status of Women (OSW) to support efforts by higher education to become more inclusive and equitable.[55] As one of its major initiatives, the OSW prepared a Gender Policy Framework that the Office of the Presidency, which has jurisdiction over the national gender program, proposed the Cabinet adopt in 2000. That framework outlined South Africa's vision for gender equality and how it intended to realize that ideal. A key recommendation of the OSW was the creation of an National Gender Machinery (NGM) for the purpose of providing a structure that would support gender empowerment and equality initiatives and laws throughout all layers of government and civil society.[56]

Other Legislation Supporting Women

The South African government passed additional legislative measures to protect women and children. They included:

- *The Maintenance Act no. 99 of 1998*, which recognizes the legal duty of both parents and, in some cases, family members to support their children and governs all the legal procedures used by Maintenance Courts, their officers, and investigators to ensure payment of maintenance by parents.
- *The Domestic Violence Act 116 of 1998*, which provides legal protection under the law from domestic abuse and introduces measures to ensure relevant entities of the state support and enact the law.
- *The Recognition of Customary Marriages Act 120 of 1998*, which makes valid customary marriages, monogamous or polygamous, prior to the enactment of this law. Marriages contracted after the establishment of the act are recognized if the spouses are both 18 or older and have both consented to the marriage, and neither are already married under the Marriage Act or Civil Union Act of 2006. However, the age requirement may be waived by the special written permission of the Minister of Home Affairs or their delegate.
- *The Promotion of Equality and Prevention of Unfair Discrimination Draft Bill of 2000*, which prohibits unfair discrimination by the government, private organizations, and individuals and forbids

hate speech and harassment. It lists race, gender, sex, pregnancy, family responsibility or status, marital status, ethnic or social origin, HIV/AIDS status, color, sexual orientation, age, disability, religion, conscience, belief, culture, language and birth as "prohibited grounds" for discrimination.

The National Gender Machinery Structure

How is the NGM structured throughout the various sectors of the South African government? Within the executive branch of the national government, the primary structures concerned with gender equality are (1) the Cabinet, (2) the OSW in the Office of the Presidency, and (3) the Gender Desks or Focal Points in governmental departments.

The Cabinet is responsible for policy making; it must approve all national policies before they are introduced to Parliament or carried out by government departments. Within the Cabinet, Cluster Committees and Clusters of Directors-General are charged with ensuring that the national gender policies outlined in the Gender Policy Framework are adopted and implemented. They make recommendations on policy and legislation as they relate to gender for discussion and approval by the Cabinet. (In South Africa the government has created clusters as a way to create an integrated approach to governance. The purpose of the clusters is to improve planning, decision-making, and service delivery and to ensure the effective coordination of government programs both at the national and provincial level.)

The OSW advises and briefs the President, the Deputy President, and the Minster in the Presidency on all issues related to the empowerment of women. It is considered the nerve center and principal coordinating structure for South Africa's gender framework. It develops national gender plans and is responsible for creating strategies for their implementation. OSW is also responsible for monitoring how those strategies and plans are carried out, as well as for serving as a liaison between the government and NGOs dedicated to women's and gender issues.[57]

The main responsibility for seeing that the National Gender Policy is actually put in place rests with the individual national and provincial government departments. All the departments are required to establish dedicated Gender Units or Focal Points to assist in the design and implementation of plans to promote women's empowerment and gender equality in their work. In addition, departments are in charge of coordinating staff gender training and education within their offices, monitoring and evaluating departmental projects and programs to determine if they are consistent with the national gender policy, and creating relationships with civil-society organizations related to gender issues.

Parliament also plays a key role in facilitating women's empowerment and gender equality. In 1996, the Joint Monitoring Committee on the Quality of Life and Status of Women was established to ensure that all legislation passed by Parliament was "engendered." The committee evaluates the country's progress in improving the quality of life and status of women. It specifically monitors South Africa's performance related to its international commitments to women's empowerment and gender equality.[58]

In addition, several women's committees and groups within Parliament focus on legislative issues. The Women's Empowerment Unit (WEU) identifies and addresses obstacles women face in participating in the lawmaking process, and the Parliamentary Women's Group (PWG), a multiparty women's caucus established in 1994, works to make Parliament more gender sensitive.[59]

Despite the creation of all these groups and bodies to further women's interests, however, their effectiveness has often been thwarted. For example, while the PWG made some great strides, and several women's caucuses were established to work on gender issues, they often ran into roadblocks: inadequate funding, limited time to meet outside the lunch hour, and hostile resistance from other members of Parliament. They also struggled as a group to agree on the key gender issues and which ones they were willing to bring forward and support.[60]

For its part, the OSW often lacked authority, resources, or power in the early years of its existence. The first person appointed as minister in charge of the office was Essop Pahad, a close friend of President Mbeki's from their days together at university. He had little experience or knowledge on the issues facing women.[61] That lack of authority, resources, and power remains problematic to this day.

Independent Statutory Bodies

Several independent statutory bodies are involved in gender issues. The constitution calls for the establishment of the *Council on Gender Equality (CGE)*, which acts as an independent statutory, advisory, consultative, and research body. It plays the primary role in advancing the empowerment of women and gender equality, with the other groups complementing its work. The CGE's main role is to monitor, evaluate, and make recommendations on all policies and practices of the government, organizations, and institutions in South Africa to ensure they promote gender equality in their work. An important part of the CGE's work is to recommend to Parliament or the provincial legislatures the adoption of new legislation that would bolster gender equality and improve the status of women. It is also responsible for developing and managing education programs that support gender equality.

South Africa recognizes women's rights as human rights. As a result, the *Human Rights Commission*is another important part of the National Gender Machinery. It works with the CGE and often receives referrals from it.

The constitution created the *Independent Electoral Commission (IEC)*to promote and safeguard democracy in South Africa. It is responsible for strengthening constitutional democracy and promoting the democratic process. It helps to involve women in the political and electoral process.

The *Public Protector's* role within the NGM is to receive complaints from individual women or groups about a government agency or official. This body has the power to investigate any case of unfair practice, impropriety, or prejudice.

The South African Law Commission is responsible for legal research and legal reform. It analyzed the relationship between Customary Law and the Equality clause in the constitution, which led to revisions to Customary Law.

The Land Commission is concerned with restitution and redistribution of land. As women's access to land is an important part of economic empowerment, this commission plays an important role for women.[62]

South Africa's NGM include a number of independent women's organizations, recognizing that the government alone cannot shift public opinion or policy without the cooperation and participation of these groups. Several bodies within the NGM—the CGE, the OSW, and the Joint Monitoring Committee—are responsible for interacting with women's organizations. The purpose is to create close and effective relationships, assist organizations with capacity building and education, provide resources, and gather input on key government initiatives.

Gender Machinery at the Provincial Level

In many ways, local governments have carried out the most important piece of the NGM. They are literally the closest to the people of South Africa, so their actions have had the most impact on their lives—especially the lives of those who are marginalized.

The country's gender policy framework calls for each of South Africa's nine provinces to establish a structure parallel to the NGM. The OSW also recommended in the national gender framework that the Department of Provincial Affairs and the South African Local Government Association (SALGA) work together to lobby local government councils to create gender structures. The OSW has asked civic and community-based organizations to get involved, as well.[63]

In response, some of the provinces have, in fact, established gender structures within their governments and legislatures or independent statutory bodies to focus on women's rights and advancement. But most local governments do not have a coherent approach to women's empowerment and gender equality, and they lack the resources to promote those objectives. Further, as discussed earlier, many of the traditional customs and laws allowed by the constitution often conflict with the national gender framework.

Thus, although South Africa's NGM is recognized as one of the best in the world, it lacks the skills, resources, and accountability necessary to be effective. In addition, the integration and coordination of efforts among government agencies, and between national and provincial governments has been challenging.

The CGE provides an example of the lack of accountability and inability to deliver among some government bodies. In April 2008, the police escorted Chana Majake, its chief executive, out of her Johannesburg office. Majake had been under investigation in 2006 after her staff accused her of mismanagement and corruption. She was cleared of the charges but was found to have failed for almost two years to deal with a sexual harassment case against one of the CGE's provincial heads. The commission immediately announced her suspension after staff members passed a no-confidence vote on her leadership. An investigation has begun to address the staff's recent charges against Majake. The former chairperson of the Parliamentary review committee, Kader Asmal, believes the commission has failed to understand its legal and constitutional mandate.[64]

To address the ongoing structural challenges of the multiagency gender machinery in advancing general equality, particularly in rural areas, in 2009 the government established the Ministry of Women, Children, and People with Disabilities in 2009. The ministry replaces the OSW, the National Office on the Status of Disabled Persons, and the Office on the Rights of the Child.[65]

Women's Progress Under the National Gender Machinery

It is clear that some women have benefited tremendously since the beginning of the reforms in 1994. In fact, a number of people believe that women generally have been liberated by South African democracy more than any other group. But it is also clear is that certain women have not benefited, and in some cases, life has become even more difficult. It is true that the government and most corporations have a significant number of women in Parliament, agencies, departments, and divisions (dictated by law), but the question one must ask is if those are women from the middle class who have simply moved to the upper-middle class.

Amina Mama examined this question in a 1995 article using the term "femocracy" to describe the phenomenon.[66] She suggested that what has been created in South Africa is actually an antidemocratic female power structure which claims to help women but, in fact, does not because it is dominated by a small group of women whose power is derived from being married to powerful men. More and more people in South Africa are considering this theory, and it could help explain why some organizations such as the Gender Commission are paralyzed by power struggles with other government agencies and have not been able to create any substantive change.[67]

Rural women in particular do not seem to be benefiting from the gender equality and empowerment laws and policies of the country, as later chapters will describe in more detail. Especially in rural areas, the prevailing attitude is that men are in charge and women should be obedient and are the weaker gender. This is reflected in the prevalence of gender violence and rape. As long as women are controlled financially, physically, and emotionally, things will continue as they are.

Orly Stern, a former human rights lawyer at the Sonke Gender Justice Network and now a consultant, believes rural women need to be taught about their rights and what to do if those rights are violated. Presently, the network has a campaign underway to do just that, but it is only taking place in the cities. Orly recognizes the difficulty of reaching people in the rural areas and also worries about the women who do know their rights but do not have the money to pursue a case or are too far away from courts and lawyers. Strengthening the police system and legal-aid organizations as well as getting reports into more remote areas would help tremendously. More mechanisms must be put in place to enforce the laws.[68]

When it comes to the entrenched problem of patriarchal attitudes, it's not clear what will change the situation. As one effort, the Sonke Gender Justice Network is also working with men and boys to understand their attitudes and, more important, to educate them and try to improve their views and conduct toward women.

Ultimately, it could be argued that South Africa's laws and policies are ahead of its cultural and social norms. Those laws and policies have created a contradiction of opportunities. On the one hand, they have begun the process of breaking down stereotypes and creating greater independence for women. On the other, women still find themselves having to exercise those choices in a context of a conservative and patriarchal society.[69]

As is often the case, laws and policies are only the first step in bringing about change. They provide structure, legal protection, and a foundation to build upon, but they alone cannot carry the weight of the task. To make real change requires personal and collective will, the relinquishment of long-held attitudes and norms, time, and resources.

The debate about gender equality among women in South Africa has called attention to the fact that what is formally written in a document does not guarantee or secure equal treatment. According to Assie-Lumumba, "What has become clear during the debates over this contested issue is that, unless there is a radical restructuring in the sexual division of labor as well as a concomitant change in the consciousness, discourse, and behavior of men and women about gender roles, women will be trapped as wives, mothers, and lovers instead of being accorded citizenship in their own right."[70]

The adoption of laws and policies that promote gender equality and women's empowerment is just the promise of what should be. It is important not to let that promise mask the reality of life for many disadvantaged women in South Africa. Moreover, as the next chapter will demonstrate, it must also be acknowledged that much of that reality is based on macroeconomic trends and policies that have driven South Africa and its people's progress, or lack thereof, over the last several decades.

Profiles of South African Women

Helen Suzman

Helen Suzman was distinctive in many ways—a white Jewish English-speaking woman from a privileged background who served in a male-dominated, Afrikaner-speaking parliament who adamantly and vocally opposed apartheid.

She was first elected to the South African Parliament in 1953 and, by 1960, had become a controversial figure, as she was the only parliamentarian, until 1974, to oppose the National Party's apartheid policies. And for 6 of the 13 years (1961–1974), she was the only woman in Parliament.

Helen also approached her opposition to apartheid in her own way. In addition to the moral arguments, she argued that South Africa's economy would suffer under apartheid, as the majority of the country's people would live in poverty and therefore not be able to contribute to the economy.

Helen not only gave speeches and fought with other members of Parliament against apartheid laws and policies, she actively worked with the poor—often meeting them in her office or in their neighborhoods, listening to their stories, and hearing first-hand of their hardships. As a result of her efforts, the police harassed her, her phone was tapped, and the BBC regularly reported on her work. It was very courageous of her to continue her opposition under such difficult circumstances, yet she persisted and became a beacon of hope to many South Africans and others opposed to apartheid. Helen was known for her fearlessness, energy, sense of humor, and commitment to the principle, "Let right be done." She also used to quote Theodore Roosevelt: "I did what I could, where I was, with what I had."

After serving in Parliament for 37 years, Helen left it in 1989, the year President F.W. de Klerk lifted the ban on liberation movements and released political prisoners, including Nelson Mandela, whom Helen visited several times during his imprisonment. She was present at the signing of the 1996 constitution and was nominated twice for the Nobel Peace Prize.

On New Year's Day, 2009, Helen Suzman died at the age of 91. Her legacy will be what Nelson Mandela called her "magnificent battle against apartheid."

Sources:
The Guardian, Helen Suzman, January 1, 2009, https://www.theguardian.com/world/2009/jan/01/helen-suzman
(accessed August 2, 2016)
SUNY Cortland, Remembering Helen Suzman: A Life of Struggle Against Apartheid in South Africa, http://www.cortland.edu/cgis/suzman/
(accessed August 2, 2016)

Winnie Mandela

In the 1950s, Winnie Madikizela Mandela became involved in the ANC. She met Nelson Mandela in 1957 when he and 155 other people were on trial following the civil disobedience campaigns carried out during most of the decade. A year later, Winnie and Nelson were married and settled in Soweto.

Their marriage was interrupted when Nelson was imprisoned for 26 years on Robben Island. Winnie was forced to raise their two daughters alone, and although she had visitation rights, she was prohibited from having any physical contact with Nelson. Winnie was also subject to a series of legal orders and banned under the Suppression of Communism Act, restricting her to a township in Soweto.

That forced her underground, where she continued to attend meetings and circulate antiapartheid materials. It was during this period that Winnie sent her daughters to Swaziland to protect them from harassment and so they could continue their education. In 1970, Winnie was placed under house arrest, but she continued to violate the order resulting in numerous charges and additional arrests.

In 1976, Winnie established the Black Women's Federation and the Black Parent Association. Those organizations became part of the Black Consciousness Movement, which rejected "white" values. It was for her involvement in those organizations and other antiapartheid activities that she was once again detained and later put under house arrest

Winnie returned home in 1986 and found herself surrounded in controversy. She publicly endorsed the use of the "necklace" method (placing a tire around the neck of a person, dousing it with gasoline, and setting it on fire) of killing dissidents and alleged police informants. She also was criticized for the behavior and acts of a group of young men who acted as her bodyguards.

In 1990, Nelson Mandela was released from prison with Winnie at his side. The following year, she was elected to the ANC's National Executive Committee but was also charged with the kidnapping and murder of a 14-year-old boy, Stompie Seipei, whom she believed was a police informant. She was found guilty of kidnapping and sentenced to six years in jail, but on appeal, her sentence was reduced to a fine.

In 1992, Winnie resigned from her ANC positions, including her position in Parliament. She also separated from Nelson, and the two divorced in 1996. When it came to her political involvement, however, she made a comeback and was elected president of the ANC Women's League in 1993. After the 1994 elections, Winnie was appointed Deputy Minister of Arts, Culture and Science and Technology. But after she was accused of financial mismanagement, Nelson dismissed her in 1995.

Winnie was charged with fraud and theft from the funeral accounts of loan applicants in 2001 and sentenced to five years in prison. But, in 2004, an appeals court judge overturned the conviction for theft while upholding the fraud charges, resulting in a three- and- a- half- year suspended sentence. She resigned as president of the ANC Women's League in 2003.

Source:
South African History Online, Winnifred Madikizela-Mandela
http://www.sahistory.org.za/people/winnie-madikizela
(accessed August 2, 2016)

Notes

1. Election Resources on the Internet: Republic of South Africa General Election Results, http://electionresources.org/za/provinces.php?election=1994 (accessed July 29, 2016).
2. From April 27, 1994 to February 3, 1997, the country was operating under an interim constitution. South African Government Information. Constitution of the Republic of South Africa, http://www.info.gov.za/documents/constitution/index.htm (accessed November 20, 2009).
3. International Monetary Fund, *Post-Apartheid South Africa: The First Ten Years* (Washington, DC: IMF Publication Services, 2005), 1.
4. Trevor C. Sehoole, *Democratizing Higher Education Policy: Constraints of Reform in Post-apartheid South Africa* (New York: Routledge, 2005), 84.
5. Constitution of the Republic of South Africa 1240.
6. Ibid., 1241.
7. Ibid. Preamble, 1243.

8. The Oxford English Dictionary http://dictionary.oed.com/cgi/entry/50195905?query_type=word&queryword=racialism&first=1&max_to_show=10&single=1&sort_type=alpha (accessed February 12, 2010). The Oxford English Dictionary (OED) defines racism as the "belief that all members of each race possess characteristics, abilities, or qualities specific to that race, especially so as to distinguish it as inferior or superior to another race or races." The term racialism defines racialism as the "belief in the superiority of a particular race." The OED records racism as a synonym of racialism. At the end of World War II, racism acquired the same connotations as racialism where "racism implied racial discrimination, racial supremacism, and a harmful intent."
9. Ibid., Chapter 1: Section 1; Founding Provisions, 1243.
10. Ibid., Chapter 2: Bill of Rights, Section 9, Equality, 1245.
11. Ibid., Chapter 9: State Institutions Supporting Constitutional Democracy, Section 187- 1331 (15).
12. Ibid., Chapter 9: State Institutions Supporting Constitutional Democracy, Section 185 and 186, 1331 (14).
13. Ibid., Chapter 1: Founding Provisions, Section 6, 1245.
14. Ibid., Chapter 2: Bill of Rights, Section 30, Languages, 1257.
15. Diane Eynon, "Interpreting the Economic Growth and Development Policies of Post-Apartheid South Africa: Its Influence on Higher Education and Prospects for Women" (Doctoral diss., University of Pennsylvania, 2010), 65.
16. Marissa Herbst and Willemien du Plessis, "Customary Law v. Common Law Marriages: A Hybrid Approach in South Africa. *Electronic Journal of Comparative Law,* 12, no. 1 (May 2008), http://www.ecjl.org/121/art121-28.pdf, 2.
17. Ibid., 5, 7, and 8. Ukuthwala is the abduction of a girl to another family household in order to force the girl's family to give permission for the marriage. More often than not, the girl has agreed to the abduction. The Recognition Act requires permission of both individuals to the marriage. Lobolo is defined in the Recognition Act as "property in cash or kind . . . - which a prospective husband or head of his family undertakes to give to the head of a prospective wife's family in consideration of a customary marriage." The validity of a customary marriage is based on the agreement to pay lobolo.
18. *Government Wooing Chiefs with New Ministry,* September 1, 2009. www.timeslive.co.za/sundaytimes/article35967.ece?service=print. (accessed November 21, 2009). The new ministry will cost an estimated R135 million a year for taxpayers. The Minister for Provincial and Local Government, Sydney Mufamadi introduced the proposal. Mufamadi's spokesman explained the new ministry is "about the work they do in communities

around improving service delivery and working together with local government in achieving that goal." It is not clear if the new ministry will be replicated in each of the nine provinces.

19. Karen MacGregor, "Shocking results from university tests," *University World News*, issue 0035 (August 16, 2009). The National Benchmark Tests Project was commissioned in 2005 by HESA. The objectives were to gauge entry-level literacy and math proficiency of students, to explore the relationship between university entry requirements and school outcomes, to assist in curriculum development, and to provide information which would help universities place students. More 13,000 students from the universities of Cape Town, KwaZulu Natal, Rhodes, Stellenbosch and the Witwatersrand, and Mangosuthu University of Technology in commerce, education, engineering, the health sciences, humanities, law, and science took the test.
20. The World Bank: Data: Prevalence of HIV, total (% of population ages 15–49), http://data.worldbank.org/indicator/SH.DYN.AIDS.ZS (accessed July 29, 2016).
21. AFROBAROMETER, *Summary of Results, Round 4 Afrobarometer Survey in South Africa* (Cape Town, South Africa: Afrobarometer, December 2008), 4.
22. AFROBAROMETER, *Summary of Results, Round 6 Afrobarometer Survey in South Africa* (Cape Town, South Africa: Afrobarometer, April 2016), 2.
23. Eynon, "Interpreting the Economic Growth and Development Policies0f Post-Apartheid South Africa: Its Influence on Higher Education and Prospects for Women," 68.
24. Julian Kunnie, *Is Apartheid Really Dead? Why Apartheid Changed Its Character in 1990* (Oxford, UK: Westview Press, 2000), 77.
25. John Weeks, "Stuck in Low GEAR? Macroeconomic Policy in South Africa, 1996–98," *Cambridge Journal of Economics*, 23 (1999), 795–811.
26. Sehoole, *Democratizing Higher Education Policy: Constraints of Reform in Post-apartheid South Africa*, 81.
27. African National Congress (ANC), *RDP White Paper*, http://www.anc.org.za/ancdocs/policy/white.htm (accessed November 21, 2009).
28. Ibid., 6.
29. The RDP White Paper is the document which sets out strategies for the implementation of RDP by establishing a policy-making methodology and outlines the government's implementation framework. However, when presented in September 1994 it had not been adopted by Parliament in order to allow further discussion and debate provided by the Base Document.
30. Republic of South Africa, *A Basic Guide to the Reconstruction and Development Program*, http://www.anc.org.za/ancdocs/policy/short.htm (accessed January 12, 2009).

31. Claude Kabemba and Tobias Schmitz, *Understanding Policy Implementation: An Exploration of Research Areas Surrounding the Reconstruction and Development Programme,* Centre for Policy Studies, Johannesburg, South Africa, research report number 73 (2001), 16.
32. Gerald Meier and James Rauch, *Leading Issues in Economic Development, 8th Edition* (New York and Oxford: Oxford University Press, 2005), 76.
33. George Mavrotas and Anthony Shorrocks, eds., *Advancing Development: Core Themes in Global Economics* (New York: Palgrave Macmillan, 2005), 235–240.
34. The 30 member countries of OECD are Australia, Austria, Belgium, Canada, Czech Republic, Denmark, Finland, France, Germany, Greece, Hungary, Iceland, Ireland, Italy, Japan, Korea, Luxembourg, Mexico, the Netherlands, New Zealand, Norway, Poland, Portugal, Slovak Republic, Spain, Sweden, Switzerland, Turkey, the United Kingdom, and the United States.
35. Mavrotas and Shorrocks, 235–240, and Omano Edigheji, "Globalization and the Paradox of Participatory Governance in South Africa: The Case of the New South Africa," *African Journal of International Affairs* 7, no. 1& 2, 1–20 (2004).
36. African National Congress, "The State and Social Transformation," discussion document (1996), http://www.anc.org.za/ancdocs/policy/s&st.html (accessed October 22, 2009).
37. Ibid.
38. Alan Hirsch, *Season of Hope: Economic Reform Under Mandela and Mbeki* (Scottsville, South Africa: University of KwaZula-Natal Press, 2005), 25. Omano Edigheji, *The Emerging South African Democratic Development State and the People's Contract,* Center for Policy Studies, Research Report 108, Johannesburg, South Africa, 2007, 10.
39. Republic of South Africa, *Growth, Employment and Redistribution: A Macroeconomic Strategy*, www.treasury.gov.za/publications/other/gear/chapters.pdf, 4.
40. Sehoole, *Democratizing Higher Education Policy: Constraints of Reform in Post-apartheid South Africa,* 82.
41. Edigheji, *The Emerging South African Democratic Development State and the People's Contract*,, 11. Silvia Federici, George Caffentzis, and Ousseina Alidous, *A Thousand Flowers: Social Struggles Against Structural Adjustment in African Universities* (Trenton, NJ: Africa World Press, 2000), 12. Antoinette Handley, "Business, Government and Economic Policymaking in the New South Africa, 1990–2000. *Journal of Modern African Studies* 43, no. 2 (2005).
42. COSATU. "Creating Jobs in South Africa: Key Issues and Strategies," April 1999, http://www.cosatu.org.za/docs (accessed April 9, 2009).

43. Edigheji, *The Emerging South African Democratic Development State and the People's Contract*, 13.
44. Organization of Economic Co-Operation and Development (OECD), *Reviews of National Policies for Education: South Africa* (Paris, France, 2008), 19–23.
45. Sehoole, *Democratizing Higher Education Policy: Constraints of Reform in Post-apartheid South Africa*, 13–24.
46. OECD, *Reviews of National Policies for Education: South Africa*, 40.
47. OECD, 320.
48. Republic of South Africa, National Plan for Higher Education in South Africa, 2001, http://www.education.gov.za/Documents/policies/NationalPlanHE2001.pdf (accessed February 18, 2009).
49. Council on Higher Education, *South Africa Higher Education in the First Decade of Democracy*, The Council on Higher Education (CHE) Pretoria, South Africa (2004). The current institutional structure of public South African higher education includes eight separate and incorporated universities (University of Cape Town, University of Fort Hare plus Rhodes University East London Campus; University of Free State plus Vista University and University of the North Qwa-Qwa; University of Pretoria plus Vista University Mamelodi; Rhodes University; University of Stellenbosch; University of the Western Cape plus University of Stellenbosch Dental School; and University of Witwatersrand); three merged universities (University of Durban-Westville plus University of Natal—now the University of Kwazulu-Natal; The University of the North plus Medical University of South Africa—now the University of Limpopo; Potchefstroom University of Christian HE plus University of the North-West plus Vista University—now the North-West University); two separate and incorporated universities of technology, or technikons (Technikon Free State plus Vista University Welkom—now Central University of Technology; Vaal Triangle Technikon plus Vista University and infrastructure and facilities of Sebokeng—now Vaal University of Technology); three merged universities of technology (Cape Technikon plus Peninsula Technikon—now Cape Peninsula University, Mangosuthu Technikon plus infrastructure and facilities of the Umlazi campus of the University of Zululand—now Durban Institute of Technology, Technikon Pretoria plus Technikon Northern Gauteng plus Technikon North-West—now Tshwane University of Technology); two separate comprehensives (University of Venda—now University of Venda for Science and Technology; University of Zululand); four merged comprehensives (Rand Afrikaans University plus Technikon Witwatersrand plus Vista University East Rand and Soweto—now University of Johannesburg; University of Port Elizabeth plus Port Elizabeth Technikon plus Vista University Port

Elizabeth—now Nelson Mandela Metropolitan University; Technikon South Africa plus Vista University Distance Education Centre—now University of South Africa; University of Transkei plus Border Technikon plus Eastern Cape Technikon—now Walter Sisulu University of Technology and Science); and two national institutes (Mpumalanga Institute of Higher Education; Northern Cape Institute for Higher Education).

50. The World Bank: Data: Proportion of seats held by women in national parliament (%), http://data.worldbank.org/indicator/SG.GEN.PARL.ZS?locations=ZA (accessed July 29, 2016).
51. World Economic Forum, Which countries have the most women in parliament? https://www.weforum.org/agenda/2015/09/countries-most-women-in-parliament/ (accessed July 29, 2016).
52. SANGONet Pulse, *South Africa Misses The Mark on Women in Politics*, May 28, 2014, http://www.ngopulse.org/article/south-africa-misses-mark-women-politics (accessed July 29, 2016).
53. Michael H. Allen, *Globalization, Negotiation, and the Failure of Transformation in South Africa: Revolution at a Bargain?* (New York: Palgrave Macmillan, 2006), 142.
54. Office on the Status of Women, *South Africa's National Policy Framework for Women's Empowerment and Gender Equality* (Pretoria, South Africa: South Africa Government, 2000), 4.
55. Reitumetse Mabokela and Kaluke Mawila, "The Impact of Race, Gender and Culture in South African Higher Education," *Comparative Education Review* 48, no.4 (2004), 396.
56. Office on the Status of Women, 10.
57. Ibid., 27.
58. Ibid., 28.
59. Ibid., 34.
60. Gisela Geisler, *Women and the Remaking of Politics in South Africa* (Uppsala, Sweden: Nordiska Afrikainstitutet, 2004), 37.
61. Pregs Govender, *Love and Courage: A Story of Insubordination* (Auckland Park, South Africa: Jacana Media Ltd., 2007), 157.
62. Office on the Status of Women, 37.
63. Program on Action on Women's Empowerment and Gender Equality, *Report on National Gender Machinery* (Pretoria, South Africa, 2005).
64. Matuma Letsoalo, "Fresh Crisis at Gender Commission," *Mail & Guardian Online*, April 24, 2008, www.mg.co.za (accessed November 17, 2009).
65. Rozenda Hendrickse, *Reshaping Power South Africa's Gender Machinery Reviewed*, Paper prepared for presentation at the International Political Science Association 22nd World Congress of Political Science: Reshaping Power, Shifting Boundaries Universidad Complutense de Madrid, Madrid, Spain, July 12, 2012, 10.

66. Amina Mama, "Feminism or Femocracy? State Feminism and Democratisation in Nigeria," *Africa Development* 20, no. 1 (1995), 37–58.
67. Eynon, "Interpreting the Economic Growth and Development PoliciesOf Post-Apartheid South Africa: Its Influence on Higher Education and Prospects for Women," 95.
68. Ibid., 94.
69. Ibid.
70. Assie-Lumumba, 145.

CHAPTER 5

Two Decades of Economic Growth and Development Policies

Given the significant economic and social demands on the new South African government in 1994, its leaders went through a process of prioritizing those demands, creating strategies to address them, and then seeking ways to finance them with the available resources. They struggled with difficult fiscal policy questions, such as how to pay down the debt inherited from the apartheid government, how to reduce the budget deficit, and how much to borrow to finance development. The answers would determine what resources would be available for social-service spending on health care, housing, education, sanitation, electricity, and water.

The new government was also facing the challenge of how to move the country onto the global world stage and accelerate economic development. It wanted to accomplish that while maintaining its independence—and not go the way of many Latin American countries, which essentially gave up their sovereignty to institutions like the IMF. The IMF frequently imposed austerity policies that required countries to implement belt-tightening measures at the expense of spending on social services—an approach the new South African government wanted to avoid given the huge social service needs of its people. Yet, at the same time, it did not want to forfeit the opportunities that foreign investment might provide or the chance to create sustained economic growth, which the country had not seen since the boom years of the 1960s.

© The Author(s) 2017

D.E. Eynon, *Women, Economic Development, and Higher Education*,
DOI 10.1007/978-3-319-53144-1_5

The ANC also realized that it could not rebuild an economy strictly on the basis of social welfare but had to try to bring poor people into the formal economy by redistributing wealth that would only come through economic growth. The government understood it was being more pragmatic than it had originally intended, yet it moved forward despite opposition and criticism from grass-root organizations, the Congress of South African Trade Unions (COSATU), and others.[1]

There are many reasons to believe that the ANC's decision to take a fiscally conservative, market-based approach to growth and development was the right decision for the time. Essentially the GEAR policy was investor friendly. It provided a sense of security for people who may have otherwise taken their money out of the country, encouraged those who had previously removed their money to reinvest, drew new investors to South Africa, and helped to develop the middle and upper classes that are thriving today.[2]

The focus at the time was to concentrate on capacity building that would allow the country to meet the demands of competing in the global economy. According to the architects of GEAR, that strategy would allow for a growth rate of 6 percent per year and create 400,000 jobs annually by 2000.[3] Although those goals were never achieved, the policy did result in increased financial reserves for infrastructure development, housing, education, and health.[4] By the end of 2000, the deficit, inflation, and consumption performance measures had improved, coming close to reaching the targets set forth under GEAR, as did the management of public funds. In addition, expenditures by the government decreased significantly due to its effective restructuring at all levels.

Yet while GEAR brought about greater macroeconomic stability, predictability, and the confidence of financial markets, it did little to resolve the major social problems afflicting the South African people—such as poverty, unemployment, and the widening gap between the rich and poor. [5]As a result, a social movement emerged in South Africa—made up largely of farm workers, shack dwellers, job seekers, and domestic workers—to campaign around the "bread and butter" issues like health and education that most affected people's daily lives. Police statistics from 1997 to 2009 show that on average, 8,000 protests occurred each year in South Africa, making it the nation with the highest number of protests, on a per-person basis, in the world. And in April 2009, *The Economist* magazine identified South Africa as the riskiest emerging market to do business in, given the number of labor strikes and protest against delivery services, which resulted in an inability of the government to provide even basic services.[6]

Meanwhile, grassroots organizations and COSATU continued to pressure the government to make economic policy changes. The 2007 resignation of President Thabo Mbeki, an advocate of GEAR, a year before the next presidential election was considered a signal from left-wing members of the ruling party who were anti-GEAR that economic policy needed to change. And that is what occurred when Jacob Zuma won the presidential election in 2009, becoming the third elected president in the post-apartheid era.

What follows is a deeper examination of the effectiveness of post-apartheid macroeconomic policies—from 1994 until recently—in meeting the economic targets set by those policies. This chapter will also consider what challenges remain and the implications for the future—particularly for young South Africans, or the "Born Frees."

1996–2005: Growth, Employment, and Redistribution: A Tale of Two Economies

Over the first decade after the new government came to power, a shift began to take place that still continues today: South Africa moved from a society defined by race to one defined by class.[7] That shift is a story of social mobility and the emergence of a black middle class in South Africa. Its seeds were sown when the GEAR policy became the basis for the macroeconomic strategy of the country. How did that occur, and how successful was it? Where did it meet the needs of the South African nation and its people, and where did it fall short?

GEAR set performance targets for the national economy that were to be achieved by 2000. As noted in Chapter 2, the results were mixed. The results of the GEAR strategy came close to established goals: it helped shrink the fiscal debt to 2.2 percent, reduce government consumption to 18 percent, and lower inflation to 5.4 percent.[8] But South Africa continued to have persistent problems with unemployment, poverty, and income disparity. While the average South African grew wealthier, distribution was uneven, and the gap between rich and poor continued to grow.

In 2000, the poorest 20 percent of households received a miniscule 1.6 percent of total national income, a smaller percentage than in 1995.[9] By 2006, the official unemployment rate was 25.5 percent, with rates much higher in the poorer provinces of Eastern Cape and Limpopo. And within those provinces, the numbers were even higher for blacks (30.5 percent) and black women (36.4 percent) in particular. Poverty was pervasive, with 61 percent of blacks classified as poor, compared to 38 percent of coloreds, 5 percent of Indians, and 1 percent of whites. About 45 percent of the population lived in rural areas where the poverty level was particularly high and people lacked basic amenities like water, sanitation, and electricity, as well as formal schooling. Those persistent problems presented the greatest challenge for the country, its citizens, and its future.

Like other governments that have adopted neo-liberal economic policies, the ANC-led South African government believed redistribution would follow economic growth. And, indeed, money did start to flow back into the country, and a new wave of economic growth and development did benefit the middle and upper classes in South Africa. The hope was that, with that growth, the government could begin to invest financial reserves into housing, education, health, and so on, and that resources would trickle down to the less fortunate in the society. But therein lies the problem for South Africa: the trickle needed to be large enough to redistribute wealth to the majority of the population, and that required extraordinary economic growth, resources, and capabilities.[10]

Criticism and debate about the macroeconomic decisions that the ANC made in 1994 and have continued to this day. For some people, the decision to abandon the RDP and adopt the economic principles promulgated in GEAR was a missed opportunity. Many South Africans, not just Communist Party or trade union members, sensed that, in 1994, the ANC and the country had had a wonderful opportunity to create a social democracy on the model of Scandinavia, where free-market capitalism and a large welfare state coexist.[11]

As was, although the rhetoric of South Africa's government, politicians and academic leaders was that of liberation, equity, and equality, they unfortunately did not deliver on those goals. By the early 2000s, not only were there high levels of unemployment, a huge disparity between rich and poor, and pervasive poverty but also corruption was creeping into the system due to increasing nepotism. In fact, the National Directorate of Public Prosecutions investigated and prosecuted top-level figures in the ANC, such as Schabir Shaik.[12] Observed Martin Hall, emeritus professor and former deputy vice chancellor at the University of Cape Town, "It is as though the government has become more focused on how to perpetuate government power for its own sake than how to use this power for transformational change."[13] Legislatively, the country looked quite democratic—but not for working class and poor, who were gaining little.[14] COSATU issued a policy statement in July 2001, noting:

> In contrast to this political progress, in socioeconomic terms the legacy of apartheid remains entrenched and, with the massive loss of jobs in the past decade, even appears to be worsening. Wealth is still concentrated in a white minority. The nature of capital remains largely the same—concentrated in the mining-finance complex—which continues to dominate the commanding heights of the South African economy. Serious inequalities persist, with signs of worsening particularly among the formerly oppressed. The number of people living in poverty is staggering. Almost half the population lives in poverty, including many of the employed—the working poor. Unemployment and underemployment are on the rise as more jobs are shed and people rely on survivalist activities to make ends meet.[15]

That reality was creating difficulties for the government. Many South Africans had been patient and supportive, believing that the ANC would and could deliver on its promise of transformational change where the majority would no longer be the economic, social, or political minority. People were willing to give the government time as long as they thought their children would be better off. But as the chance of achieving the promise began to fade, people became increasingly frustrated.

That frustration and disillusionment was evident in the 2009 election when, for the first time, a splinter group, the Congress of the People (COPE), emerged from the ANC to compete against it in the election.[16] South Africans began to question what the ANC had accomplished for them, as more people than ever before experienced decreases in their quality of life and became so poor that they were eligible for government social grants.

In rural areas, economic activity had actually decreased since 1994; the only bright side was that social policy payouts had grown.[17] Observed Thomas Koelble, a professor in the Graduate School of Business at the UCT:

> When you drive through Zambia or Malawi, you see people trading on the street corners all along the trade routes. But when you drive through the Eastern Cape, you see little economic activity at all. Those are not good signs![18]

The high unemployment rate in 2006 of 25.5 percent had remained relatively stable over the following three years.[19] But stability did not indicate a turning tide—instead, the number of people who were actively looking for a job had decreased significantly. For example, the number of people who did not actively look for employment in the month of July 2009 increased by 302,000, bringing the total to 1.52 million people. The unemployment rate remained steady because those "discouraged workers" had simply stopped looking for jobs and reduced the number of people registered as unemployed.[20]

Who were those unemployed? Fully 70 percent were under the age of 35, and many had not ever held a job before. The fact that a significant number people in the country between the ages of 18 and 35 had never been employed—individuals who were in the prime of their lives and peak years of productivity—was an economic and social time bomb. [21] In most countries, 60 percent of working-age people work, but in South Africa only 40 percent were working in 2009.

Unfortunately, job creation in South Africa continued to be a major economic challenge over the years, despite the end of apartheid. In 1994, the government initially set an annual target of 2.9 percent job growth in the formal sector. Between 1995 and 2003, the actual rate was 2.5 percent, but only if jobs in the informal sector were counted.[22]

Moreover, a big part of the problem in South Africa was the mismatch between the supply of labor, which was—and still is—mainly unskilled, and the demand for skilled labor. It is one thing for a worker to lack skills in a particular industry, but many South Africans could not find jobs because they simply couldn't read or write at a level necessary to perform basic tasks and function properly in the workplace. And for those who found employment despite those limitations, wages were often so low that it wasn't worth their while to go to work.[23]

In addition, an estimated 300,000 jobs remained unfilled due to the shortage of skilled workers in specific sectors: engineering, information, communication, technology, and, to some extent, the financial industry. While 27 million people were unemployed due to lack of jobs, large corporations were at the same time complaining of a shortage of skills and a brain drain because people with those skills and knowledge were leaving the country—partly because many young university graduates were being recruited away by global companies.[24] Without enough skilled workers, companies were not going to set up shop, and certain industries could not prosper.

That, in turn, also meant that the government, but mainly the private sector, had to seek those skills from outside the country's borders.[25] It also had an influence on the rate of foreign investment in the country, which limited growth.[26]

Moreover, while the shortage of skilled labor certainly contributed to unemployment and difficulty in creating jobs in the formal sector, the reality was there were just not enough jobs for the millions of unemployed in the country—even if each one of them were skilled.[27] Given that reality, a new attitude took hold in the government in the early 2000s when it came to the unemployable people in the country. According to Crain Soudien, the acting vice chancellor at the UCT:

> The basic approach, by the government, and I've heard them say so, is that this large reserve of unemployable people in the country, you can do nothing about. They're so under-skilled, and it will take so much investment to be able to turn that situation around, that the best the country can to do is to provide reasonable safe nets for them. And it's a kind of patronizing policy, which effectively, in some ways, condemns the poor, and that's a problem.[28]

In essence, two economies were operating in the country: one that was globalized, industrialized, and modern, and another where people lived on the margins with little skills and no full-time employment.[29] Thus, the country hit an impasse economically and socially. Industry could not expand because it lacked demand for orders; demand for orders was low because, without skilled labor, industry lacked the capacity to fill them.

Yet, at the same time, the country had huge numbers of chronically unemployed workers, as the government continued to struggle with how to move those workers into the skilled category. Critics of the market economy would bring up this problem as evidence that it was time for the government to use industrial engineering, in the same way that the Soviet Union, Korea, and China have utilized social and economic engineering.[30]

Affirmative Action and Its Aftermath

Unemployment and the difficult economic circumstances reflected and reinforced the long-entrenched, gaping inequities between black and white, rural and urban, and male and female South African workers. In

1998, the ANC-led government passed the Employment Equity Act (EEA), the first labor legislation to promote employment equity and affirmative action at the workplace. The objective of the legislation was to "achieve equity in the workplace by promoting equal opportunity and fair treatment in employment through the elimination of unfair discrimination and to implement affirmative action measures to redress the disadvantages in employment experienced by designated groups and to ensure equitable representation in all occupational categories and levels in the workforce." [31] Under the act, "designated groups" consisted of blacks, colored, and Indians who were citizens of the country before April 1994 or who had been prohibited from becoming citizens due to apartheid laws and policies. The government recognized that affirmative action was needed to give people equal access to employment and the opportunity to fulfill their potential.

The act did not include quotas but allowed for preferential treatment in the recruitment, selection, and promotion of previously disadvantaged groups of people. It affected: (1) employers with 50 or more employees, (2) employers with 50 or fewer employees with a turnover rate higher than specified in the act, (3) municipalities, and (4) government organizations. It required them to eliminate policies or practices that "unfairly discriminate" (not defined in the act) based on race, gender, sex, pregnancy, marital status, family responsibility, ethnic or social origin, color, sexual orientation, age, disability, religion, HIV status, conscience, belief, political opinion, culture, language, and birth or any other arbitrary ground.[32]

While affirmative action was successful in creating a public sector workforce that better represented the overall population, it also created challenges. During the apartheid years, white Afrikaners working in small municipalities dominated a large and thriving civil service. After the passage of affirmative action legislation, black staff members replaced many of those civil servants, but they were not trained to run systems or departments. Thus, the employment of members of underrepresented groups in the civil service grew over the years, but many new hires lacked the skill level necessary to effectively perform their jobs.[33]

That created high levels of dissatisfaction with the delivery of government services, resulting in social problems and civil unrest.[34] Nadine Petersen, a professor of education at the University of Johannesburg in 2009, commented:

> Our civil service is imploding. It's about the ability to deliver. You've had people put in positions on a quick basis to get them jobs, to get the right people in with the right kind of faces into these positions, but they're not able to deliver. Those are systemic issues.[35]

People disagreed as to when affirmative action should end. South Africans increasingly expressed frustration with the system as they felt black people were getting all the top jobs but were being pushed through with no merits.[36] Other concerns were that affirmative action wasn't helping the majority of black South Africans—just a small portion—and thus creating a culture of entitlement. South Africans who originally supported affirmative action but believed it had run its course were among those critics.[37] Harold Herman, an emeritus professor of comparative and international education at the University of Western Cape, noted in 2009:

> I know a lot about affirmative action. I've taught it, and I have supported it. But, I have spoken persistently at graduations and elsewhere about the culture of entitlement that is now happening in this country. It's become a big problem. The people who are benefiting from it are the upper middle class and the bourgeoisie. The people who are *not* benefiting from it are the working class.[38]

The fear among many South Africans was that the continuation of affirmative action would lead to a complete culture of entitlement based on race. However, most people thought that affirmative action should be continued among black rural women, who remained underrepresented in all areas of employment.[39] And while some government officials, academics, business leaders, and leaders of NGOs believed a number of the affirmative action policies would be dropped within the next five years, the Employment Equity Amendment Act of 2013, signed by the President Zuma in January 2014 and effective in August 2014, actually strengthened such policies. The following are key amendments to the act:

- Expands the meaning of "unfair discrimination" based on gender, race, religion, sexual orientation etc. by including the language "on any other arbitrary grounds."
- Requires employer to demonstrate that differences in wages or employment conditions for the same work or work of equal value are based on fair criteria—for example, skill and experience.

- Limits the use of psychometric tests by employers to only those certified by the Health Professionals Council of South Africa or any organization authorized to certify the tests.
- Allows employees to take unresolved disputes to the Commission for Conciliation, Mediation, and Arbitration (CCMA) under these conditions: sexual harassment, when an employee earns less than the threshold prescribed under section 6(3) of the Basic Conditions of Employment Act, No. 75 of 1997 (BCEA), or when all parties involved in the dispute agree to go to arbitration. It also allows for repeal of an arbitrator's decision to the Labor Court. Prior to the amendment all disputes were filed with the Labor Court.
- Includes a scenario where burden of proof rests with the employee. Prior to the amendment, regardless of dispute, the burden of proof was with the employer. Under the amendment, the burden of proof remains with the employer if the discrimination dispute is based on race, gender, sexual orientation, and the like. However, if the discrimination dispute is based on arbitrary grounds, the proof of burden is with the employee.
- Increases the maximum fines and allows the Minister of Labor to adjust fines to offset the effects of inflation without approval from the Minister of Justice.[40]

Broad-Based Black Economic Empowerment

The second major piece of legislation to address employment inequities was the Broad-Based Black Economic Empowerment (B-BEE) Act of 2003, created to encourage the voluntary transfer and redistribution of assets dominated by white-minority investors to black investors and the promotion of black participation in business management and operations. An integral part of the legislation was the measurement of a company's progress in providing black South African's empowerment in four areas: (1) direct empowerment through ownership and control of an enterprise and its assets, (2) management at the senior level, (3) human resources development and employment equity, and (4) indirect empowerment through preferential procurement, enterprise development, and corporate social investment. The legislation required all government bodies and public companies to abide by and apply these codes of good practice to win government contracts.[41] It called for white-owned and managed firms to turn management and ownership over to black businessmen and for the new black capitalists to pay market price for their acquisitions. Many companies believed if they didn't comply, it would only be a matter of time before the government would nationalize them. The goal of B-BEE was to have 25 percent black ownership of South African companies by 2014.

In the early years of its implementation, it appeared that B-BEE might even exceed that goal. In 2006, the value of B-BEE deals totaled 56 billion rand, and by 2007, it had jumped to 96 billion. At that rate, some experts predicted that more than half, or 52 percent, of South African privately held businesses would change ownership by 2016.[42]

Similar advances occurred at the board of director level. In 1992, only 14 (1.2 percent) of the directors of the top 100 Johannesburg Stock Exchange companies were black; that number had increased to 156 black directors (13 percent) by a decade later, in 2002. After the passage of B-BEE in 2003, 432 black directors served on all 472 companies listed on the Johannesburg Stock Exchange, and the following year, 435 did, representing 16.6 percent of the total.[43]

In 2015, the officials in charge of B-BEE extended its mandates to include subcontractors and small and medium enterprises (SMEs), as well as increased its oversight and sanctions for noncomplying organizations. In recent years, there has also been a movement toward providing more direct support to black entrepreneurs in the form of assistance with business plans and subsidized access to finance and management training programs—allowing more blacks to create, manage, and control businesses and organizations.[44]

The jury is still out, however, as to whether the B-BEE has been a success. The government wanted to engineer a more representative role for the black majority under the program. Yet polls have shown that most South Africans have viewed it as benefitting only a small portion of the population: a handful of politically connected black tycoons who have made fortunes at companies who were obliged to conduct "equity sales."[45] The criticism of the program has been—and continues to be—that the only beneficiaries have been the senior members of the ANC.[46]

The following story provides an example of how many people regard the B-BEE program. In June 2009, First Rand Bank, the nation's second largest financial services group, announced the appointment of Sizwe Nxasana as the bank's next chief executive. He is the first black chief executive of the bank. But analysts raised concerns about the appointment, saying the decision to appoint Nxasana was influenced by politics, considering he joined the group less than four years previously and had no hands-on banking experience.[47]

B-BEE policies were created to reduce inequalities and encourage and support black entrepreneurship, which was restricted during apartheid. The policies were also designed to incentivize organizations, via a point system, to increase and include throughout the operations of an organization—management, leadership, and ownership—people who had been historically disadvantaged. Yet while government leaders created the affirmative action and B-BEE policies to correct gross inequities in employment and business opportunities, people have increasingly criticized those policies, saying that they benefit just a few South Africans—those who are politically well-connected—and create a culture of entitlement. The debate and predictions about the future of such policies will continue, as the impact of the current revisions to the B-BEE legislation, yet unknown, play out over time.

2005–2010: The Accelerated and Shared Growth Initiative of South Africa

In 2005, in response to prolonged poverty, unemployment, jobless growth, low earnings, and a shortage of skilled workers, the South African government introduced the Accelerated and Shared Growth Initiative of South Africa (ASGISA) and the Joint Initiative on Priority Skills Acquisition (JIPSA). It launched ASGISA as a complementary economic plan to GEAR, with the objective to halve poverty by 2010 and unemployment by 2014 through accelerated growth of 4.5 percent or higher through 2009 and at least 6 percent from 2010 through 2014.[48] In ways, ASGISA brought economic policy back to the basic tenets established under the 1994 RDP: that the government should not only spur economic growth through opening up the domestic market and increasing the efficiency of the economy, but it should also create, steer, and fund economic policies that would improve the quality of life for the poor and reduce inequalities through a redistributive process.[49] ASGISA identified six constraints that were blocking accelerated growth, one of which was the shortage of key skills, and called for the development of a separate initiative to address that specific problem.

Three months later, the government also introduced the JIPSA and identified five high-priority skills: (1) engineering; (2) city, urban, and regional planning and management skills; (3) artisan and technical skills; (4) management and planning skills in health and education; and (5) mathematics, science, and language competence in public schooling.[50]

ASGISA and JIPSA focused specifically on the skills in science, technology, engineering, math—or the STEM fields—that were and remain a major blockage to economic growth and job creation. The two initiatives were an attempt to bring direct funding to the development of those skills, in alignment with specific sectors of the economy.[51]

In the end, JIPSA was a massive state infrastructure project that failed to achieve its objectives, especially given that it fell short in the training and development of the less technically oriented jobs that were in drastic shortage in the country, such as boilermakers, fitters, and turners. Jenni Case, associate professor of chemical engineering and former director of undergraduate studies at the UCT, expressed her frustration with the program: "I heard people saying the other day that JIPSA was a damn screw-up that never went anywhere. It's easy to write big amounts of money for infrastructure to get people training, but it's not enough. In a sense, the state has failed."[52]

Many people believed the initiatives were unsuccessful because they were initiated about two years before the end of President Thabo Mbeki's term, when the economic and political environment began to shift and the focus turned to developing new economic strategies related to education, health, and safety.[53]

By 2008, many South Africans viewed GEAR and the ancillary economic policies and programs related to it, such as ASGISA and JIPSA, as roadblocks to employment opportunities, social services, and a better way of life that were all promised in 1994 with the advent of a new South Africa. The fundamental challenge continued: how to maintain strong conditions for economic growth and development while improving the social and economic well-being of a significant majority of the population.

2010: A New Path Toward Growth

When Thabo Mbeki was ousted as president of South Africa in September 2008, some economist and investors worried that the new government would change the country's economic policies at a time when they thought continuity was required to keep the nation on track toward meeting its economic and social goals. Jabu Moleketi, the deputy finance minister at the time of Mbeki's ouster, was quoted as saying, "In this current environment, to talk about fundamental change of economic policy is suicidal."[54]

However, many other people in the working class, trade unions, and Communist Party expected the government to revise the policies adopted under GEAR, especially given that Jacob Zuma, the recently elected president, had relied heavily on the COSATU and SACP during his presidential campaign.[55] COSATU was becoming vocal in its demands that Zuma enact more populist economic policies. The unions and the unemployed, 23.5 percent of the population at the time, expected Zuma to turn things around and finally create needed jobs. Their expectations were understandable, as Zuma had made job creation the cornerstone of his campaign.

As poverty, unemployment, and housing shortages increased, and the gap between the rich and poor widened, COSATU, SACP, and other South African citizens continued to pressure the government to re-evaluate the nation's macroeconomic policies.[56] Polls and surveys revealed South Africans' growing dissatisfaction with the economic direction of the country, and people began increasingly expressing their concerns and demands through demonstrations, strikes, and open criticism of the government.[57]

Thus Zuma's challenge was to balance the interests of the unions that helped him get elected with those of foreign investors who were worried he would move the country politically and economically to the left. In May 2009, just a few weeks after the election, Matthew Phosa, the ANC treasurer, was in London meeting with foreign investors to discuss the newly elected government's intentions for the country. Phosa told those in attendance that President Zuma intended to keep his campaign promises to make social and institutional changes that would tackle poverty, unemployment, and economic inequalities—but that he would also keep spending within the country's means. He went on to say the government would not "lurch to the left" to please trade unions or the Communist Party.[58]

Yet the problem was that the new government still did not appear to have a strategic, comprehensive, or coordinated plan to address the country's persistent problems related to unemployment and poverty, as well as the lack of housing, health care, and education for the majority of South Africans.[59] Instead, it seemed as if the government would continue to propose, drive, and support ad hoc individual policies, initiatives, and projects, and that it would shift its focus primarily toward improving service delivery. That said, although Zuma's approach at the moment did, in fact, seem to concentrate on service delivery, the broader goal was to give people a sense of ownership of the social space they found themselves in.[60] According to ANC Treasurer Phosa:

> Our view is that we have beautiful policies. There is cash. But the skill level in the public service is very low. If you have no project managers to implement policy you will not deliver. The government will lay off lazy officials and strive to improve civil services training and performance.[61]

Then, in May 2009, following a major recession in the United States and elsewhere around the globe, South Africa announced it was also officially in a recession—for the first time in 17 years. The economic data were not good: GDP fell by 6.4 percent, manufacturing by 22 percent, and mining by 33 percent. Construction was the only sector to show improvement, which was not surprising since the country was preparing for the 2010 World Cup.[62] Job losses were also severe: employment dropped by a million jobs from the end of 2008 to the middle of 2010.[63]

It should be noted, however, that even though the recession deeply impacted South Africa, many people believed the fiscally conservative policies that the previous administration had adopted allowed the country to weather the global economic downturn better than other countries. During that downturn, they recognized that some good work had been put into the development and management of the country's economic growth and development policies. [64]

Within a month after the formal declaration that South Africa was in recession, President Jacob Zuma unveiled at his inaugural State of the Nation Address on June 3 a new economic framework for the country, "The New Growth Path." Referring to it in that speech, he said: "The creation of decent work will be at the centre of our economic policies and will influence our investment attraction and job creation initiatives. In line with our undertakings, we have to forge ahead to promote a more inclusive economy."[65]

The framework identified the key jobs (agro-processing, mining, tourism, and business services) and priority sectors (capital equipment for construction and mining, metallurgy, heavy chemicals, pharmaceuticals, software, green technologies, and biotechnology) on which the government would concentrate its efforts over the next few years. It targeted infrastructure development, particularly in rural areas, and regional integration as key strategies in the creation of new jobs.[66]

Zuma pledged to create 500,000 jobs by the end of the year and set out plans to add a total of 14 million jobs by 2014, offering hope to "young people, the rural poor, and women." Yet many economists were skeptical that the economy had the strength to create 500,000 jobs within six months, let alone millions within just five years.[67]

In May 2010, President Zuma appointed an advisory National Planning Commission composed of 26 members who were selected from outside government and were considered experts in their various areas. He tasked the commission to draft a National Development Plan (NDP) that would include an assessment of South Africa's achievements and challenges since 1994 and, from those findings, recommend future priority areas. The commission presented its "Diagnostic Report" in June 2011, in which it identified nine primary challenges, including public health, public services, education, infrastructure, corruption, unemployment, overreliance on natural resources in the economy, continued concentration of the poor within areas of the country, and a deeply divided country.[68]

After extensive review and a period for public comment, four additional areas were added to the original nine. They included a "focus on the rural economy, social protection, regional/world affairs, and community safety." [69] President Zuma, his cabinet, and the ruling party approved the plan following further public review and comment, and in December 2012, during his State of the Nation Address, Zuma introduced his new plan.

2013: The National Development Plan

The key objectives of the NDP were to eradicate poverty and to significantly reduce the inequalities that had only grown since 1994 by achieving more than 5.7 percent growth in GDP and by adding 11 million new jobs by 2030.[70] It was an ambitious plan—one requiring economic reform, coordination across all sectors and government initiatives, the ability of the government and others to implement such policies, and a means to effectively respond to uncertainties in a global economy.

To date, things have not gone as hoped. In 2014, the economy's growth deteriorated to 1.5 percent, down from 3.2 percent in 2011. That slowdown was due in part to falling global commodity prices and China's weakening growth, as it is one of South Africa's largest trading partners and employs over 30,000 South Africans in the 140 companies it owns in the country. However, it also reflected the government's failure to buffer itself against fluctuations in commodity prices (coal, ilmenite, vanadium, chrome, manganese, vermiculite palladium, rutile, and zirconium) during periods of boom and bust.[71] There were also long, costly, and at times violent strikes in the platinum mining sector. Economists estimated that those strikes resulted in a 2 percent decrease in growth in the first quarter of 2014 and slower growth in the third quarter. A lack of new electric capacity and unplanned maintenance, leading to power outages, also caused economic disruptions.[72]

By the end of the first quarter of 2015, the growth rate increased to 1.9 percent while the mining sector began to recover from the strikes, and the financial and business service sectors experienced strong growth. But in the second quarter, things began to deteriorate again, as the effects of a severe drought decimated agricultural production. In fact, South Africa experienced the worst drought in almost 30 years, pushing approximately 50,000 more people into poverty. Not surprisingly, it was low-income South Africans living in rural and farming communities who carried the heaviest burden as a result of the drought and had the largest percentage-point increase in poverty.[73]

Unemployment rates also remained high during this period, hitting 26.4 percent—the highest since 2004—before dropping to 25.5 percent by the third quarter of 2015. As many as 5.4 million people were unemployed, of which 40 percent had been new entrants to the labor force. Despite job losses and high unemployment, however, wage increases continued at a higher rate than inflation.[74]

By October, government leaders acknowledged that growth rates were not at the targeted levels and revised their projections downwards to 1.5 percent in 2015, followed by 1.7 percent in 2016, and 2.6 percent in 2017. However, even those lower targets were overly optimistic, as growth in 2015 was only 1.3 percent, and economists expected that the growth rate would continue to deteriorate to 0.8 percent in 2016 and 1.1 percent in 2017.[75] If such projections hold true, South Africa will make little progress in reducing poverty.

Given those projections and current state of the economy, it will be difficult to meet the targets set forth under the NDP of an annual growth rate of 5.4 percent. The economy would have to grow by an annual rate 7.2 percent after 2017, which seems unlikely.[76] Economists have based those projections on the fact that agriculture will undoubtedly continue to struggle as the implications from the drought continue to play out. In addition, the mining sector anticipates future work disturbances, demand from China will most likely continue to lag, and commodity prices are expected to remain low. Moreover, with new government ministers in charge of the key portfolios of mining and finance, there is uncertainty and weakening investor confidence.

The "Born Frees"

Meanwhile, South Africa has the greatest gap between the rich and poor of any country in the world. [77] Unfortunately, the contrast between the First and Third World in South Africa is particularly marked, and that gap between rich and poor has proved especially difficult to close. Up until a few years ago, teachers at the University of South Africa were still talking about some of the students' assignments coming in with candle wax on them.[78] So on the one hand, some people live a very comfortable lifestyle while, on the other, a significant number of South Africans do without even the most basic amenities.

Today the black middle class represents about 10 percent of the total population of South Africa; its members are often referred to as the "black diamonds" of the country.[79] They are the first generation of black middle class that is providing the foundation for future generations.[80] Only an estimated 2.6 million of South Africa's 39 million blacks, who make up about 80 percent of the total population, earn at least 6,000 rand a month. It may not sound like much, but it is more than half of what other black South Africans make.[81] The way of life for these black middle-class South Africans is worlds apart from the majority of their countrymen and women.

Of great concern is that inequality continues to grow despite government interventions to lessen it. In 1993, the poorest 10 percent of the population held 0.6 percent of total income, while the richest 10 percent accounted for 72.7 percent of it. In 2007, the numbers were 0.6 percent and 72.5 percent, showing a slight improvement, with a Gini coefficient of 66. Today that coefficient stands at 63.4, despite all the government initiatives and programs to close the gap between rich and poor in the nation. The disparity is most worrisome when looking at rural areas, where the inequities are at their most extreme. [82]

Of a total national population of 54 million, about half are children, teenagers, and young adults who were born after 1990—the year in

Nelson Mandela was released from prison. Although 85 percent are Africans, they are often referred to as the "born frees" and seen as the "post-racial generation" in that they look beyond racial boundaries.[83] While a third of the children live in a household where no one is employed, "born frees" increasingly are children born into middle-class homes who are growing up in a richer environment than their parents. However, unemployment rates are higher among younger people, women, and blacks. Among black male "born frees" between the ages of 15 to 24, unemployment is now running at 53 percent and for females that percentage is even greater at 61 percent—which compares to an unemployment rate of just 17 percent for white youth. Not surprisingly, when surveyed, 61 percent of "born frees" cite unemployment as the country's most important issue.[84]

This generation is also facing other challenges:

- Approximately 3 million of the country's 18 million children are orphans;
- Just 40 percent of the boys and 49 percent of girls can expect to live to be 65 years old;
- Antiretroviral drugs are available for only 25 percent of the one million people born with HIV/AIDS;
- Close to a third of the country's prison population is composed of young people between the ages of 14 and 25; and
- Only 30 percent of born frees support the ANC, while 49 percent support the Economic Freedom Fighters (EFF) and 14 percent the Democratic Alliance (DA).[85]

In June 2009, President Zuma stated South Africa must close the gap between rich and poor and address the issue of poverty. He went on to say that ignoring those issues would only lead to serious problems and consequences: "If that happens you are certainly sitting on a situation that will explode one day."[86] Part of the problem for South Africa is the inability of the economy to create jobs with incomes that allow the poor to accumulate wealth. Most of the new jobs have been added in the informal economy and do not even provide enough income to alleviate poverty.[87]

To date, the country has contained social pressures by throwing a wide and deep safety net over the problem. In 1994, the government spent 10 billion rand on social grants for 2.6 million South Africans. By 2003 the government was spending 38.4 billion rand for 6.8 million people.[88]

Today, a quarter of all South Africans are receiving welfare grants.[89] As important as social grants are as a way of ensuring that people have bread on their table, that approach does not address the root problem but instead only increases the number of people on welfare.[90] Social grants do not transform lives nor deal with the basic issue created under the apartheid system: a culture that thought less of certain people and took away their dignity.[91]

And, in fact, policy makers and other experts are increasingly recognizing that social grants will not bring about the fundamental change necessary to move people out of poverty and address the enormous economic disparity in the country. According to the University of Cape Town's Crain Soudien:

> It's that disparity that I think the leadership in this country misunderstands every single day. It doesn't realize how the bottom of the socioeconomic ladder is not something that you can simply in a politely way appease. You can't just say to people, here's a social grant. With this new GEAR policy, if you simply feed this community with those kind of handouts, you're not dealing with the social fears and concerns that this community has inherited from apartheid, which we need to actively turn around, in a whole range of ways.[92]

What apartheid basically did was to alienate a large portion of the population, giving them little sense of investment in the society. That is reflected in a township culture where many people take whatever they can from the local government and feel no obligation to move toward independence; their goal is simply to survive.[93] The challenge in South Africa, as in other parts of the world, is to fully empower people to take charge of their lives and make meaningful contributions—not just rely on the government.[94]

The macroeconomic growth and development strategies of South Africa are closely linked to improvement of the higher education system and to gender equity, as the government considers both to be instrumental to the county's economic and social progress. The government looks to higher education to produce skilled workers who can bring the country into the globalized, knowledge-based economy of the twenty-first century. And it looks to women, who represent half the country's population, to participate in that economy. Chapters 7 to 9 will explore the implications of the government's macroeconomic policies on both the higher education system and the women of South Africa.

Profiles of South African Women

Gil Marcus

Gil Marcus was born in 1949 in Johannesburg, South Africa, one of four children whose parents were antiapartheid activists and members of the South African Communist Party (SACP). While her parents were born in South Africa, her grandparents were Jewish immigrants from Lithuania. In 1969, Gil's parents went into exile in the United Kingdom, taking their children with them. The following year, while in exile, Marcus joined the SACP and the ANC, where she worked in the Department of Information and Publicity and later became the department's deputy secretary when she returned to South Africa. In 1976, she completed her Bachelor of Communications in Industrial Psychology as a correspondence student at the University of South Africa.

When the ban against the ANC was lifted in 1990, Marcus returned home. She established the ANC Department of Information and was elected to the National Executive Committee and the National Working Committee, positions she held until 1999. During that period, she was also elected to Parliament (1994–1998) and served as the chairperson of the Joint Standing Committee on Finance. In 1996, she was appointed Deputy Minister of Finance and, three year later, she became the Deputy Governor of the South African Reserve Bank—the first female to do so.

In 2004, Marcus stepped down as Deputy Governor and joined the Gordon Institute of Business Science as a professor of Policy, Leadership and Gender Studies, where she continues to teach today. In 2007, she became chairman of the Barclay's Africa Group Ltd., a position she held until 2009, and also a nonexecutive director of Gold Fields.

In 2009 President Jacob Zuma announced the appointment of Gil Marcus as Governor of the South African Reserve Bank—again as the first women to do so. She took office when the global financial crisis hit and South Africa was experiencing high inflation and its first recession in almost 20 years. Marcus served in the role until November 2014, at the end of her five-year term. Her tenure as governor has been described as one of stability. The benchmark rate (the minimum interest rate investors will seek for investing in a non-Treasury security) was adjusted only six times compared to 17 times in the previous five years.

After announcing her departure, Marcus shared some thoughts about the future. She said she believes that monetary policy and low interest rates, while important, are not the only answer to economic growth. There must be structural reforms, as well.

Sources:
Mail & Garden, *Marcus to step down as Reserve Bank Gov*ernor, September 18, 2014
http://mg.co.za/article/2014-09-18-marcus-to-step-down-as-reserve-bank-governor (accessed November 16, 2016)
Penwell Dlamini, Monetary policy is not the panacea for SA's growth, says Marcus, Mail & Guardian, June 6, 2013
http://mg.co.za/article/2013-06-06-sa-needs-clear-action-to-stabi lise-economy-says-marcus
(accessed November 16, 2016)
South African Reserve Bank, Gil Marcus profile
https://www.resbank.co.za/AboutUs/Documents/ProfileofGillMarcus.pdf
(accessed November 16, 2016)

Vuyokazi Felicity Mahlati

Vuyokazi Mahlati is an entrepreneur, business leader, and activist who is currently serving as one of the 26 commissioners on President Jacob Zuma's advisory National Planning Commission. The commission was tasked in May 2010 to draft an National Development Plan (NDP), which was to include an assessment of South Africa's achievements and challenges since 1994, and from those findings, recommend future priority areas. In this role, she chairs a working group on the Capable and Development State and Spatial Transformation. She is also the deputy chairperson of a panel of experts charged with establishing the Integrated Urban Development Framework for the country.

She is the founder of Siya TV, which has created a platform for what she calls "Africa's voice and youth creativity." For example, through the acquisition of a pay-TV license and engagement with Digital Terrestrial Television in rural South Africa, a high-tech broadcast facility was established to train young people to work in broadcasting and also become entrepreneurs. The company is a 100 percent black-owned, with 40 percent owned by the rural community. Mahlati has also been a member of various boards of directors, including

Lion of Africa Insurance Company, the Financial Markets Advisory Board, the Financial Services Board Licensing Committee, Alexkor Mining, and Umbono Capital. In addition, she has served as chairperson of the South African Post Office board of directors, which includes the Post Bank.

Mahlati has focused on issues related to people with disabilities, children, and women. Her activism in those areas led to her participation in the research process informing the drafting and creation of South Africa's constitution and UNICEF's first report on the status on women and children in South Africa. Today, she serves as president of the International Women's Forum (IWF) South Africa, an organization composed of more than 6,500 women leaders from 35 countries, and as global director of the IWF Leadership Foundation Board.

Mahlati earned her Ph.D. in Public and Development Management from Stellenbosch University and a M.Sc. in Social Policy and Planning from the London School of Economics. She is the recipient of the 2008 Black Management Forum Presidential Award, as well as the Black Business Executive/ABSA Kaelo (Guidance and Wisdom) Award.

Sources:

The National Planning Commission website, *Profile Dr. Vuyokazi Felicity Mahlati*,

https://nationalplanningcommission.wordpress.com/npc-commissioners/dr-vuyokazi-felicity-mahlati/

(accessed November 18, 2016)

Makamba Online, *Interview with successful businesswoman Dr Vuyokazi Mahlati*, January 6, 2016,

http://makambaonline.com/index.php/2016/01/06/interview-with-successful-businesswoman-dr-vuyokazi-mahlati/#.WC97VeErJBw

(accessed November 18, 2016)

International Women's Forum South Africa website, *Dr. Vuyo Mahlati*,

http://www.iwfsa.co.za/index.php/iwf-members/members-gallery/item/54-dr-vuyo-mahlati

(accessed November 18, 2016).

Notes

1. Eynon, "Interpreting the Economic Growth and Development PoliciesOf Post-Apartheid South Africa: Its Influence on Higher Education and Prospects for Women," 90.

2. Ibid., 91.
3. Organization of Economic Co-Operation and Development (OECD), "Development in Non-Member Economies," in *OECD Economic Outlook 2008* (Paris, France: OECD, 2008), 221–223; R.W. Johnston, *South Africa's Brave New World: The Beloved Country Since the End of Apartheid* (New York: Penguin Group, 2009), 412; Richard Knight, *South Africa: Economic Policy and Development* (New York: Shared Interest, 2001), http://www.richardknight.com (January 14, 2009); Knight, Richard, *South Africa 2006: Challenges for the Future* (New York: Shared Interest, 2006), 3, http://www.richardknight.com (January 14, 2009). Growth rates from 1996 to 2007 were as follows: 1996 4.2 percent; 1997 2.5 percent; 1998 0.7 percent; 1999 1.9 percent; 2000 3.1 percent; 2001 -2.7 percent; 2002 3.6 percent; 2003 2.8 percent. Growth averaged 5 percent between 2004 and 2007. Growth slowed to 4.2 percent in the first half of 2008 with projections of 3.3 percent by yearend, 3 percent in 2009 and 4.2 percent in 2010. In 2001, the government announced the creation of 1.1 million jobs between 1996 and 1999 but the majority were in the informal sector. 400,000 jobs were lost in the formal sector between the same years. Between 2001 and 2006, more than 1.1 million jobs have been created, a 10 percent increase. In the formal sector, 960,000 more people were employed and in the informal sector, 495,000.
4. Eynon, 91.
5. South African History Online, South Africa's Key Economic Changes Since 1994–2013, http://www.sahistory.org.za/article/south-africa%E2%80%99s-key-economic-policies-changes-1994-2013 (accessed August 06, 2016).
6. Farook Chotia, "Analysis: Zuma's Challenges," *BBC News Online*, April 25, 2009, http://news.bbc.co.uk/2/hi/africa/8018267.stm (accessed April 25, 2009).
7. Eynon, 104.
8. Statistics South Africa, South Africa Labour Force Survey, March 2003, http://www.statssa.gov.za, (accessed November 12, 2009). The targets included a reduction in the fiscal deficit to 3 percent of GDP, reduction in government consumption of GDP to 18.1 percent, and maintain an inflation rate of 6 percent. Each of these targets were met or exceeded with the fiscal deficit at 2.2 percent, government consumption at 18 percent, and inflation at 5.4 percent.
9. OECD, *Reviews of National Policies for Education: South Africa,* (Paris: OECD, 2008), 28–31; Statistics South Africa, "General Household Survey 2005," *Statistical Release PO318* (Pretoria: Statistics South Africa, 2006), 32.
10. Eynon, 93.
11. Ibid.

12. Ibid., 94.
13. Ibid.
14. Ibid.
15. Congress of South African Trade Unions (COSATU), Policy Statement, July 2001; Richard Knight, *South Africa: Economic Policy and Development.*
16. The Economist, "Briefing South Africa's Elections: Voting for the People's Man," April 18, 2009, 23–25.
17. Eynon, 95.
18. Ibid.
19. OECD, *Reviews of National Policies for Education: South Africa,* 30; Statistics South Africa, "General Household Survey 2005," 35.
20. Nasreen Seria, "South African Jobless Give up Hope as Economy Shrinks (Update 3)," http://bloomberg.com (accessed November 17, 2009).
21. Eynon, 95.
22. Statistics South Africa, South Africa Labour Force Survey, March 2003, http://statssa.gov.za (accessed November 12, 2009).
23. Eynon, 98.
24. Ibid., 97.
25. Ibid.
26. Alan Hirsch, *Season of Hope: Economic Reform Under Mandela and Mbeki* (Scottsville, South Africa: University of KwaZula-Natal Press (2005), 172.
27. Eynon, 98.
28. Ibid.
29. Hirsch, *Season of Hope: Economic Reform under Mandela and Mbeki*, 172.
30. Ibid., 97.
31. Mpfariseni Budeli, *Employment Equity and Affirmative Action in South Africa: a Review of the Jurisprudence of the Courts since 1994*, Conference on "Twenty Years of South African Constitutionalism," page 7, New York Universityhttp://www.nylslawreview.com/wp-content/uploads/sites/16/2014/11/Budeli1.pdf (accessed August 08, 2016).
32. Ibid., 8.
33. Eynon, 101.
34. Ibid.
35. Ibid.
36. Ibid.
37. Ibid.
38. Ibid., 102.
39. Ibid.
40. Polityorg.za Legal Briefs, "Employment Equity Act Amendments Effective from 1 August 2014 also Affects Smaller Businesses," August 6, 2014, http://www.polity.org.za/article/employment-equity-act-amendments-

effective-from-1-august-2014-also-affects-smaller-businesses-2014-08-06 (accessed August 08, 2016).

41. South Africa Department of Trade and Industry, "Black Economic Empowerment," http://www.southafrica.info/business/trends/empowerment/bee.htm. (accessed November 30, 2009).
42. South Africa Department of Trade and Industry.
43. Hirsch, *Season of Hope: Economic Reform Under Mandela and Mbeki*, 228.
44. OECD, Economic Surveys, "South Africa," (July 2015), 15.
45. Tom Burgis, "First Rand Picks South Africa's First Black Bank Chief," *Financial Times*, June 10, 2009, www.ft.com (accessed June 10, 2009).
46. Robert Guest, "The World's Most Extreme Affirmative Action Program," *Wall Street Journal*, December 26, 2004, www.wsj.com (accessed November 30, 2009).
47. Ibid.
48. World Bank, "Country Partnership Strategy for the Republic of South Africa for the Period 2008–2012," Report no, 38156-ZA, (December 12, 2007), 5.
49. African National Congress (ANC), *RDP White Paper*, http://www.anc.org.za/ancdocs/policy/white.htm (accessed November 21, 2009).
50. Deputy President of South Africa, "JIPSA Report on Activities in 2007," Pretoria, South Africa, April 2008, www.thepresidency.co.za (accessed November 14, 2009).
51. Eynon, 99.
52. Ibid., 100.
53. Ibid.
54. Tom Burgis, "South Africa Warned Against Sharp Policy Shifts," *Financial Times*, http://www.ft.com (accessed December 17, 2008).
55. Florence de Vries, "Zuma Job Target Met with Disbelief," *Business Report*, June 4, 2009, www.busrep.co.za (accessed June 4, 2009).
56. Dugger, "South Africa's Jobless Hope Zuma Delivers Work"; Farook Chotia, "Analysis: Zuma's Challenges"; Matthew Richmond, "Finance & Labor: South Africans are Unsatisfied," *IOL*, June 2, 2009, www.iol.co.za (accessed June, 2, 2009).
57. Nasreen Seria, "South African Jobless Give up Hope as Economy Shrinks (Update 3)"; Scott Johnson, "Fleeing from South Africa: Fourteen Years After Apartheid, Why Are the Best and the Brightest Leaving Africa's Most Successful State?" *Newsweek*, February 23, 2009, http://www.newsweek.com/id/184783/output/print (accessed February 16, 2009); AFROBAROMETER, *Summary of Results, Round 4 Afrobarometer Survey in South Africa* (Cape Town, South Africa: Afrobarometer, December 2008), 7; Matthew Richmond, "Finance & Labor: South Africans are Unsatisfied"; News24, "Striking Doctors Get Ultimatum," June 26, 2009, http://www.news24.com (accessed June 26, 2009).

58. Financial Times Online, "Zuma Official Vows No Lurch to the Left," http://www.ft.com (accessed May 1, 2009).
59. Eynon, 117.
60. Ibid.
61. Financial Times Online "Zuma Official Vows No Lurch to the Left."
62. Staff Reporters, "Economy in Free Fall-Treasury," May 25, 2009, SABA, Reuters, AP, www.busrep.co.za (accessed May 25, 2009).
63. Economic Development Department, Republic of South Africa, The New Growth Path: Framework, November 2011, 15.
64. Eynon, 116.
65. Economic Development Department, Republic of South Africa, The New Growth Path: Framework, November 2011, 4.
66. Ibid., 24, 29.
67. Eynon, 115.
68. H. Zarenda, *South Africa's National Development Plan and Its Implications for Regional Development* (Stellenbosch, South Africa: Tralac Trade Law Center, 2013), 1.
69. Ibid., 2.
70. OECD, 7.
71. World Bank, "South Africa Economic Update: Promoting Faster Growth and Poverty Alleviation Through Competition," *South Africa Economic Update*, 8th Edition (Washington, DC: World Bank Group, 2016), 2.
72. OECD, 9.
73. Ibid., 2.
74. Ibid.
75. Ibid., 5.
76. Ibid., 25.
77. World Bank, 11.
78. Eynon, 104.
79. Ibid.
80. Ibid.
81. *The Economist*, 24.
82. Ebrahim-Khali Hassen, *South Africa: Budget 2009: Great Transformation or Illusion Leading to Delusion* (Johannesburg: The South African Civil Society Information Service, 2009), http://allafrica.com/stories/200902120773.html (accessed November 17, 2009).
83. Kane-Berman, J. *Born Free but Still in Chains: South Africa's First Post-Apartheid Generation* (Johannesburg, South Africa: South African Institute of Race Relations, 2015), 1.
84. Ibid., 9.
85. Ibid., 12.

86. IOL, "Close the Gap Between Rich and Poor-Zuma," www.iol.co.za (accessed June 7, 2009).
87. Eynon, 105.
88. Hirsch, *Season of Hope: Economic Reform under Mandela and Mbeki,* 105.
89. Celia W, Dugger, "South Africa's Jobless Hope Zuma Delivers Work," *New York Times,* June 11, 2009, www.nytimes.com (accessed June 11, 2009).
90. Eynon, 106.
91. Ibid.
92. Ibid.
93. Ibid.
94. Ibid., 107.

CHAPTER 6

The Present State of Higher Education

In October 2015, student protests erupted throughout South Africa's public universities in response to a10.5 percent tuition increase proposed by President Jacob Zuma. While for the most part peaceful, the protests forced some institutions to shut down. Such student demonstrations on campuses and in social media (#FeesMustFall) sparked a national debate about the value of higher education and who has access to it.

The proposed tuition hike would have prohibited many current students from continuing with their studies. It would also have denied many others the opportunity to even enroll in higher education—particularly black students who have continued to struggle to afford college, given that the average income of households headed by blacks has been only about one-sixth that of the average income for those headed by whites.[1] In response to the protests, President Zuma announced there would be no increase in 2016. Yet he also did not give any explanation of how the government would cover the estimated $1.1 billion cost to operate all the institutions in the system, let alone how it planned to fund higher education over the longer term. And despite his pledge not to increase tuition in 2016, the students continued to press the government to address their demand for free education beyond the 2016 academic year.[2]

Student protests broke out again a year later, in September 2016, when Blade Nzimande, the head of the Department of Higher Education and Training, announced his proposal to allow public universities to set their own tuition fee increases, recommending that such fees not exceed 8

© The Author(s) 2017
D.E. Eynon, *Women, Economic Development, and Higher Education*,
DOI 10.1007/978-3-319-53144-1_6

percent. This time, however, the demonstrations turned violent. At the University of Witwatersrand, police shot rubber bullets and threw stun grenades at protestors, and the University of KwaZulu-Natal and the University of Cape Town (UCT) had to cancel classes.[3]

In response to the protests, officials at the Department of Higher Education and Training convened a forum on October 3, 2016, to create a "fee-free" funding model for students from poor and working-class families. The forum was convened to seek a way to end student unrest and keep the universities open as protests turned violent and disruptive. Speaking at that forum, President Zuma announced a 2017 "fee-free" pilot program for students from families who earn less than $43,200 a year. That means that, in 2017, the South African government will support an estimated 75 percent of university students. Zuma also asked that a newly formed Presidential Commission on Inquiry into Higher Education Funding be given the time to finish its work—beyond the pilot program—in identifying lasting solutions to higher education funding.[4]

Students have also demonstrated on campuses about other issues besides higher tuition fees, such as improving institutional cultures, the creation of curricula more relevant to students' needs, the hiring of more black academics and administrators, and the removal of colonial symbols.[5] In March 2015, for instance, students at the UCT protested on the campus and in social media (#RhodesMustFall), demanding the removal of a statue of Cecil John Rhodes, the British imperialist who made his fortune mining diamonds and who donated the land for the campus. Those protests led to additional rallies and the occupation of administrative buildings at the country's most prestigious universities.

Why have these protests occurred now? Perhaps this is the beginning of a second wave of transition in the country, as the "Born Free" generation has come of age and is increasingly frustrated with the slow pace of economic and social change. The demonstrations signal a pervasive sense among students and others that the post-apartheid government's promises of greater equality and access to higher education have fallen significantly short.

When he served as president of South Africa (1999–2008), Thabo Mbeki met frequently with university vice chancellors to convey his expectations for higher education and the role it should play in transforming the country in a post-apartheid era. Through these interactions, he made it clear that he expected universities to organize themselves around national initiatives related to economic growth and development—notably the GEAR program—as he saw higher education as the engine to economic growth.[6]

However, in hindsight, some faculty members and administrators have come to believe such an approach has had a negative impact on universities by "starving" them of the funds needed to redress the inequities that have continued to exist.[7] Many people have the sense that higher education has become commoditized, and corporate jargon has crept into the system whereby students are referred to as "clients," programs need to be "marketed," and staff and faculty member are "managed," according to Yvonne Shapiro, Director of the National Learners' Records Database, South Africa Qualifications Authority (SAQA).[8]

While people hold varying views on how GEAR has influenced the higher education system, a consensus among policy leaders seems to have emerged that the RDP, if pursued instead of GEAR, would have improved the system in a fundamental way by redressing the inequalities of apartheid. The thinking goes something like this: if the country were operating under the macroeconomic policies of the RDP, universities would not be functioning according to the market-related, student-fee system that they are today. Under the current system, universities set fees according to their perceptions of the market, while under the RDP, the government would have, in contrast, regulated fees in order to maximize access.

According to Harold Herman, emeritus professor of comparative and international education at the University of Western Cape, in countries like the United Kingdom, for example, tuition and fees are held to a certain level, but South Africa has no such regulation.[9] RDP would not only have regulated tuition and fees but would also have provided more funding for higher education in general. The shift to GEAR has also encouraged and increased competition among South African higher education institutions, leading to questionable results. As institutions have sought to recruit better students and faculty members, and pursue new research opportunities, it has increased costs, which are often passed along to students in the form of tuition fees. That has led, in turn, to the continued stratification of students as those higher tuition fees have created barriers to access for the poor, who are predominately black.

Not surprisingly, as higher education's role in meeting the economic growth and development goals of the country has expanded, so has the controversy surrounding the sector.[10] One of the core debates in the country today, as in the United States, is the question of whether higher education serves a broader public good or simply empowers certain individuals to advance financially.

South Africa has unquestionably spent considerable thought, time, effort, and resources to restructure and transform its higher education system. This chapter looks at the state of the higher education system today. It examines lingering issues, provides an overview of key performance indicators such as retention rates, and describes the performance of higher education institutions after the consolidation and merger of many universities, colleges and technikons.

Lingering Issues

Despite all the legislation, initiatives, and policies that have been put in place since 1994, the higher education system is still struggling with some of the same issues it faced more than 20 years ago. Those issues include, but are not limited to, access and participation, affordability and funding, student preparedness, racial relations on campuses, institutional cultures, and languages.

Access and Participation

Access to the higher education system for historically disadvantaged South Africans has been a high priority for the government since the end of apartheid. But while such access has improved, a second goal—that of ensuring that the racial profile of the student body reflects the profile of the South African population in general, as established in the 1997 White Paper—has proved more difficult to achieve.

In 1993, a report from the vice chancellors' association, the HESA, showed that black, colored and Indian people made up 89 percent of the population yet only 52 percent of those enrolled in higher education. Black South Africans alone represented 77 percent of the population, but they made up just 40 percent of enrollments. In comparison, white South Africans accounted for 11 percent of the population but represented 48 percent of enrollments. [11]

In 2001, the National Plan for Higher Education (NPHE) set a target enrollment rate of 20 percent of the South African population aged 20–24 over the next 10 to 15 years.[12] By 2008, or seven years later, 17 percent of that population had enrolled in higher education, and the headcount of enrollments across the system had grown from 744,489 in 2004 to 799,490.[13]

And between 2008 and 2013, the most recent year for which data is available, all institutional types experienced an increase in enrollments, with distance education growing by 7 percent, universities of technology 6 percent, traditional universities by 5 percent, and the comprehensives by 4 percent.[14]

Despite the increase in enrollments, however, the average annual growth rate for first-time undergraduates between 2006 and 2013 was only 1.7 percent, compared to an average annual growth rate of 4.7 percent for the categories of undergraduate students who had previously been in the university system.[15] Moreover, the racial profile of the student body has continued to be a challenge. While the percentage of black students enrolled increased significantly from 1995 to 2008—from 49 percent to 64 percent—that was still 15 points less than the percentage of black people in the country (79 percent). Colored students were also underrepresented—they made up 9 percent of South Africa's population but only had a 6 percent enrollment rate. Meanwhile, Indian and white students were overrepresented in higher education, with Indian students representing 7 percent of those enrolled (compared to 3 percent of the population) and white students representing 22 percent of those enrolled (compared to 9 percent of the population).[16]

By 2013, the enrollment rate of South Africans between the ages of 20 and 24 had reached 20 percent. Yet black and colored students have continued to remain underrepresented in higher education in proportion to the total national population. The enrollment of black students has increased to 70 percent, but it is still 16 percent less than the total population of blacks in the country (80 percent). And for colored students, the numbers remain the same as they did in 2008. They make up 6 percent of total enrollments yet account for 9 percent of the population. Meanwhile both white and Indian students have continued to be overrepresented.[17]

It's also important to consider which students enroll in which institutions or types of institutions. In historically black institutions, the student population remains predominately black. At historically white universities, the impact on the enrollment of black students across these institutions has varied, but the proportion enrolled remains lower than their proportion of the total population.

All that said, looking at the numbers alone, it might be assumed that the goal of making higher education more accessible to historically disadvantaged South Africans is slowly being met—and will, in fact, be reached in the coming decade or so. But the most important underlying trend is that access is improving not by race but by economic class. In other words, traditional universities have become overwhelmingly institutions for the middle class—a relatively small percentage of the overall population. And for people who are not part of that middle-class life, access to education has not materialized. The system is still leaving behind the majority of the black community[18]—a tough truth that the South African government must confront and address.[19]

To put the level of inequality that exists in the higher education system in perspective, Martin Hall, emeritus professor and former vice chancellor of the University Cape Town, has used the shopping mall as a metaphor. Like a shopping mall, he says, the university is open to everyone, but only those who have money come in and truly participate.

In South Africa, only eight million of the 48 million citizens have the means to participate in the formal economy, and unfortunately, the situation at universities is similar. As a result, 40 million people are excluded from opportunities that come from higher education.[20] And in that way, the government's policies and initiatives to increase access for historically disadvantaged South Africans have not been as successful as they have often been portrayed.[21]

Looking ahead, the government's National Development Plan (NDP) has set new targets for 2030: a 25 percent enrollment rate and a growth in total headcount from 983,698 students in 2013 to 1.6 million by 2030. Yet officials have provided little detail on how they plan to meet those targets.[22] What is clear is that the government will need to make difficult decisions about its priorities and how best to use its resources—especially in light of the continuing social and political upheavals on campuses.

Affordability and Funding

The basic fact, of course, is that students can't have access to higher education and graduate unless they can financially afford it—which many people in South Africa cannot. For example, the cost of education in South Africa rose nationally by 53 percent from March 2010 to March 2015. What that means is that for every R100 a household spent on higher education in 2010, it would have to pay out R153 in 2015.[23]

The cost of education as a percentage of total household expenditures had already increased from 2 percent in 1994 to 4 percent in 2008, representing a real expenditure increase of 60 percent. Moreover, rich and poor households have had to spend a vastly different percentage of their total household expenditures on education, with the poorest households paying on average twice as much of their incomes on education.[24]

To try to address such financial challenges, the South African government's support for higher education increased from R11 billion in 2006 to R26 billion in 2013. But the government's investment, while appearing to be significant, has actually been declining in terms of per-student costs and as a percentage of its budget and the country's GDP.[25] The National Student Financial Aid Scheme (NSFAS) has calculated that, in 2007, the average full cost of study[26] ranged from R25,983 to R49,253 with an average of R35,806.[27] By 2013, that cost had nearly doubled to R60,710.[28]

The result has been growing pressure on universities to create alternative revenue streams through, typically, tuition increases, donations, research grants, and contracts. Yet despite the efforts of various higher education institutions to offset declining government funding, such revenues often fall short, putting increasing pressures on university budgets. That, in turn, has forced students to shoulder more of the costs and incur ever-larger debts. In fact, the government's share of covering the cost of higher education declined from 49 percent in 2000 to 40 percent by 2012, while that of students increased from 24 percent to 31 percent. [29]

The availability of financial aid, or the lack of it, is also a concern. In 2004, 13 percent of all students enrolled received grants from the NSFAS, and by 2007, that percentage had increased slightly to 15 percent. The majority of the grants (93 percent) went to black students, with 4 percent going to colored students, 2 percent to white students, and 1 percent to Indian students. As noted in NSFAS' 2014–2015 annual report, 415,000 students were assisted throughout the higher education system.[30]

But while the number of grants has increased slightly, the number of students who apply for grants but have been declined for them has also been growing much faster.[31] That is why, even though the NSFAS announced it would increase allocations for financial aid, from R5.1 billion in 2013 to R6.6 billion in 2016–2017, student protests continued. Current students' growing needs for financial assistance, coupled with the government's target of 25 percent enrollment by 2030, will only increase the demand for funding through loans and scholarships.[32]

NSFAS has worked to ensure that poorer, rural students with academic potential are able to participate in higher education, so it established criteria for receiving financial aid that considers both the student's academic merit and family income. Frequently, due to extended periods of unemployment, a black rural family has no real income—only a social grant or pension. The bursary usually covers most of the tuition and often times is greater than the income of a poor family in a year, making it difficult to determine what percentage of family income goes toward higher education.[33]

Another significant problem, which will be discussed in detail in the next chapter, is that students—especially poor black students from rural areas—often divert bursary money for their studies to their impoverished family back home. Even if the student receives a substantial bursary, he or she may send as much as 80 percent of it back home to help his or her family. It isn't uncommon to find students who haven't eaten in days because they have sent their money home.

In June 2008, the vice chancellors' association, HESA, told Parliament that while the "explosion" in the number of students accessing the higher education system has been positive, the increasing financial burden on families is contributing to high dropout rates.[34] Often the pressures on black students to help pay for family expenses at home are so great that they work one or two part-time jobs and eventually must opt out of school because they are unable to keep up with their studies.[35]

That is why a tuition hike can also greatly jeopardize students' ability to continue with their studies. For first-generation university students, the entire family, community, or village provides support for them to attend college. For example, every student at Cedar City Campus, a private university located in the center of Johannesburg, is on a scholarship; officials there seek out smart underprivileged children and bring them to the university. But not all expenses are covered by the scholarship, and the entire village or community pays for the rest. Given the continuing jumps in tuition and school-related expenses, these students will have a very difficult time finding the means to come back to university next year.[36]

In a Student Pathways Study conducted by the Human Sciences Research Council, 70 percent of the students who dropped out of university were from low-income families, and of those, 73 percent were black and just 12 percent were white.[37] In essence, poor students who can enter the higher education system but are unable to complete their studies and graduate, return to a cycle of poverty—but this time, with the added burden of the student loan debt they might well have picked up along the way.

The South African constitution specifies rights and access to education. Those are formal rights, but they have not been realized in practice. The challenge for South Africa's education system is how to make the transition from formal rights and goals in the constitution to real outcomes. For substantive change to occur, there need to be institutional changes—and, perhaps most important, the resources to make them happen.

Student Preparedness

Another problem that continues to plague the higher education system is the lack of student preparedness. The HESA commissioned the National Benchmark Test Project in 2005 to assess the entry-level literacy and mathematics proficiency of students entering higher education. By evaluating the relationship between university entry requirements and students' proficiency as they left their K-12 schools, institutions hoped to gain information that would help them place students in the right courses and improve their institutional curricula.

The initial results, based on a pilot project, revealed that only 7 percent of first-year college students were proficient in mathematics and only a quarter fully quantitatively literate. In fact, fewer than half had the academic literacy necessary to be successful in a university.[38] A mismatch existed between, on the one hand, the government's goals and expectations for the higher education system and, on the other, the performance of the primary and secondary schools that feed into that system.

Such results were cause for concern for several reasons: (1) the lack of student preparedness plays a role in student dropout rates, and (2) with the government's current emphasis on students graduating in science, engineering, and technology, inadequate levels of quantitative literacy are particularly challenging.[39]

In response to such poor learning outcomes, the Department of Education launched a three-year "foundation for learning strategy" in March 2008.[40] It identified the main problems, in order of priority, that K-12 students experienced: a lack of books, high tuition and fees, inadequate facilities, large class sizes, a shortage of educators, and poor teaching.[41]

Government officials and educators have tried many new ideas to improve student preparedness. They have implemented programs, projects, and even special schools to help children succeed academically. In certain schools in the South African townships, for example, a teacher has been assigned to track each student through secondary education. Every time that a student misses a homework assignment or is late for school, the teacher reminds and encourages him or her. Not surprisingly, students at those schools have a 94 percent success rate in secondary school and perform better on college entrance tests.

Disappointingly, however, more than 98 percent of those students drop out after the first semester at the university—perhaps because no one follows and guides them once they get there. And although such students obviously have the talent to perform in the higher education system, this particular method of helping them to succeed has proven to be too resource-intensive to be sustainable.[42]

Teachers in particular have been held responsible for the lack of student preparedness. In his first State of the Nation speech in June 2009, President Jacob Zuma warned teachers that they needed to take their jobs seriously; additional training would be made a prerequisite to any promotions. He also shared what he believed were the government's nonnegotiable expectations, saying, "Teachers should be in school, in class on time, teaching with no neglect to duty, and no abuse of pupils."[43] Yet teacher performance in the primary and secondary sectors of education continues to be an issue, as schools lack the capacity and/or willingness to prepare and incentivize teachers to improve their teaching, or to try to meet the shortage of good teachers by recruiting new ones.

In particular, many black students still feel they are not well prepared for university studies at elite universities, even though those institutions have become more racially integrated, and find it challenging to be in a predominately white environment for the first time. Unfortunately, the statistics demonstrate a high failure rates among black students. For example, at the UCT, an elite and historically white institution, 82 percent of white students completed their degree in five years, while only 48 percent of blacks did.[44]

Racism on Campuses

Racism may also be playing a part in the failure rates of black students in the South African higher education system. It remains a highly charged issue, and incidents continue to flare up in very public ways. Among the most telling is that of the "Reitz Four," which occurred in 2009 when four white students filmed a racist video at the University of the Free State. The case illustrates the continued struggle for race reconciliation and tolerance in South Africa.

The shocking video shows four white students forcing four black female custodians and one black male custodian to run and drink urine.[45] The incident is now referred to as the "Reitz Four"—the name of the all-male residence hall where the four students lived. It resulted in the creation of the Mandate of the Committee into the Transformation in Higher Education (MCTHE), chaired by Crain Soudien, the acting vice chancellor of the UCT.[46] The MCTHE was composed of nine academics appointed by former Minister of Education Naledi Pandor. Using questionnaires and visiting all 23 of the country's universities, the committee members concluded that the intolerance behind the Reitz incident was typical of "pervasive racism" among students, staff members, and senior administrators throughout historically white universities.[47] The committee also found that historically black universities were guilty of sexism, ethnic discrimination, xenophobia, and racism—for example, colored students at certain institutions refused to share rooms in the residence halls with black South African students.[48]

The allegations made to the committee via interviews and the questionnaires were not verified, which led to a fair amount of criticism of the report's findings and recommendations, especially those that were more far-reaching. As an example, the report stated that the "entire academic syllabus was divisive and Euro-centric . . . to put it bluntly, a white project . . . and the committee recommended the curriculum be 'Africanised.'"[49] Soudien anticipated, as did the rest of the committee members, that they would receive "lots of flak" and knew the report "was vulnerable because at no stage have we been able to verify what people were claiming."[50]

Shortly after Reitz Four video became public in early 2009, but before the MCTHE released its report that May, Professor Jonathan Jansen, previous dean of the faculty of education at the University of Pretoria, was selected to become the first black vice chancellor of the University of Free State.[51] Jansen is a renowned education professor and a much-published scholar who has explored issues of racism and reconciliation.[52] In his statement of intent, Jansen said that Free State had to "find a way of integrating classroom life while at the same time ensuring the promotion of Afrikaans, an important cultural trust of the institution, as well as

Sesotho and other indigenous languages." He went on to say that the university had to bring faculty, staff, workers, students, and the parents behind "a compelling vision of transformation that works in the interest of all members of the university community."[53]

Yet it wasn't long before Jansen found himself in the middle of controversy and was accused of being a racist. On the day of his inauguration speech as the new vice chancellor in October 2009, he announced, "in a gesture of racial reconciliation, and the need for healing," that the University of the Free State would withdraw its charges against the four students. He went on to say "the deeper issues of racism and bigotry that conflict our university—and many others—will not be resolved in the courts." Based on this decision, the four students would be allowed to continue their studies, the workers who were abused in the video were to be compensated financially, and the Reitz all-male residence hall would reopen and set an example as "a model of racial reconciliation."[54]

Archbishop Desmond Tutu was quick to release a statement of support for Jansen's announcement, but that did not quiet the uproar that came in the wake of it. Two days after Tutu's endorsement, South African Minister of Higher Education Blade Nzimande called on Jansen to suspend his decision saying it was "insensitive and taken without consultation." Nzimande requested a report be submitted in two days on the process that Jansen had used to come to his decision, claiming Jansen had never spoken to him or his staff about the matter.[55] And the next day, Parliament announced its displeasure over the Reitz Four decision.

Then, just 10 days after Jansen's announcement to withdraw university charges against the four students, the University of the Free State announced the reopening of university discussions about the incident and what action, if any, to take with the students. The next day, Thebe Meeko, chair of the ANC Youth League at the university, was quoted in the national daily newspaper, *The Times,* threatening Jansen with physical harm and saying: "Like President Jacob Zuma when he said the police must meet fire with fire, the shoot-to-kill approach must also apply to all the racists, including Jansen—because he is a racist. He must know that we have removed more powerful people than him before. Jansen is equally a criminal like those four racists. We will shoot to kill racism and those who are racist. Jansen must go."[56]

Within two days, however, Julius Malema, national ANC Youth League President, went to the University of the Free State to meet with Jansen. Upon leaving the campus, he announced his full support of Jansen and his remaining as vice chancellor, saying, "We do not agree with any call that he must go." And in a meeting with the students, he also said, "We cannot feed Jansen to the enemy."[57] Five days later, the ANC issued a statement of support for the University of the Free State's plan for transformation as called for by Jansen and the opening of further university discussions.

The outcome was the reinstatement of two of the four students; the other two have had since graduated. All four faced charges in criminal court. In February 2011, the four former Reitz students, during a public reconciliation ceremony before 300 people, apologized and expressed deep regret for their behavior and the harm it caused to the five workers at the university. On behalf of the group, one of the workers accepted their apology.

In addition, before the reconciliation ceremony, a court settlement was reached that guaranteed job security for the workers and the establishment of a human rights institute at the university. To ensure the women's job security, the university agreed to pay their salaries for five years and to provide funds and training to help them establish a cleaning company. That allowed the women to continue to receive income while starting their business and ensured they did not have to come back to the university, given the circumstances.

This story illustrates how fragile race relations still are in the country, specifically within the higher education system. It also reflects, to a certain degree, the lack of tolerance and the ease in which old and damaging patterns of interaction between black and white South Africans reemerge. In such an environment, it is difficult to get beyond rhetoric and resolve issues in a way that allows everyone to move forward.

The MCTHE final report concluded, "Transformation is clearly a challenge facing all South African higher education institutions." Yet one of the key barriers to such transformation has been a lack of implementation of the comprehensive policies created by all the universities to address discrimination. According to the report, the continuing prevalence of racism and sexism on campuses is due to the dearth of information, awareness of the policies, and institutional will to implement the policies.[58]

Institutional Culture

Racial incidents have also stimulated protests that have called attention to the cultural and social environments of higher education institutions. To date, the most visible protest occurred at the UCT when students began the "Rhodes Must Fall' movement. That protest, like similar ones, has generated heated debates about the Eurocentric foundation upon which many higher education institutions were built. The demonstrators are calling into question everything from the norms, values, rituals, symbols, and practices of the institution to the curriculum—protesting that black experiences, culture, knowledge, ideas, and traditions are not represented.

It should also be recognized, however, that no South African university is without its challenges when it comes to creating an institutional culture that fully embraces and promotes the principles of diversity, inclusivity, multiculturalism, and equality. While racism continues to create a sense of alienation for many students at historically white universities, there are also reports of sexism, homophobia, patriarchy, and tribalism at historically black universities.[59]

Language Matters

Language continues to pose a problem for students and professors alike. Although English is used in public engagement and economic interaction, and is the language of teaching in most of South African universities, only 5 percent of South Africans claim it as a first language. In addition to English and Afrikaans, people speak nine local languages in South Africa. That means that most university students have to learn in a language that is their second or third one.[60]

The question, then, is why not ratchet up of the teaching of English throughout all levels of the education system—and long before students arrive at the university? A likely answer is that many people hold strong feelings in the post-apartheid era about the need to preserve native languages, even though that clearly creates significant problems for students.

On the one hand, every South African has the constitutional right to use their language of choice as well as the right to basic education and adult basic education. On the other, as the National Benchmark Tests Project shows, for people entering into the higher education system, the right to one's language of choice can result in significant disadvantages for oneself and the higher education system. For instance, there are costs to the students who must hire tutors to help them to complete assignments in their own language. Faculty members who have to break through a language barrier to connect with students also face difficulties.

By the third grade, teachers are supposed to start teaching students in either English or Afrikaans. As a result, by the time a student is ready to enter the higher education system, their choice of university is limited on the basis of language. A student who went through primary and secondary school speaking English would not survive in the University of Pretoria, where classes are taught in Afrikaans.

The state has recognized and tried to address the issue, mandating that, starting in the third grade, students be taught in English or Afrikaans. But, in fact, many teachers don't know English or Afrikaans, so they continue to teach in native languages.[61] Indeed, the issue of language is a problem for virtually everyone who comes to a university from a rural area. Getting into any higher education institution from a rural school is a big challenge.[62]

Several educational foundations have created special programs to help students who are struggling with language barriers and to work with teachers on how to connect with those students. One such organization is the Zenex Foundation, which has given more than R237 million to the education sector to develop programs that increase the capacity of South African schools to improve mathematics, science, and language teaching. In addition, many universities are offering extra tutoring to help students who are having academic difficulties with their language skills. The tutors work with students in their own language to help them complete reading and written assignments.[63] Still, much work needs to be done.

Student Success: Retention and Graduation

Given all these issues, how successful has South African higher education been since the end of apartheid in the early 1990s? An important indicator of success in any higher education system is the number of students who graduate from its institutions. And, unfortunately, South African graduation rates have been and continue to be disappointing.

To be fair, however, when assessing those graduation rates, one must keep in mind that the government's primary focus has been on increasing access to the higher education system—with much less emphasis placed on retention and graduation. That focus is beginning to change.

In 2000, the South African Department of Education conducted a cohort study that, five years later, tracked students who entered the higher education system in 2000 through 2004 five years later. By the end of the study period, only 30 percent of first-time entering students had graduated. As many as 56 percent had left their original institution and 14 percent remained in the system.[64]

The category "left without graduating" does not take into account those who may have left one institution, enrolled in another, and eventually graduated. The Department of Education estimates that approximately 10 percent of the students who fall into this category have transferred to another institution. Assuming 70 percent of the transferring students eventually graduated, the overall graduation rate for cohort 2000 would increase from 30 percent to 44 percent. Yet that still means that the South African higher education system lost at a minimum of 65,000 of the students who enrolled in 2000.[65]

Moving ahead to students who entered college between 2004 and 2007, the overall graduation rate dropped to close to 16 percent, or significantly lower than the graduation figures cited in the Department of Education study cited above. The graduation rates across institutional types shows that the comprehensive universities have been the least successful, with graduation rates of 11 percent, compared to graduation rates of 22 percent at traditional universities and 20 percent at universities of technology, or technikons.[66]

The decrease in graduation rates of students who entered from 2004 to 2007 can be attributed, to a certain degree, to the growth in enrollment rates. While the comprehensive universities have had lower graduation rates, that trend may in part be because many more students are enrolling in them. The graduation rates of students who entered traditional universities in 2006 showed a similar relationship to enrollment rates: they increased even though enrollment rates declined that year, only to fall again in 2007 as enrollment rates rose. And while the universities of technology showed consistent improvement in their graduation rates, the number of students who enrolled from 2004 to 2007 decreased.

Even allowing for higher enrollments, however, the low graduation rates are cause for concern. In 2011, only 27 percent, or about one in four students, completed their degree in the allotted time, and researchers estimated that up to 55 percent would never graduate.[67] Indeed, graduation rates across the various types of institutions in the higher education system are generally poor, with some performing worse than others. Less than half, or 48 percent of students who entered traditional universities in 2011 graduated within a five-year period, with an estimated 45 percent never completing college at any institution. As for distance education, only 6 percent of students who enrolled graduated within a five-year period, with an estimated 78 percent never graduating.

Such data clearly shows that more students have failed and dropped out of the system than have graduated.[68] The sad fact is that the system is taking in undergraduate students knowing they only have a roughly 30 percent chance of graduating in five years.

What's causing this problem? While many elements contribute to lower retention rates—especially for black students—some key factors are the low expectations that many higher education institutions have for their students and the lack of attention that they pay them. That can especially be the case in some of the historically white institutions like the UCT or Wits University.[69]

At the most fundamental level, the problem is one of inadequate resources. Many students lack adequate housing or transportation to and from their off-campus living quarters. It is not uncommon to find many students crammed into one room because of the exorbitant prices that landlords charge, knowing they are students and need a place to stay. Such students also often don't have money to travel back and forth between school and the places where they're staying. And many of them don't know any better because they come from rural areas and have never had to deal with these issues. All these factors contribute to dropout rates.[70]

What is particularly troubling is that, despite the growth in the number of black students entering the system, the government has invested little time, attention, or money in ensuring their success within it. While accounting for 63 percent of all students reenrolled across the system, black students represent just 57 percent of all higher education graduates. In contrast, the graduation rates of colored and Indian graduation students are equal to the percentage of such students' enrollment, and whites students' graduation rates are greater than the percentage of those enrolled.

The enrollment and graduation rates of black students have increased since 2004, but a gap between enrollment and graduation continues to exist.[71] In 2011, 41 percent of black students graduated after six years and 59 percent dropped out. Among white students, 55 percent graduated in six years and 45 percent dropped out.[72]

Part of the trouble seems to be that the government has focused on student enrollment while neglecting retention and graduation. Under the current government-funding model of block grants to institutions, 70 percent of a university's grant goes to subsidize undergraduate enrollments, 16 percent to increase graduation rates and completion, and the remainder to postgraduate work and research. Given the country's low retention and completion rates, the debate about whether government funding should give equal weight to both enrollment and outcomes is increasing.[73]

The fact is that, once students enter the higher education system, institutions must create conditions and programs that will help students be successful. As part of that, they must pursue avenues to help ease the financial burden placed on students and their families. Otherwise, the system will continue to experience high failure rates.

In sum, the South African higher education system has expanded significantly over the years, but it has also experienced low growth rates for first-time undergraduates, low participation rates among blacks and colored students, high dropout rates, and low completion rates. That means that the shortage of highly skilled people needed to fuel and contribute to the country's economic and social development will continue.

This is an inefficient use of the country's resources and as such an opportunity to reexamine and identify ways in which to facilitate better outcomes through curriculum reform, high-quality teaching and learning environments, and increased accountability for educational outcomes.

Reconfiguring the Higher Education System

Since 1994, the higher education system has been going through a restructuring process. The Higher Education Act of 1997, which brought higher education under one centralized system, and the government's 2004 White Paper, calling for the reorganization and merger of higher education institutions, have been the two key policy initiatives driving that process.

What has happened consistently since 1997, with the Higher Education Act and a series of amendments to it, is the strengthening of central state control over the higher education system. To date, the number of institutions in the system has been reduced from 21 to 11 universities, and from 15 technikons to 5 universities of technology and 6 comprehensive universities (which were often created by the merger of universities and technikons).[74] In total, 14 higher education institutions have closed. In addition to the closing of the some universities and the technikons, most of the 100 teacher training colleges have been absorbed into the new structure.[75]

All that has led to greater government oversight of the funding of the 23 public higher education institutions that now exist, including the University of South Africa, a completely online university. A key to coordination across any system lies in the way that revenues from the government are actually handled. This shift to centralized control over funding is linked to the economic policies of GEAR, which has mandated the strengthening of science, technology, and engineering sectors of higher education. By having more control, the government has been able to allocate funds into programs that are focused on those key sectors.[76]

As described in previous chapters, the South African government has viewed, and continues to view, the higher education system as a key player in its efforts to create a skilled workforce—one that can contribute to economic growth and job creation. That higher education is a priority for government is evident in President Jacob Zuma's move in 2009 to split the Ministry of Education in two and form a separate Ministry of Higher Education and Training, with many of the Department of Labour's initiatives around skill development coming under the umbrella of the newly formed ministry. At the same time, the government has been providing funding for higher education institutions to enroll more students in fields of study related to science, technology, and engineering.

In fact, one of the immediate outcomes of the mergers has been the ability of universities to expand into new areas of study, setting up research units that did not exist before. The University of Pretoria is a good example.[77] Students there have benefited from the changes, which have expanded degree offerings and created more of a university atmosphere. They can now choose from a larger pool of professors and a wider range of courses.[78]

A new higher education qualifications framework also went into effect in January 2010 in response to the consolidation of the higher education system. The new system sets common qualifications, ensures consistency across different institutions, and allows for transferability among institutions. At the same time, according to the former Minister of Education, Naledi Pandor, the guidelines will allow for diversity and innovation by each of the institutions and provide "ample scope to design educational offerings to realize their different visions, missions and plans, and to meet the varying needs of the clients and communities they serve."[79] The framework establishes minimum admissions requirements, allowing the universities to set their own policies beyond those minimums. It also lets them recognize students' prior learning and work-related qualifications as part of the application process.

By putting every institution under the same umbrella of quality as defined and monitored by the Council on Higher Education (CHE), the single system has helped to address the problem of quality in the smaller institutions that were historically for colored and black students. The CHE has implemented a system of quality with peer review and other mechanisms to monitor and increase the level of quality in all the schools.

Rooting Out Inequities

The government's desire to redress the inequities that had taken root from the days of apartheid and the colonial education system has helped drive its mergers of universities. The National Commission on Higher Education (NCHE) pursued the establishment of a single system, believing that the move would address "inherited inequities, inefficiencies" and allow it to "plan and manage increased access."[80] But, thus far, it has not been able to reach those goals.

Under the apartheid system, South African higher education institutions could be categorized as one of two main types: Historically Advantaged Institutions (HAIs) and Historically Disadvantaged Institutions (HDIs). Mostly white South African students attend the HAIs, and mostly black students attend the HDIs.[81] One of the recommendations in the 2004 White Paper was to merge most of the HDIs, using efficiency measures as a way to combine institutions. Yet, once implemented, those mergers resulted in the disappearance of HDIs, which had long served disadvantaged and rural communities—leaving somewhat of a vacuum in their place.[82]

The government has certainly tried to make money available for the historically disadvantaged and poorer schools by shifting money away from advantaged ones. But those richer and better institutions have always been supported by the social and economic capital that existed in their circles. They have been able to tap into parent and alumni networks to fill in any gaps in financial support in ways that institutions in the rural areas and in the townships cannot.

Thus, unfortunately, the issues of inequity, inefficiency, and, to a lesser degree, access continue to challenge the higher education system. The reality is that, although the mergers began in 2005, the process of consolidating, merging, and creating new institutions sometimes takes years of effort before the desired results are achieved. For many institutions, it has been a difficult process for the students, faculty members, and administrators.

The fact is that restructuring, especially by way of merger, is difficult under the best of circumstances. Imagine the complexity of merging South Africa's higher education institutions given the history of education under the apartheid system. It is astounding to think that every single higher education institution in the country has gone through or is still going through the stress, uncertainty, and the complexity of this procedure, with some still working on the problem years later.[83]

Many Challenges

The process of restructuring began when former Minister of Education, Kader Asmal (1999–2004) came into office and quickly began "ripping stuff apart or putting them together in new ways that a lot of people found extremely stressful."[84] Asmal essentially told people who would merge with whom and how they were to do it. Many did not respond well to all the changes he mandated.[85]

One of the key challenges in any merger is bringing different institutions with different cultures, systems, and people together to form one cohesive institution with a shared culture and purpose. Management of the process is key, and in many cases, the mergers have not been managed very well. Different work ethics, institutional processes, faculty qualifications, and pay are but some of the issues that can arise.[86]

An example of the challenge of merging two institutions that had fundamentally different missions, student bodies, and curricula is the University of Johannesburg, which was created in 2005 from the merger of what was called Rand Afrikaans University and an underfinanced technical school located nearby. Rand Afrikaans was a traditional higher education institution that was established to serve working-class Afrikaner students under the old apartheid government. It was a relatively well-endowed university that catered specifically to students in that class.

The technical school, prior to its merger with Rand Afrikaans, had itself incorporated a small section of another institution, which was previously disbanded and broken up into different parts; this piece was established as the technical school's western campus. Each of the two institutions, before merging as the University of Johannesburg, had a distinct and homogenous student body. One institution had a white and relatively privileged student body and the other a black, far less affluent, student body.[87]

Some of the difficulties that faculty and staff members have experienced have related to problems around perceptions of academic standing. Each institution, as well its professors and administrators, was operating under a different system of remuneration and way of operating. That, in turn, influenced how people from the two institutions have perceived the process. As a result, they have struggled with how to accommodate each other.[88]

There have also been issues of faculty expertise and questions as to where faculty members from the two merging institutions would teach in the new institution.[89] Some people thought that those at the larger, formerly white, institution received "special treatment" in terms of teaching loads, research opportunities, and promotions.[90]

In the years since the establishment of the University of Johannesburg, relationships among faculty members have definitely improved. The upper management of the university, as well as the middle management, has made a deliberate attempt resolve issues of equity and make sure the environment is inclusive.[91]

That said, other challenges have remained. As a result of the merger, some believe that certain people have been placed on the same level as others but do not have the same experience, work ethic or expertise[92] and, in fact, that they lack the qualifications required of an academic at a university. For example, senior lecturers from both institutions now work at the university, but while those from one have been expected to and do publish, those from the other have never published and can't work at the level expected. This creates animosity and an unpleasant work environment for all involved.

The response from the University of Johannesburg has been to try to help those who are lagging to catch up. The university is now embarking on a drive to ensure that all staff members have, at a minimum, a master's degree.[93] That is certainly a long-term solution and will serve the university well in the future. The problem is how to deal with the issue in the short term.

In addition, the mergers have put higher education institutions in a situation where they are jockeying for position within the hierarchy. The top management of each institution sets objectives for growth and change according to the type of institution they want to become, and it is then up to the faculty and staff to achieve those ambitious goals. This is taking a personal toll,[94] as academics are increasing finding it difficult to fulfill a growing number of responsibilities and duties. Class sizes have expanded tremendously, research is becoming increasingly important to many institutions, community service obligations have expanded, and members of various departments must now also generate funding.[95]

It appears the comprehensive universities, where the focus is on teaching and bachelor's degrees and technology qualifications, have experienced the most difficulty. The mergers created challenges related to curriculum, institutional identity, and "market relevance."[96] Part of the problem was that, after the mergers, the universities did not have a clear idea of what they were or how to deliver on the government's mandate. The temptation was to copy the model and approach of traditional universities. The danger is that institutions will spread themselves too thin: by trying to do everything, they will do nothing well.[97]

One of the biggest challenges for the comprehensive universities is how to respond to market needs. They must expand the number and type of their course offerings, providing a variety of programs from undergraduate to doctoral degrees, and a mix of types of knowledge, including technical, vocational, career-oriented, and professional. They must choose what they are going to be—and that may be multiple institutions within one organization[98]

Racial Imbalances

One of the main objectives of restructuring the higher education system was to create racial balance across all types of institutions. Under apartheid, there were two institutional types: universities and technikons. The majority of black South Africans were enrolled in technikons.

Following the end of apartheid, black enrollment percentages in universities began to increase, growing from 50 percent in 1995 to 53 percent in 2003. And in technikons, black enrollment grew from 47 percent to 77 percent during the same period. Meanwhile, the enrollment percentages of white students dropped at universities from 38 percent to 32 percent and at technikons from 41 percent to 14 percent.[99]

Beginning in 2004, data was available for enrollment rates by the three institutional types established as a result of the reorganization of the higher education system: universities, comprehensive universities, and universities of technology. When looking at enrollment rates across the three types of institutions by race, Africans make up 50 percent of the students at universities, 63 percent at comprehensives, and 77 percent at universities of technology.

Of the three, the universities of technology come closest to representing the overall population. The representation of black South African students at the comprehensives also moved toward a more representative profile of the overall population; this may be attributed to the incorporation of technikons into these universities during the mergers. But when looking across all institutional types, white and Indian students were overrepresented and colored and black students underrepresented.[100]

By 2013, black students represented 84 percent of those enrolled in universities of technology, 84 percent of those in comprehensives, 57 percent in traditional universities, and 71 percent of those enrolled in distance education. In comparison, white students represented 6 percent of those enrolled in universities of technology, 10 percent enrolled in comprehensives, 27 percent in traditional universities, and 16 percent in distance education. Black students' enrollment in comprehensive universities has increased by more than 20 percent since 2004, while white students' enrollments continue to decrease as a percentage of total enrollments across all institutional types. [101]

A Strong and Successful System?

There is no doubt the reforms made in the higher education system were all necessary and good in terms of bringing some kind of equity and evenness into the governance structure. However, higher education and government officials need to examine the results closely in order to determine why some reforms have resulted in positive change while some have not, and still others have made matters worse.[102]

For example, one key focus of higher education policy has been on improving access to higher education for all South Africans. As mentioned previously, the government set a target rate of 20 percent enrollment by the year 2015. While the country is trending toward that number, significant questions have arisen about who is enrolling and the quality of the education they are receiving. Today, universities are swamped with students—in some cases, their enrollments have doubled—resulting in large classes and leading to a growing concern over the caliber of the graduating students.[103]

The reconfiguration of the higher education system was an attempt to create a differentiated system by orchestrating extensive institutional consolidation and mergers and also by creating mechanisms whereby the state required institutions to offer specific qualifications and courses of study. It was also a way to "right" the inequalities that existed in the higher education system after decades of apartheid rule. But one of the continuing concerns is that, even with the reconfiguration, those institutions that were historically disadvantaged will continue to be so as a result of the ongoing lack of funding and institutional capacity.

People also question higher education institutions' ability to maintain high standards of quality while at the same time meeting the expectations for opportunity and change, as well as their capacity to acquire the financial resources required to implement and sustain all the government initiatives. The plans are good, and the democratic aspects of reform welcome. Yet there is growing uneasiness among faculty members and administrators that such plans could lead to a breakdown in the higher education system—as the government struggles to find solutions to funding shortages and, at the same time, tries to ease the increasing financial burden on working-class and poor families that send their children to university.[104]

Fields of Study

The 2001 NPHE set enrollment target rates by field of study as

- 40 percent in the humanities and social sciences,
- 30 percent in business and commerce, and
- 30 percent in science and engineering.[105]

The enrollment rates in the humanities and social sciences dropped from a peak of 58 percent in 1995 to 42.3 percent in 2005, slightly higher than the target of 40 percent but significantly lower than the 1995 figure. At the same time, enrollments in the fields of study in business, commerce, science, technology, and engineering almost doubled during that same time, although they remained below the NPHE target rates.[106]

In 2010, the newly formed Ministry of Higher Education and Training set new target rates:

- maintaining the 30 percent target for science and technology,
- increasing business to 33 percent, and

- combining the humanities and education while significantly reducing the target to 37 percent.[107]

By 2013, all fields of study showed absolute growth in terms of number enrolled. Yet the percentage of students enrolled in business decreased slightly from 29 percent in 2008 to 28.4 percent, while those enrolled in science and technology increased from 28 percent to 28.8 percent, and those enrolled in the humanities (including education) decreased slightly from 43 percent to 42.5 percent.[108]

Restructuring the Ministry of Education

In his first day of office in 2009, President Zuma announced the creation of a Ministry of Higher Education and Training with Bonginkosi Emmanuel "Blade" Nzimande, also the secretary-general of the South African Communist Party (SACP) as its head.[109] The splitting of the National Department of Education into two ministries, not just one for both K-12 and higher education, was expected. In December 2007, at the ANC national conference, policy priorities in higher education were identified, including the creation of such a higher education ministry. This new ministry would oversee all universities and colleges and encompass 1.5 million people including students and staff.[110] Other policy priorities highlighted at the time included reopening teacher colleges that were incorporated into universities, revisiting institutions that were merged during the 2005 restructuring process, and offering free undergraduate education.[111]

Public reaction to the creation of a Department of Higher Education and Training was mixed. Some people welcomed the division of basic and postsecondary education, given that the size and complexity of each sector had made it extremely difficult for one minister to effectively run both. In addition, they believed that a Department of Higher Education would bring more attention and management to skills training.[112] Other observers were concerned about the lack of planning related to the split, the cost of creating a separate department, and the ability to staff the department with qualified people—which had been difficult enough under a single ministry of education.

The new department takes responsibility for higher education, colleges, and all postliteracy adult education, including workplace skills development. Workplace skills development includes the infrastructure of the Sector Education and Training Authority (SETA) the National Skills Authority, and the National Skills Fund,[113] which was transferred from the Department of Labour to the new DHET.[114]

The Department of Labour had been trying for quite some time to identify the critical skills needed in the South African workforce. The preference was for developing these skills within the country and to only go outside the country when needed. The sense was, according to Yvonne Shapiro of SAQA, that they have been "chasing their tails for a very long time."[115]

Interestingly enough, the original macroeconomic policy of the ANC, the RDP, envisaged the combination of education and training to redress some of the practices under apartheid, which relied on unskilled labor. Many South Africans were never formally trained or had formal qualifications under the old system. With the split of the education department, the RDP's original plan for aligning higher education and training will finally happen. If business and industry need particular skills, they have to come to higher education. The hope is that the move will give universities and the higher education system in general a way to ensure students are acquiring the skills needed for industry and economic growth.[116]

During a public lecture at Wits School of Public and Development Management, Blade Nzimande stated that people should stop thinking about education and training as two separate things and recognize they are part of an integral whole. He explained why the ministry was taking over skills training from the Ministry of Labour: in essence the two departments could not get along, respective institutional interests clashed, and each department thought too narrowly—leading to a lack of cooperation between the two. Minister Nzimande went on to say DHET is the "glue"[117] that will hold everything together. For him, the goal is to prepare post-school youth for the labor market and to help them to further develop the "skills, values, and ethics needed to participate usefully in the social, political, and cultural life of their communities and society as a whole."[118]

Nzimande believes one of the key obstacles to the country's development is the shortage of skilled workers. He sees higher education and training playing a critical role in helping with economic growth and the creation of more jobs. He acknowledges that much improvement is needed in the quality of education and the capacity to educate and train more young people.[119]

Nzimande referenced a recent report, commissioned by former Minister of Education Naledi Pandor, which looked at post-compulsory school provisions. The report showed that 2.8 million (41 percent) of the country's 18- to 24-year-olds are neither employed, enrolled in educational institutions, nor participating in a workplace-training program. Nzimande attributed this to "very limited access to post-school education and training opportunities, poor resources, the lack of financing, and the restricted availability of jobs."[120] He referred to the situation as a "huge waste of human capital."[121]

Nzimande believes that workers' prior learning, and not just formal university entrance qualifications, should be taken into consideration during the admissions process. He also has stated that experienced workers should not have to take metric exams, as this barrier doesn't allow young people to reach their full potential. And he is has called on universities to modify the tests so that more students might gain access.[122]

Postgraduation Employment Rates

An important indicator as to whether or not the Department of Higher Education and Training has been successful is to examine postgraduation employment. Unfortunately, the exact percentage of students who do graduate and get absorbed in the labor market is unknown, as the NSFAS does not track this and many other outcomes.

What is known is that, while 344,000 people with degrees, diplomas, or certificates are unemployed, the country is still experiencing a significant shortage of skilled workers. And although graduates have better employment opportunities, there are still an estimated 470,000 vacancies for management and professional positions.[123] Further, while the proportion of whites with skilled jobs has risen by almost 20 percent since the end of apartheid, it has only risen by 3 percent for blacks.[124]

In a speech his budget speech in May 2015, Minister Nzimande promised to continue the push for the transformation of the higher education system in response to various recent student protests. He mentioned the need to change the demographics of the academy, from faculty to staff, to transform the curriculum, to eliminate racism and sexism, and to improve success rates.[125]

Mixed Results

In sum, when it comes to higher education in South Africa, the picture is mixed. Institutional change is difficult under the best of circumstances, and South African leaders are clearly placing huge expectations on higher education. There is a sense that it will be the cure-all for building the human capital needed to spur economic growth and development, unemployment, a better life, professional mobility, and equality. That is a heavy burden to carry. The South African higher education system has made impressive progress, but the reality is that the apartheid system has been difficult to break completely and the transformational change called for in the constitution difficult to attain.

A number of challenges continue to confront South African higher education moving forward, including (1) ensuring that standards are maintained as the government continues to press for increased enrollment rates, (2) preparing rural and poor South Africans students for higher education, (3) addressing the issue of affordability and the increasing financial burden on students and families, and (4) creating initiatives and programs that better support the economic growth and development strategies of the country.

It should be recognized, however, that no other part of the world has completed this comprehensive a restructuring program—with the possible exception of Eastern Europe, which went through the same sort of restructuring after the collapse of the Communist Bloc. When weighing the successes and failures of South Africa's system, it is important to remember what it has tried to accomplish in the short time since the end of apartheid: not just a change in course requirements but also an entirely new curriculum, new campuses, and a new educational bureaucracy. In short, despite the continuing challenges, South Africa's higher education system has, in many ways, made great strides.

Profiles of South African Women

The Women Who Led the #FeesMustFall Protest

Young women have been leading the "Fees Must Fall" movement, and two are of particular note: Nompendulo Mkhatshwa, president of the University of the Witwatersrand (Wits) Student Representative Council

(SRC), and Shaeera Kalla, the council's past president. The #FeesMustFall campaign began at Wits University when students rejected the government's 10.5 percent tuition fee increase for academic year 2016. In October 2015, both Mkhatshwa and Kalla led a student march to the ANC headquarters in Johannesburg, where Mkhatshwa spoke on the students' behalf and delivered a memorandum of the students' grievances to ANC secretary-general Gwede Mantashe. Mkhatshwa, Kalla, and the Wits students were credited with sparking the protests that lead to the closing of universities across the country.

Nompendulo Mkhatshwa

Nompendulo Mkhatshwa is an undergraduate student at Wits University, a part-time researcher at the ANC headquarters in Johannesburg, and leader of the Progressive Youth Alliance (PYA). At the height of the #FeesMustFall campaign, Mkhatshwas was the president of the SRC, an ANC activist, and widely regarded as one movement's leaders.

Nompendulo has since become a divisive figure among Wits student protestors and others within the movement. One of the most prominent faces in the media, she appeared on the cover of the popular magazine, Destiny in December 2015. She and the magazine were criticized for drawing attention to one person, therefore detracting from the thousands of students who were involved in the movement.

She also lost credibility when, hours after President Jacob Zuma announced a tuition freeze for 2016, she called for an end to the nationwide university shutdowns. Although she has not been as visible since falling from favor with students, she has represented them at the fees commission, has worked with police and within the courts to help secure the release of students arrested during protests, and has met with university management to discuss and negotiate students' demand for free education.

Shaeera Kalla

Shaeera Kalla was born in Pretoria, the youngest of five children. Growing up, she attended many protests with her parents and other adults—as Kalla described it, not a common practice for young Muslim Indian woman. She credits being Muslim as one of the primary reasons she is involved in social justice movements, as she believes it is inherent in the teachings of the Quran.

Kalla holds a Bachelor of Commerce degree, majoring in philosophy, politics, and economics from Wits University and is now a postgraduate political science student. She joined the Wits Palestine Solidarity Committee, the Workers Solidarity Committee, and South African Students Congress (SASCO) while an undergraduate and served as the Student Representative Council in 2014.

For Kalla the #FeesMustFall movement was more than a protest against fees—it was a way for students to express their anger and frustration at their universities, which they believe to be anti-black and poor. Students believe that universities' Eurocentric curriculum and commodification of education needed to be changed.

In October 2016, Kalla was struck at close range by 13 rubber bullets during a protest at Wits University. She was shot in the back while walking away from police.

Sources:

Emily Corke, *#FEESMUSTFALL: Student FEMALE LEADERS SHOWED DISCIPLINE, Eyewitness News Website, November 15, 2015.*

http://ewn.co.za/2015/10/25/FeesMustFall-Female-leaders-of-the-campaign-showed-disciple (accessed November 20, 2016)

S'thembile Cele and Staff reporters, *The women who led the #FeesMustFall protest*, October 25, 2015

http://city-press.news24.com/News/New-activist-generation-Profiles-20151025 (accessed November 20, 2016)

Devaksha Vallabhjee, #MbokodoLead: The women leading the #feesMustFall movement, October 27, 2015

http://www.marieclaire.co.za/hot-topics/mbokodolead-women-leading-feesmustfall-movement (accessed November 20, 2016)

Govan Whittles, *The rise and fall of Nompendulo Mkatshwa, the Wits SRC president*, Mail & Guardian Website, October 20, 2016

http://mg.co.za/article/2016-10-20-00-the-rise-and-fall-of-nompendulo-mkhatshwa-the-wits-src-president (accessed November 20, 2016)

Notes

1. John Campbell, and Ralph Bunche, "Slow Progress for South Africa's 'Born-Free' Generation." *Council on Foreign Relations*, December 18,

2015, http://www.cfr.org/south-africa/slow-progress-south-africas-born-free-generation/p37393 (accessed June 15, 2016).

2. Nicky Falkof, "South Africa's Student Revolt,"—*The New York Times*, October 25, 2015, http://www.nytimes.com/2015/10/26/opinion/south-africas-student-revolt.html?_r=0 (accessed June 10, 2016).
3. Christine Hauser, "Fees Must Fall: Anatomy of the Student Protests in South Africa," *The New York Times*, http://www.nytimes.com/2016/09/23/world/africa/fees-must-fall-anatomy-of-the-student-protests-in-south-africa.html?emc=eta1 (accessed October 11, 2016).
4. Munyaradzi Makoni, "Government Stakeholder Forum Fails to End Student Unrest," *University World News*, October 7, 2016, http://www.universityworldnews.com/article.php?story=20161007154826650 (accessed October 11, 2016).
5. Elizabeth Redden, "In South Africa the Struggle for Free Tuition – And Fundamental University Transformation – Continues After Massive Student Protests," *Inside Higher Education*, November 18, 2015, https://www.insidehighered.com/news/2015/11/18/south-africa-push-continues-free-tuition-and-adequate-support (accessed June 18, 2016).
6. Eynon, 122.
7. Ibid.
8. Ibid., 124.
9. Ibid., 129.
10. Ibid.
11. Karen MacGregor, "The HESA Presentation to the Portfolio Committee on Higher Education and Training Is Titled 'South African Higher Education in the 20th Year of Democracy: Context, Achievements and Key Challenges,'" University World News Global Edition Issue 317, April 27, 2014, http://www.universityworldnews.com/article.php?story=20140425131554856 (accessed August 3, 2016).
12. Ministry of Education, *National Plan for Higher Education in South Africa*, February 2001, 19.
13. The Council on Higher Education (CHE), *"Vital Stats, 2013"* Pretoria, South Africa, 2015, 3.
14. Ibid., 33.
15. Nico Cloete, *Another Self-Destructive South African Policy, Center for Higher Education Trust (CHET)*, January 2016, Cape Town, *South Africa*, 4.
16. The Council on Higher Education (CHE), *"Vital Stats, 2013,"* 4.
17. Ibid.
18. Eynon, 138.
19. Ibid., 137.
20. Ibid.

21. Ibid.
22. Cloete, 4.
23. Stats South Africa, "Education Costs Outstrip Inflation," April 22, 2015, http://www.statssa.gov.sa (accessed October 22, 2016).
24. Organization of Economic Co-Operation and Development (OECD), *Reviews of National Policies for Education: South Africa* (Paris: OECD, 2008), 98.
25. Reflections on Higher Education Transformation, Discussion Paper prepared for the second National Higher Education Transformation Summit, 2015, South Africa, 20.
26. Department of Education, *Information on the State Budget for Higher Education 2007* (Pretoria: Department of Education, 2007), 25. The NSFAS assesses the cost of students to study by adding the registration fee per student, to the average cost of tuition and the average cost of residence. The average cost of tuition is calculated as the tuition fee income divided by the number of enrolled students and the average cost of residence is calculated as the residence fee income divided by the number of students in residence.
27. South Africa Council on Higher Education, *Higher Education Monitor: The State of Higher Education in South Africa,* 28.
28. The Council on Higher Education (CHE), *"Vital Stats, 2013,"* 94.
29. Department of Higher Education and Training (DHET) 2010: Audited financial statements of the universities for the period 2000/01 to 2011/12, Moving Forward: Trends in annual reporting by South African public universities—September 2014 Report of the Ministerial Committee for the Review of the Funding of Universities—October 2013, released February 2014 OECD Indicators: Education at a Glance 2014 National Development Plan 2030, Our future—Make it work, 2012.
30. National Student Financial Aid Scheme, 2014/15 Annual Report: NSFAS Toward a Student Centered Approach, Cape Town, South Africa, 17.
31. Ibid.
32. Reflections on Higher Education Transformation, Discussion Paper prepared for the second National Higher Education Transformation Summit, 2015, South Africa, 20.
33. Eynon, 146.
34. Karen McGregor, "South Africa: Debate Moves on from Access to Success," *University World News,* March 15, 2009, http://www.universitynews.com/article.php?story=20090313111607177& (accessed March 24, 2009).
35. Eynon, 146.
36. Ibid., 148.

37. Karen MacGregor, "South Africa: Student Drop-out Rates Alarming," *University World News*, October 28, 2007, http://www.universityworldnews.com/article.php?story=2007102510.php?story=20071025102245380 (accessed November 17, 2009).
38. Karen MacGregor, "South Africa: Shocking Results from University Tests," *University World News*, August 16, 2009, http://www.universityworldnews.com/article.php?story=20090816 (accessed November 17, 2009).
39. Eynon, 153.
40. OECD, 57.
41. Department of Education, *Monitoring and Evaluation Report on the Impact and Outcomes of the Education System on South Africa's Population: Evidence from Household Surveys* (Pretoria: Department of Education, September 2006), 40.
42. Eynon, 154.
43. News 24, "Zuma Reads Teachers the Riot Act," June 8, 2009, www.news24.com (accessed June 8, 2009).
44. Campbell and Bunche, "Slow Progress for South Africa's 'Born-Free' Generation".
45. YouTube, Reitz Racist Video Bloemfontein, March 5, 2008, www.youtube.com/watch?v=F4jq_sucA34 (accessed November 20, 2009).
46. Eynon, 149.
47. Ibid.
48. Ibid.
49. *The Times*, "South Africa's Universities of Shame," May 17, 2009, http://www.thetimes.co.za (accessed May 17, 2009).
50. Ibid.
51. Karen MacGregor, "South Arica: First Black Leader for Free State," *University World News*, March 15, 2009, http://www.universityworldnews.com/article.php?story=20090315085644 70 (accessed April 10, 2009).
52. Dr. Jansen is one of South Africa's leading—and most outspoken—intellectuals. A former biology teacher, he went on to obtain a master's degree from Cornell University in the US and a PhD from Stanford. He was dean of education at the University of Pretoria from 2001 to 2007, and a Fulbright Scholar to Stanford in 2007–08. Jansen's recent books are *Knowledge in the Blood* (2009) and he co-authored *Diversity High: Class, Color, Character and Culture in a South African High School* (2008).
53. MacGregor, "South Arica: First Black Leader for Free State."
54. *Mail & Guardian Online*, "UFS Drops Racist Video Charges," October 18, 2009, http://www.mg.com.za/article/2009-10-18-ufs-dropsracist-video-charges (accessed November 10, 2009.

55. *Mail & Guardian Online*, "Suspend Reitz Decision, Ministry Tells Jansen," October 21, 2009, http://www.mg.com.za/article/2009-10-21-suspend-reitz-decision-ministry-tells-jansen (accessed November 10, 2009).
56. Karen MacGregor, "South Africa: Vice-chancellor Faces Death," *University World News*, November 1, 2009, http://universityworldnews.com/article.php?story=20091101 (accessed November 2, 2009).
57. *Mail & Guardian Online*, "Malema: 'We cannot feed Jansen to the Enemy,' October 29, 2009, http://www,mg,co,za/article/2009-10-29-malema-we-cannot-feed-jansen-to-the-enemy (accessed November 10, 2009).
58. South Africa Council on Higher Education, *Higher Education Monitor: The State of Higher Education in South Africa*, 85.
59. Reflections on Higher Education Transformation, Discussion Paper prepared for the second National Higher Education Transformation Summit, 2015, South Africa, 12.
60. Eynon, 155.
61. Ibid., 156.
62. Ibid.
63. Ibid.
64. Ian Scott, Nan Yeld, and Jane Herdy, "South Africa Council on Higher Education," *A Case Study for Improving Teaching and Learning in South African Higher Education,* Higher Education Monitor no. 6 (October 2007); Centre for Higher Education Development, University of Cape Town, South Africa, 12.
65. Ibid., 12.
66. Ibid., 34–35.
67. Ibid.
68. Cloete,4.
69. Eynon, 143.
70. Ibid., 147.
71. Cloete, 30.
72. Reflections on Higher Education Transformation, Discussion Paper prepared for the second National Higher Education Transformation Summit, 2015, South Africa, 10.
73. Cloete, 8.
74. OECD, 338. Comprehensive universities were expected to combine formative and career-focused technological higher education through student access to a wider variety of courses with different entry requirements, student mobility between career-focused and formative courses, expanded research opportunities that linked applied research to basic research. It was thought that with this increased scope and capacity they would be able to meet regional needs.

75. Eynon, 157.
76. Ibid.
77. Ibid., 162.
78. Ibid.
79. Karen MacGregor, May 4, 2008, "South Africa: New qualifications Framework," *University World News,* http://universityworldnews.com/article.php?story=20080501171728596& (accessed March 3, 2009).
80. Thiven Reddy, *Higher Education and Social Transformation: South African Case Study*, Report to the South African Council on Higher Education, Pretoria (February 2004), www.che.ac.za, 35.
81. Silvia Federici, George Caffentzis, and Ousseina Alidous, A *Thousand Flowers: Social Struggles Against Structural Adjustment in African Universities* (Trenton, NJ: Africa World Press, 2000), 101.
82. Ibid., 101.
83. Eynon, 163.
84. Ibid., 159.
85. Ibid.
86. Ibid., 160.
87. Ibid.
88. Ibid.
89. Ibid.
90. Ibid.
91. Ibid.
92. Ibid.
93. Ibid.
94. Ibid.
95. Ibid.
96. OECD, 338.
97. Karen MacGregor and G.Maslen, "Comprehensive University Reality 'fraught and complicated,'" *University World News: Special Africa Edition,* January 29, 2008, www.universityworldnews.com/article.php?story=20080129095613996 (accessed December 20, 2009).
98. OECD, 338.
99. South Africa Council on Higher Education, *Higher Education Monitor: The State of Higher Education in South Africa*, 2007, 20.
100. Ibid., 20–21.
101. The Council on Higher Education (CHE), *"Vital Stats, 2013,"* 33.
102. Eynon, 159.
103. Ibid., 82.
104. Ibid., 83.
105. Ministry of Education, 27.

106. Organization of Economic Co-Operation and Development (OECD), *Reviews of National Policies for Education: South Africa* (Paris: OECD, 2008), 344, Figure 8.3.
107. I. Bunting, C. Sheppard, N. Cloete, and L. Belding, "PERFORMANCE INDICATORS IN SOUTH AFRICAN HIGHER EDUCATION 2000–2008 Summary Report," Center for Higher Education Trust (CHET), Cape Town, South Africa, 14.
108. The Council on Higher Education (CHE), *"Vital Stats, 2013,"* 25.
109. Karen MacGregor, "South Africa: Communist Takes Charge of Higher Education," *University World News*, May 24, 2009, 1.
110. Ibid., 2.
111. Ibid.
112. Eynon, 166.
113. SETA stands for Sector Education and Training Authority. SETA organizations were established by Minister of Labor Membathisi Mdladlana in 2000. There are at 23 SETAs operational in South Africa. The main function of a SETA is to improve workforce skills—to bring new skills to the employed, and help those wanting to be employed in a given sector acquire the skills they need. SETAs follow the National Skills Development Strategy; their goal is to ensure that people learn skills that are needed by employers and communities, Training must be to agreed standards within the National Qualifications Framework wherever possible, CTFL SETA. http://www.ctflseta.org.za (accessed November 29, 2009). National Skills Authority: The 29-member National Skills Authority was established in the Skills Development Act and is made up of representatives from business, labor, government and community organizations. Its main function is to advise the Labor Minister about a national skills development strategy and its implementation, http://www,southafrica,info/business/economy/policies/labourbodies,htm (accessed December 5, 2009). National Skills Fund: The National Skills Fund (NSF) was established in 1999 under the terms of the 1998 Skills Development Act, to support the implementation of the National Skills Development Strategy (NSDS), "The Act seeks to address the structural deficiencies of the labour market, and develop a workforce that can respond to the modern economic environment, taking into account the equity considerations that are peculiar to South Africa," *National Skills Fund Strategic Projects 2006–2009*, Department of Labour, Republic of South Africa, 1, http://www.labour.gov.za.(accessed December 5, 2009).
114. Blade Nzimande, "The Post-School Education and Training System: Some Issues of Policy," public lecture by the Minister of Higher Education and Training, July 23, 2009, Wits School of Public and Development Management, Pretoria, South Africa, 1.
115. Eynon, 166.

116. Ibid., 167.
117. I Blade Nzimande, "The Post-School Education and Training System: Some Issues of Policy," public lecture by the Minister of Higher Education and Training, July 23, 2009, Wits School of Public and Development Management, Pretoria, South Africa, 3.
118. Ibid.
119. Ibid., 4.
120. Caiphus Kgosana, "All Deserve University Education-Nzimande," *IOL*, www.iol.co.za (accessed July, 1 2009).
121. Kgosana, "All Deserve University Education-Nzimande;" Centre For Higher Education Transformation, *Responding to the Educational Needs of Post-School Youth: Determining the Scope of the Problem and Developing a Capacity-Building Model*, First Draft Synthesis Report (Wynberg, South Africa: Centre for Higher Education Transformation, June 2009).
122. Kgosana, "All Deserve University Education-Nzimande."
123. Kane-Berman, J. *"Born Free But Still in Chains: South Africa's First Post-Apartheid Generation* (Johannesburg, South Africa: South African Institute of Race Relations, 2015), 24.
124. Ibid.
125. Reflections on Higher Education Transformation, Discussion Paper prepared for the second National Higher Education Transformation Summit, 2015, South Africa, 20.

CHAPTER 7

Women and Higher Education: The Successes and Challenges

On August 28, 2007, Deputy President Phumzile Mlambo-Ngcuka told those present at the 4th annual Women's Parliament Conference in Cape Town, "Educate a woman, you educate a nation."[1] His remarks reflected the government's commitment since 1994 to increase women's access to higher education and its belief that the education of women is a key factor in the country's future. And in many ways, the government's initiatives, plans, and laws related to women and education have succeeded: women's enrollment and retention rates in higher education have risen significantly.

In spite of those accomplishments, however, many women still have limited access to higher education, and for those who have managed to enter the system, challenges remain. Further, the combined effect of race, class, and geographical location create inequities among groups of women in South Africa. Acknowledging those differences allows for a closer examination of the challenges and how to move beyond them.

Unfortunately, however, when discussing race, retention, and higher education, women are usually hidden in the discussion and black women's stories in particular are lost.[2] Moreover, the available data on gender and higher education lump all women together rather than looking at access and retention by race, socioeconomic status, or geographical location. While policy makers recognize to some degree that certain women have benefited significantly more than others, the lack of qualitative and quantitative data helps to support the view that all South African women are created equal and have similar challenges and opportunities.

© The Author(s) 2017
D.E. Eynon, *Women, Economic Development, and Higher Education*,
DOI 10.1007/978-3-319-53144-1_7

The following chapter clearly illustrates that this view is skewed and that, in fact, for many women, access and retention continues to be out of reach. It will also describe the progress that has been made since 1994 in bringing more women into the higher education system, their enrollment in fields of study considered vital to South Africa's economic growth and development, and the difficulties they still face in their pursuit of higher education.

The Promise Fulfilled? It Depends

South African women, particularly black women, have historically obtained lower levels of education than men. For example, in 1998, data on educational achievement by gender and age group revealed that more women ages 25 years and older had no education at all compared to men in the same age category. Specifically the data showed that, in that category, 18 percent of all women and 23 percent of black women had no education compared to 12 percent of all men and 16 percent of black men. In addition, black women had the greatest lack of education: compared to 22 percent of all women, 28 percent of black women had not completed a minimum level of education for basic literacy.

The post-apartheid government recognized the problem and began efforts to increase girls' and women's access to education through various policies and initiatives as described in previous chapters.[3] As a result of those efforts, the percentage of black women with no education has been cut almost in half—from 28 percent to 14 percent—yet is still considerably higher than the 1 percent of white women without any education.[4]

But there is still a long way to go when it comes to educating particularly black women from rural areas. The pipeline of women who have high school degrees and are eligible to enter higher education suggests that the inequities between black and white women not only exist today but could very well remain: only 22.7 percent of black women have the equivalent of a high school degree compared to 40.7 percent of white women.

Going forward, what is the potential for black women to attend a university and obtain a postsecondary degree? Because higher education data, while disaggregated by gender, does not provide enrollment data by specific groups of women in terms of race, socioeconomic status, or geographical location—all factors that influence one's ability to access higher education—it's difficult to have any definitive answers. This is what we do know.

Fields of Study: The Move Toward Nontraditional Programs

Women as a group have made marked progress in higher education over the past decades. In their effort to create the human capital necessary for South Africa to compete in a global knowledge-based economy—to generate economic growth and development, and to create jobs—the government and universities have been working to increase the number of female students, especially those enrolled in science, technology, engineering, and mathematics, or STEM fields. Unless women, who constitute just over half of the country's population,[5] are consciously recruited and trained, the government's objectives for increasing the number of engineers and scientists cannot be met.[6]

South African corporations have supported such efforts—and, in fact, have been ahead of the government in recognizing the need to increase the potential pool of students in STEM disciplines. In the 1980s, the University of Cape Town (UCT's) engineering program was predominately white and male. A few colored students attended on "permits," but they were a clear minority. By the mid-1980s, corporations saw the need for trained black engineers and began encouraging and supporting universities like UCT to produce more of them. They worked with universities to help students who came from less-qualified schools to prepare for the university and to open up access to engineering.

Jenni Case, associate professor of chemical engineering and former director of undergraduate studies at UCT, arrived at the university in the 1990s. According to her, given the success of their partnership with corporations, the demographics of the chemical engineering classes at UCT then were not very different from what they were in 2008—with approximately 30 percent white students and the rest primarily black students. The general increase in black students in the chemical engineering program also brought a greater number of black female students.[7]

Since then, women have made significant advances in these fields of study, even though men still continue to dominate with 55.5 percent of enrollments—the same rate of enrollment in 2008—while the rate of change for women during the same period increased by not quite one percent.[8] But even though the percentage of women enrolled is less than that of men, when breaking down the category into more detail, one finds that more than twice as many women than men are enrolled in industrial arts, trades, technology, health care, and health sciences. Women also made up a higher percentage of those enrolled in life sciences and physical sciences. The greatest gender imbalances are in engineering and engineering technology, where only 24 percent of the students enrolled are women, and in health care and health sciences, where only 32 percent of the students are men.[9] Similar to enrollment patterns, more men graduate than women in science, engineering, and technology—but even there, just by a small margin.

Meanwhile, in education, 75 percent of the graduates are women; in human and social sciences, 66 percent of graduates are women; and in business, commerce, and management, 57 percent of graduates are women.[10] All that suggests that women are still being tracked into specific careers that are "feminized" and remain in professions that pay less and have less social status than men's.[11] For example, in 2013 women made up 75 percent of all those enrolled in education as a field of study and 64 percent of those enrolled in the humanities.[12]

Sharmala Govender, CEO of Big Brothers and Big Sisters, lectures part-time, first-year students in the department of psychology at the University of Johannesburg. Most of her students are female. She notes: "You look at any field pertaining to human activity or social development or community services, and it will be 90 percent female. You will get the one or two odd males sitting there, but most of the time, it's only out of curiosity."[13]

Still, as more women enter into STEM fields, people are more willing to accept their participation in those programs.[14] Even better, young girls are becoming increasing confident in their ability to pursue such fields. Policy makers and educators have reported that it is not unusual to hear young girls say they are going to be aeronautical engineers—and that these young women are excited about pursuing such careers.[15]

That said, convincing women they can, in fact, fulfill the skills required in historically male-dominated disciplines of science, engineering, technology, and math is vital given that, women still tend to gravitate toward the humanities, which are biased in favor of women.[16] The government could do more to target women and provide more funding opportunities and special preparation programs for them in the STEM fields. It is not uncommon to hear a female scientist say that she stumbled into engineering, science, math, or technology. Thus, it would also help to identify these young women earlier, while in high school, and to match them with a mentor. Mentoring as a social-service engagement would go a long way to encouraging more women to consider those fields of study.[17]

Female Enrollment and Graduation Rates
In 1995, for the first time ever, more women were enrolled in higher education institutions than men, and in the following decades since then, women's enrollment rates have continued to rise vis-à-vis men's.[18] By 2014, female enrollment rates rose to 58.2, while enrollment rates for males continued to drop, accounting for only 41.7 percent enrollments.[19]
At the masters' level, however, the percentage of men enrolled remains higher than the percentage of women, even though the latter grew to 49 percent in 2013, representing a 2.5 percent increase over five years. And the largest gender gap in post graduate enrollment rates comes at the doctoral level, where men represent 56.3 percent of those enrolled. That represents a decrease of 1 percent since 2008, while women have seen a 1 percent increase to 43.7 percent of doctoral enrollments.[20] Again, the numbers are trending positively, but the rate of change for women, particularly at the doctoral level, has been slow.
As with enrollment rates, women are outperforming men at the undergraduate level when it comes to graduation rates.[21] In 2013, 60 percent of bachelor degrees awarded went to women.[22] The situation is less rosy, however, at higher levels: women received only 49.5 percent of the master degrees and just 43.6 percent of the doctoral degrees awarded.[23]

Hidden Yet Entrenched Inequities

That more women in South Africa are entering universities and going into STEM fields is cause for optimism. Without doubt, female enrollment rates have increased since the end of apartheid—so much so that there is growing concern at the undergraduate level about the continuing drop in male enrollment rates. But while more women are entering higher education, the students who account for that growth are disproportionately white women.[24] A significant number of women still lack access to higher education, particularly those who are black and from rural areas.[25]

In 2011, almost 36 percent of the South African population lived in rural areas with women between the ages of 15 and 64 years old accounting for just under 60 percent of that[26] rural population.[27] Black women represented 96 percent of all women living in rural areas.[28] They are the ones who have not gained access to higher education. Some people would say it is difficult to give everyone in the country equal opportunity, yet South African black rural women represent a significant percentage of its population and human capital. It only makes sense to see to it that rural women have same chance for upward mobility within the educational system that other groups of women, particularly white women, have had.[29]

A first step is to recognize that women in rural areas have different and more difficult challenges than other women. Issues of transportation and language restrict them. What's more, they don't have access to basic tools like the Internet, email, or computers—all of which makes it extremely difficult to communicate outside their villages or gain access to information.

To deal with such problems, community-based programs have been sending student groups out to rural areas to teach women about educational opportunities that are available and how to access them. As part of this effort, they use vehicles equipped with technology that allows access to the Internet so they can assist these rural women with applications for enrollment and financial aid.[30]

While such programs have helped poor rural women gain access higher education, the magnitude of the problem requires a more strategic and comprehensive plan, as well as the investment of more resources. So far, however, none of that has materialized—perhaps again in part due to a lack of understanding of the issue and the specific challenges that women face, given the dearth of data on female undergraduates related to race, socioeconomic status, and geography.

Indeed, it's becoming increasingly apparent that South Africans are not accustomed to framing policy discussions around gender and rarely consider women as a separate category, let alone think about sub-categories of women. Jenni Case at the UCT expressed it in this way:

> We're not used to framing the discussion in terms of women. I can talk about the difficulties of black students and white students, and women are often hidden within that. And when you consider a middle-class white woman from a family of three generations of tertiary education compared to a black woman from a township whose mother is a domestic worker and whose father is a security guard, they obviously would see themselves as facing quite different challenges.[31]

Meanwhile, the rural women who, in fact, have been able to enroll in universities have often had to adjust to many changes, including city life. For many of those women, it is the first time they have lived outside their communities and away from their families. They are becoming more independent, and mature; they are finding jobs, and sending money back home. It is a new virtuous cycle for those who succeed.[32] Unfortunately, however, not many women fall into that category for reasons that we'll explore later in this chapter.

The growth in women's enrollment is certainly due in part to the efforts of the government and the various laws and gender-specific initiatives that have been put in place over the past 22 years. Other factors are also at play, including a shift in attitudes about the value and need to educate women. For example, local communities in South Africa still hold an influence over how people think and what they do. Increasingly, those communities are understanding the reasons why women need to be educated and, as a result, they are encouraging women to go to the university.[33] People are also more aware of the opportunities that higher education can open up for women.[34]

Still, while that change in attitude has had a positive influence on young women's interest in pursuing education, many are at a loss to know how to access the system. They are often the first in their family to do so,[35] and they lack role models to help them make decisions about what to study, where to stay, how to pay for school, or simply what to expect. Oftentimes the questions, effort, and frustration seem to far outweigh the opportunity.[36]

Thus, although enrollment and graduation rates among women have been improving significantly, it is important to understand the many and complex challenges that women—especially poor, black and rural women—continue to face in South Africa's higher education system.[37]

The Continuing Challenges

In many ways, the problems women encounter in the higher education system mirror those they face outside of it. And as within the broader society, different women experience worse problems depending on their race, class, and where they grew up.

According to Bev Thaver, associate professor of education at the University of Western Cape, it is important to separate women into groups when discussing their success in higher education:

> You may find that retention levels for white women may be higher than they are for black women. For it is the architecture of the past that continues to

> influence what happens in the present. I mean, the old kind of Gramscian term, you know. The past has put a high mortgage on the present.[38]

In 2008, Minister of Education Naledi Pandor announced the establishment of the previously mentioned Ministerial Committee on Progress Towards Transformation and Social Cohesion and the Elimination of Discrimination in Public Higher Education Institutions in response to the Reitz Four incident, discussed in Chapter 6. The main purpose of the committee was to investigate discrimination in public higher education institutions, with a particular focus on racism, and to make recommendations on how to eliminate discrimination and promote social cohesion. In the case of some of the historically white institutions, such as the UCT or Wits University, the committee heard reports of young black women who went to former white or multiracial elementary and secondary schools, where they performed well—sometimes better than white students. During their first year at the university they continued to be on par with the white students, but then during the second year, as the white students passed to the next level, they were channeled into foundation classes where they often had to pay extra tuition.[39] As a result, these black female students have become frustrated by the experience and have concluded that the environment is not necessarily supportive.

Crain Soudien, acting vice chancellor at the UCT, spoke with many black women during the committee's visits across the university system and recalled an interview with one of them in particular. It illustrated for him just how complex the university experience can be for a black woman and the lasting impression it can make on her life:

> In fact, she has a lot of worldly experience, and her children are these incredible, new-era products, and they're living in Australia and Switzerland—all over the world. But she herself is still having to kind of come to terms with the fact that she's a supplicant in this space (university). So she has to continually be kind of doffing her cap and being this posture of almost asking for favors all the time. And it's complicated because she knows very well what the possibilities of what this space might provide. But she still feels a sense of inferiority. It's that complexity that I have think that we're not sufficiently attuned to.[40]

A number of issues contribute to that complexity that should be explored, including patriarchal attitudes, family pressures, a lack of financial support, sexism, sexual assault and safety, and unwanted pregnancies. Each is described briefly below.

The Patriarchal System

The university setting and its structures often present the first challenges to female students. When women enter the higher education system, they find themselves within an environment defined by patriarchal attitudes. As Crain Soudien has noted, higher education institutions remain "geared towards the production of masculine privilege."[41] Women need to navigate that space, often with little preparation, leaving them feeling isolated and self-conscious. That is particularly true for rural black women, who frequently come into the system with even less preparation in how to cope than their white counterparts.[42] To survive, they must be alert, self-aware, and somehow hold their own.

Venitha Pillay, professor of education at the University of Pretoria, highlighted the challenges that the patriarchal nature of universities has created for women:

> I think the biggest issue is that all our higher education institutions are *extremely* patriarchal institutions. In a way, that it is so engrained, and so much the norm, that nobody actually sees it. Women themselves don't even see it. [43]

A by-product of this patriarchal attitude is that, in some cases, people don't expect much of women in terms of their performance. That view, in combination with lingering racist attitudes, makes it particularly difficult for black female students. University lecturers used to say that blacks were not intelligent enough to major in programs like mathematics, and, especially if you were a woman, they made you feel as if you were wasting your time and everyone else's. Unfortunately, those attitudes prevail today: during visits to universities across the higher education system, the Committee on Progress Towards Transformation and Social Cohesion and the Elimination of Discrimination in Public Higher Education Institutions learned of incidents in which lecturers placed low expectations on black people—and black women in particular.[44] Such attitudes continue to create significant challenges to female students, especially those enrolled in STEM programs.[45]

The resignation of a professor at KwaZulu Natal University illustrates just how pervasive not only racial but also patriarchal attitudes are in higher education. The professor decided to resign rather than being led by a female head of the department, saying quite candidly that, given his upbringing and culture, he could not take orders from a woman.[46]

Competing Family Demands

Many students' families communities hold patriarchal attitudes, as well. It is not uncommon to hear stories about woman who withdraw from college due to family pressures and expectations. That is especially true for female students who come from rural areas, as customary and tribal laws and traditions still rule everyday life. In many of those communities, men continue to come first.[47]

For instance, if a family can afford to send a child to a university, it will probably send the boy. If it sends both a son and daughter, and someone is needed back home, the chances are high the girl will be the one asked to drop out and return home. And, if the family's finances change and it can no longer afford tuition or transportation for both children, again it is the girl who is expected to leave the university.

Customary gender roles put additional stress on female students. In general, there is a huge amount of pressure on a woman to provide care at home and to support their family.[48] Many women who commute to college must learn to reprioritize tasks so that the provision of the family meals, cooking, and other domestic duties take a backseat to reading for the next day's class or studying for an exam. The student's entire family must learn to accept these new educational priorities,[49] and sometimes the difficulty in doing that creates significant tensions.

Even after women graduate from the university, they are not immune to such pressures. Jenni Case of the UCT told the story of a black female student who graduated with a master's degree. She married her college boyfriend soon after graduation. The pressure from her family was to fulfill her traditional gender role was so strong that she had to give up a scholarship to study for her Ph.D. overseas in order to start a family. She felt she had no other choice.[50]

While all students from poor families and rural areas are expected to come home from the university if their family is experiencing difficulties, this expectation seems to be most prevalent among black women. There are many stories of young black women who have done very well in college, who have shown tremendous progress and received financial support to continue their studies, including full residence scholarships at the university. But in the midst of that success, their families have called them back home to earn money and provide support. The family's attitude has been that the young woman is needed right away and can't be tucked away in residence learning to be this thing that would get her to earn money later.[51] Unfortunately, that story is not uncommon: in the 2014 General Household Survey, 21.8 percent of women, compared to just 1 percent of men, said that family commitments were the reason they left their university studies.[52]

Inadequate Financial Support

As mentioned in the previous chapter, insufficient financial support is also a major factor contributing to dropout rates for women as well as men—and especially for poor black female students who come from rural areas. Because of the high level of unemployment in those students' rural hometowns, they often send back home to their family as much as 80 percent of the scholarship money meant to maintain them at the university.[53] As a result, it isn't uncommon for such students to lack adequate funds for meals or for traveling back and forth to their campuses.[54] And because many of the fathers of these students have left home to work in the cities, young female students must often take care of immediate family needs—not only by sending money home but also by securing a job while in school or simply returning home to work.[55] All of these financial concerns disrupt their studies and can ultimately ruin their opportunity to graduate with a college degree.

Sexual Assault and Safety Issues

Beyond educational and financial challenges, the university setting also creates a whole new set of social ones. The sophistication level of women when they enter the higher education system is a factor, especially for those who are coming from a rural area to an urban area. Life at a university can be quite a culture shock for many young women. For the first time, they have no parental guidance, and beyond the university itself, no authority figure to whom they must answer. They enter a new, fascinating, and unfamiliar place that tests their values in many areas, including sexuality and sexual relations, which can often put women in difficult situations.

Sharmala Govender, CEO of Big Brothers, Big Sisters of South Africa, described the situation:

> It's a whole new experience being at university, and there are boys everywhere. Young women will have relationships, sometimes many relationships, increasing the likelihood of picking up HIV/AIDS. It's all the secondary issues that now come into play. And this is what affects woman the most because men don't have to go through all this as a woman does. They leave their homestead much earlier than a woman does. She only leaves when she's ready for higher education; other than that, she doesn't step foot out of there. Women enter the system very immature.[56]

It is not uncommon to hear stories about violence against women on university campuses, including murder. Those are horrible and real stories, and the kind not expected to be associated with an academic institution. But, in actuality, the campus environment does not always respect the rights and the dignity of women.[57] Women find themselves victimized in the very system that is supposed to be promoting knowledge and civility.

Maria Phalime, author and former deputy director of 2010 FIFA World Cup at Provincial Government, learned first-hand what it felt like to be a woman on a campus and how she worried about her safety and that of her friends:

> Strangely, the university was not a safe place. I remember that, during my Varsity days, there was fear around going out at night and going to parties—which is what a university's partly about, really. Those are your party years. But in my circle of friends, there were experiences of rape and abduction.[58]

In fact, one of the key findings to emerge from the work of the Committee on Progress Towards Transformation and Social Cohesion and the Elimination of Discrimination in Public Higher Education Institutions was the prevalence of sexism and the sexual harassment of female students on campuses. In the committee's view, "the impact of sexism is as pernicious as that of racism. If you are black and a woman it is doubly painful."[59]

Students described to the committee frequent situations of sexual harassment in the form of sexual favors that lecturers often expected of female students in exchange for good grades. Rape and violence were also common on many campuses, although such incidents were often kept quiet as a result of entrenched institutional culture and the lack of enforcement of the policies established to protect people.

Rhodes University, a historically all-male institution, that is today co-ed, is an example of one where institutional culture and lack of enforcement of policies perpetuate violence against women.[60] During the committee hearings, students from that institution reported that a culture had developed over time at Rhodes that undervalued women. They described how university officials had met complaints of gender inequality, sexism, and sexual harassment with resistance and a "denial of responsibility." Cases of rape were not made public, records weren't kept, and women who were abused or assaulted were not encouraged to report the incidences.[61] The committee concluded: "There is no doubt, given the endemic rape and sexual harassment in South African society, that it is equally prevalent in higher education institutions. It is therefore cause for concern that sexism and sexual harassment have not featured significantly in the institutional submissions." In other words, institutions had avoided acknowledgment of the issue. [62]

The material culture that exists on many campuses further complicates women's lives. Women feel pressured to have the right clothes, the right cell phone, and other items that define status. In fact, one way that older men on campuses gain power over younger women is by becoming "sugar daddies" and providing material possessions to them. That puts such men in a position to make sexual demands on the woman and leaves her in a position of weakness. In such situations, for example, the woman is not able to insist that the man use a condom or be tested for sexually transmitted diseases, which can result in unwanted pregnancies and/or the transmission of HIV/AIDS.[63]

In addition, the threat of violence outside of the university can have ramifications on students and faculty members on the campus, as it can discourage women from coming to classes or restrict the times they feel safe to do so. Nadine Petersen, professor of education at the University of Johannesburg, recalls her experience teaching an evening class;

> I teach a class in the evenings, and two-thirds of my black students, particularly women, have to leave at a particular time halfway through the class. Already they're at the disadvantage because of language and other issues, and then they have to leave halfway through the class because they have to get public transport at a particular time. If they miss that transport, they've had it.[64]

According to Petersen, the problem affects the ability to students to maneuver around the campus, to access library facilities after hours, or to simply travel between the university and home.[65] In an attempt to deal with the safety issues she has described, many of the women make arrangements with a particular taxi driver to be picked up as a group at a certain time because South Africa does not have a safe or reliable public transportation system.

Unwanted Pregnancies

As if all those challenges were not enough, a growing number of young women become pregnant while at university, although exact statistics on the trend and reasons for it are hard to come by.[66] Such a growth in unwanted pregnancies is rather surprising in the age of HIV when unprotected sex is a very dangerous proposition. While the universities have been trying to educate students about the need to protect themselves, the message is clearly not getting across. It is especially perplexing given what many female students have to do just to get into a university. With some, it seems an act of self-sabotage: giving up an opportunity for advancement by becoming pregnant.

At the same time, gender roles probably play out at the university in the same way they do at home. Just because a young woman or man attends a university does not necessarily mean that she or he is going to change their attitudes about sex and allow the woman greater say about the use of contraception.[67]

If a woman does become pregnant, she is under considerable pressure to give birth to the child. Thus, for students who become pregnant during their studies, the challenge is to ensure that the home environment provides enough support to allow them to continue studying. Unfortunately, that is usually not the case, as social mores usually pressure women to become caregivers for their own children.[68] That social obligation, along with the lack of assistance for women who become pregnant, makes it unlikely that they can return to the university.[69] And even if a woman is able to stay in school, she must then juggle two obligations: studying and parenting. Although attitudes vary, men are not typically active in helping out in the home. Without support, a young, pregnant woman's obligations usually force her ultimately to drop out.[70]

Yvonne Shapiro, director at SAQA, expressed her frustration with the growing number of young women who become unexpectedly pregnant during their higher education learnership programs, which include financial support and are designed to prepare talented students in a particular field of study:

> I have been frustrated three times with students who have become pregnant during their learnership. What has been upsetting for me is things like timing – people coming into the learnership and then getting pregnant fairly early on and completely distracting themselves. During the first cycle of the learnership program that we ran, there were three pregnancies, and two of the students then failed outright, and the other one sort of borderline passed, and then the poor thing also miscarried, which was very unfortunate for her.[71]

For Shapiro, the behavior of these young women is irresponsible; they are throwing away an opportunity:

> They failed the exams and then left. And that was just me seeing three people out of the 10 of my intake of that year. I think I had six women and four men. So half the women of my intake did that. And I do think that those sorts of issues do affect women more than men- and not just pregnancy but various kinds of other health issues.[72]

Universities are trying to help students who become pregnant by offering counseling services, including assistance for students who must leave the university to have a baby but can come back later and finish their degree. Some universities have special dormitories in which a student can leave a child under the care of a nanny during the day.[73] The government and NGOs also run programs designed to help students who become pregnant. Yet, in the end, while women from upper-class families tend to return, the likelihood that a rural woman will do so is still relatively small.[74]

Racism, sexism, the competing demands of family, sexual harassment and abuse, the inability to go to classrooms to study at night due to fear of violence, and pregnancy—these issues are all cited as contributing factors in reducing retention and success rates for women.[75] The Committee on Progress Towards Transformation and Social Cohesion and the Elimination of Discrimination in Public Higher Education Institutions has brought such issues to the surface. Resolving these highly complex problems will be difficult as they are endemic to South Africa as a whole.

Many of the issues are also intertwined, making it hard to untangle the causes and find simple solutions.

But policy makers and university leaders must begin to deal with these difficult and painful problems soon. They are already well aware that higher education has a significant role to play in lifting up women in South Africa. Yet despite their previous efforts to improve opportunities for women, the results have been mixed. When viewed strictly by the numbers, the situation for South Africa's women in higher education is good. Women's access and retention rates continue to increase, and more women are entering into traditionally male dominated fields of study, such as science, engineering, technology, and math. But all the issues just described make the university a very difficult environment for many women.

Moreover, on closer examination, it becomes apparent that poor, black, and rural women are not making the same progress as other women. If academics and other higher education leaders wish to gain a clear picture of the situation, they must look at gender from a multidimensional perspective. Women are white, black, rich, poor, and everything in between. How do these differences influence their ability to access higher education and their likelihood of success once in the system? What are their shared experiences?

Until South Africa's political and education leaders ask—and answer—these and other questions, it is premature for them to declare victory in their efforts to increase women's access and retention in the higher education system.

Profiles of South African Women

Irene Moutlana

Irene Moutlana is the vice chancellor and principal at the Vaal University of Technology (VUT). She earned her master's degree and doctor of education degrees from Harvard University as a Fulbright Student. She began her career as a high school teacher until she entered higher education as a lecturer and is today a central figure in the South African higher education system. Moutlana is known for her dedication to the development of South Africa's students, as is reflected in her institution's commitment to offer students an education on par with the Massachusetts Institute of Technology (MIT).

Prior to her appointment as vice chancellor in 2008, she was the interim deputy vice chancellor of research, innovation and technology at the Nelson Mandela Metropolitan University (NMMU) and a vice rector at the then Academic at Port Elizabeth Technikon. During that time, she was also a community developer and was nominated for Business Woman of the Year (2002). As a result, some people were surprised when she accepted the position at VUT; the institution was plagued by scandals and staff upheavals, and was known for a lack of high academic standards.

Today, under Moutlana's leadership, VUT has redefined itself. It draws students from all over Africa with its world-class facilities (labs and lecture halls) and strong focus on research and innovation. And, given the institution's close proximity to a strong industrial region, it has been able to create partnerships with local companies in the heavy-metal and petrochemical industries and to attract experts in science, engineering and technology. Over the course of Moutlana's tenure, VUT has received awards for financial management and governance in the management of the National Student Financial Aid Scheme (NSFAS) funds and has grown its international partnerships in research and student exchange. And its engineering qualifications now have international standing, with accreditation through the Engineering Council of South Africa (ECSA).

It took time and the creation of a new vision and strategy to transform the institution to what it is today: a University of Technology. In order to do that, Moutlana sought the advice and counsel of external strategists—people who could make an objective assessment of what the institution needed to do and how best to create a vision of shared leadership to implement the new strategy.

Moutlana's appointment has not been without controversy. On November 29, 2012, she was suspended until an investigation into alleged financial mismanagement could be conducted. The investigation focused on the 2010 awarding of two contracts to consultants who assisted in the development of a new strategy for the institution. The Minster of Higher Education and Training disbanded VUT's council as they were also implicated in the financial mismanagement. Moutlana was found guilty of personally influencing the awarding of the contract and for allowing the consultants to overspend on the project by almost three times the original amount. She was not found guilty of corruption or of personally benefiting from the awarding of the contracts. In June 2013, Moutlana returned to her position as vice chancellor and principal.

When Moutlana's first five-year term was due to end in December 2013, VUT's new council extended it for another three years. In 2014, she was appointed the deputy chairperson of the South African Technology Network (SATN). Five South African Universities of Technology established SATN in 2006 to promote the development of national education and training policies that support the work and contributions of their institutions.

Sources:
Mail& Guardian Website, *The Jewel of the Vaal*, May 27, 2011
http://mg.co.za/article/2011-05-27-the-jewel-of-vaal
(accessed November 21, 2016)

Bongani Nkosi, *VUT vice-chancellor suspended over corruption allegations*, November 29, 2012 Mail & Guardian website
http://mg.co.za/article/2012-11-29-vut-vice-chancellor-suspended-over-corruption-allegations
(accessed November 21, 2016)

IOL News Website, *Vice-chancellors' contract extension angers critics*, September 29, 2013
http://www.iol.co.za/news/south-africa/gauteng/vice-chancellors-contract-extension-angers-critics-1584185

Notes

1. Lynn Anzia, *Women News Network*, August 28, 2007, http://womensnewsnetwork.net/2007/08/28/percentE2percent80percent9Ceducate-a-woman-you-educate-a-nationpercentE2percent80percent93-south-africa-aims-to-improve-its-education-for-girls (accessed May 9, 2009).
2. Ibid.
3. Sally Baden, Shireen Hasim, and Shelia Meintjes, *Country Gender Profile: South Africa*. Report prepared for the Swedish International Development Office (Sida) Pretoria, South Africa; Bridge Development, Institute of Development Studies, University of Sussex, UK, (July 1998), 41.
4. STATS South Africa, Census 2011, October 30,2012, Pretoria, South Africa, 35.
5. Ibid., 3.
6. Eynon, 181.
7. Ibid., 182.
8. The Council on Higher Education (CHE), *"Vital Stats, 2013"* Pretoria, South Africa, 2015, 26.
9. Council on Higher Education, 2.
10. Ibid., 27.

11. Eynon, 183.
12. The Council on Higher Education (CHE), *"Vital Stats, 2013,"* 26.
13. Eynon, 183.
14. Ibid.
15. Ibid., 184.
16. Ibid.
17. Ibid.
18. Council on Higher Education, *Higher Education Monitor: The State of Higher Education in South Africa,* HE Monitor no.8 (October 2009), 22; Organization of Economic Co-Operation and Development (OECD), *Reviews of National Policies for Education: South Africa*. (Paris: OECD, 2008), 71.
19. The Council on Higher Education (CHE), *"Vital Stats, 2013,"* 3.
20. Ibid., 20.
21. Council on Higher Education, 33.
22. The Council on Higher Education (CHE), *"Vital Stats, 2013,"* 19.
23. Ibid., 21.
24. Eynon, "Interpreting the Economic Growth and Development Policies of Post-Apartheid South Africa: Its Influence on Higher Education and Prospects for Women,"179.
25. Ibid.
26. Ibid.
27. STATS South Africa, Census 2011, October 30,2012, Pretoria, South Africa, 4.
28. Michael Allen, *Globalization, Negotiation, and the Failure of Transformation in South Africa: Revolution at a Bargain?* (New York: Palgrave Macmillan, 2006), 134.
29. Eynon, 180.
30. Ibid.
31. Ibid., 181.
32. Ibid., 179.
33. Ibid., 178.
34. Ibid.
35. Ibid.
36. Ibid., 179.
37. Eynon, 186.
38. Ibid., 189.
39. Ibid.
40. Ibid., 150.
41. Ibid.
42. Ibid., 187.
43. Ibid.

44. Ibid.
45. Ibid.
46. Ibid.
47. Ibid., 188.
48. Ibid.
49. Ibid.
50. Ibid.
51. Ibid.
52. Statistics South Africa, General Household Survey 2014, July 2015, Pretoria, South Africa, 20.
53. Ibid., 190.
54. Ibid.
55. Statistics South Africa, General Household Survey 2014, July 2015, Pretoria, South Africa,, 20, Eynon, 190.
56. Ibid., 191.
57. Ibid.
58. Ibid., 192.
59. Ministry of Education, South Africa, *Report of the Ministerial Committee on Transformation and Social Cohesion and the Elimination of Discrimination in Public Higher Education Institutions,* November 30, 2008, 44.
60. Eynon, 192.
61. Ministry of Education, South Africa, *Report of the Ministerial Committee on Transformation and Social Cohesion and the Elimination of Discrimination in Public Higher Education Institutions,* November 30, 2008, 45.
62. Ministry of Education, South Africa, *Report of the Ministerial Committee on Transformation and Social Cohesion and the Elimination of Discrimination in Public Higher Education Institutions,* November 30, 2008, 46.
63. Eynon, 193.
64. Ibid.
65. Ibid., 194.
66. Ibid.
67. Ibid.
68. Ibid.
69. Ibid.
70. Ibid., 195.
71. Ibid.
72. Ibid.
73. Ibid.
74. Ibid., 196.
75. Baden et al., 42.

CHAPTER 8

Women's Prospects

Since 1994, the South African government has created and passed legally binding initiatives to promote gender equality, establishing a national gender machinery to implement and monitor those initiatives. The emphasis has been on increasing the representation of women in multiple institutions and creating an environment where women's voices can be heard. The government has done this by creating formal structures and laws in an effort to bring concerns for gender equity into the mainstream.

Those laws, bills, and commissions focused on gender equality and the empowerment of women in the post-apartheid government have served an important purpose. The question remains, however: how effective have they been in achieving their objectives? Do patriarchal, cultural and social norms still have a strong influence on women? If so, how can South Africa and women themselves balance those norms with the progressive gender framework that the government has set forth?

One could reasonably assume South African women have made great strides since the end of apartheid rule as beneficiaries of many government initiatives to further their equality and empowerment. It is a reasonable assumption but not an entirely accurate one. This chapter discusses how opportunities have opened up for women, explores the factors influencing a woman's ability to pursue these opportunities, and describes the conflict South African women often experience in their pursuit of empowerment and success.

© The Author(s) 2017

D.E. Eynon, *Women, Economic Development, and Higher Education*,
DOI 10.1007/978-3-319-53144-1_8

Women's Opportunities: Advancement and Progress…For Some

As described in Chapter 5, the post-apartheid government passed the Employment Equity Act of 1998 (EEA) and the Broad Based Black Economic Empowerment Act of 2003 (B-BBEE) to bring employment equity and balance into the private and public sectors. These acts were aimed at engineering a more representative role for the black majority, in particular women, youth, and people with disabilities.[1] The EEA also included affirmative—action measures to redress the disadvantages in employment that designated groups (Africans, Colored, and Indians) had experienced.

In many ways, women now have the opportunity to do things that they never could before. They have made significant advances since 1994, in large part due to the government's initiatives on their behalf. Today, a group of highly successful black businesswoman is adding value to the private sector, while powerful black women leaders are also taking important roles in the government and academe.

In the private sector, some women are leading the most powerful and influential institutions in the country. They include

- Salukazi Dakile-Hiongwane,[2] CEO of Eqstra Holdings Limited and founding member and chief executive of Nozala Investments;
- Phuti Malabie,[3] named by the *Wall Street Journal* as one of the "Top 50 Women to Watch in 2008" and executive and CEO of Shanduka, a black-owned and managed investment company; and
- Nonkuleleko Nyembezi-Heita,[4] former CEO of Arcelor Mittal South Africa Limited, a subsidiary of the world's largest steelmaker, and *Forbes*'s 97th most powerful woman in the world in 2011.

In the public sector, women such as Nkosazana Dlamini-Zuma,[5] former Minister of Health, Minister of Foreign Affairs, Minister of Home Affairs, and chairperson of the African Union; and Thuli Madonsela,[6] South Africa's Public Protector, who focuses her time and attention on ending mismanagement and misappropriation of funds and ensuring good governance, are powerful examples of women who have and continue to influence the country's policies and practices at home and abroad. Then there's a woman who is in a category all of her own: Mamphela Ramphele —a doctor, academic, author, and businesswoman whose achievements are even more remarkable given many occurred during apartheid and despite the government's efforts to suppress and marginalize black South Africans.

Many of these women have been able to work through the system's obstacles and gain recognition for their efforts.[7] The South African constitution's specific commitment to redress gender imbalances and promote the representation of women in electoral politics—and its identification of women in general and black women in particular as needing affirmation in the work place—have resulted in increased opportunities for women.[8]

Where women, and particularly black women, were more or less disenfranchised in the years leading up to the end of apartheid, they are now becoming important players in the South African economy. The state created specific requirements in the finance, management, science, engineering, and technology sectors, which has opened up many opportunities for women as well as men. Women who have some level of education, skills, and training are positioned to take advantage of those opportunities.[9]

But, as discussed in Chapter 8, the number of women graduating from such educational programs is still relatively small. As a result, women with these skills, particularly black women, are rare and sought after.[10]

Indeed, black South African women who are educated are "gold"[11] at the moment. Corporations want to recruit such women for management and ownerships positions, and they are increasingly placing them in top positions or on boards as they recognize the importance, as Sharmala Govender CEO of Big Brothers Big Sisters says, of having a "black image and keeping up the status of being a progressive and open organization."[12] In the words of Maria Phalime, author and former deputy director of 2010 FIFA World Cup at Provincial Government, "It pays, so to speak, to be a black woman in South Africa in certain respects."[13] Indeed, some of the top companies in the country have a significant number of black women in upper management and on their boards.[14]

Corporations are also empowering women *within* their companies, especially black women. If a company sees that a person has the potential but not the skills, they will pay for her to go through a training program and then place her in a higher-level job. In that way, companies are both improving the skill sets of their employees and fulfilling affirmative-action requirements.[15]

At the same time that black women as a category have been given a special boost in corporations, white women have advanced, as well. In fact, white women have an advantage in that they know how to play "the game"[16] in the corporate sector—which is an entirely new space for many black women, given that race and class marginalized them during the apartheid years. Thus, white women have been able to move into leadership positions much more easily than black women.[17]

More must be done to ensure greater representation of black women in senior management positions,[18] but women generally are doing better than men at all levels. As Gillian Godsell of the Wits School of Public and Development Management says, "If a women has an education and some skills that will enable her to compete in business, the world is her oyster."[19]

The Uphill Battle for Rural Black Women

Despite all the good news for some South African women, however, many others face still face significant obstacles. On the whole, the general black population has not benefited from government and corporate policies. It's all good to write about it on paper, but the reality is that few people have had the benefits that have occurred for a small percentage of women.[20] The vast majority of women are still employed in semiskilled and unskilled labor.[21]

Women who live in urban areas and don't work in the private sector are often doing clerical, menial, domestic, and cleaning work. In many households in rural areas, the men have left to work in the mines or industries located in cities, returning only once a year for holidays. That means that women are running the house and everything else, given South Africa's patriarchal society, where the role of a woman has long been to be a housewife first. In terms of black culture, women were expected to be housewives and many had to work the land, which was not the case with the colored and the white culture. So, it is an uphill battle to get employment equality for these women.[22] They are doing all the farming, mostly on a subsistence level, and selling whatever surplus they can produce. In essence, these women are earning money and finding their way to feed and clothe their children. They are engaged in the informal economy, chipping away every day, without options for changing their situation.[23] Poor, uneducated, and living in the rural areas, they don't even know that opportunities exist.[24]

Many rural black women have no access to any paid work at all and must rely on state grants. A woman who wished to enter the formal economy would have to go to an urban area and try to find domestic work, which pays little.[25] As Harold Herman, emeritus professor of comparative and international education at the University of Western Cape, put it: "I think rural women have enormous challenges. First, they must get out of their traditional role, which is a subservient one, and second, they must bridge the gap, the rural-urban divide, that we have in our society."[26]

Thus, despite all the efforts, including affirmation action, that the government and private sector have taken to engage more women in the formal economy, the situation is far from rosy for many women in South Africa when it comes to employment and economic advancement.

The Numbers Tell the Story

The statistics do not paint a very favorable picture of women's employment in general. The unemployment rate has been and remains much higher for women than men according to data from South Africa's Human Sciences Research Council Center for Poverty, Employment, and Growth.[27] From 1995 to 2014, women across all races had higher unemployment rates than their male counterparts. In 2014, the national unemployment rate was 5.4 percent higher for women than men, with black women most likely to be unemployed.[28]

In addition, unemployment rates among groups of women—particularly between black and white South African women—are uneven. In 2014, black female South African unemployment rates were 30.2 percent compared to only 6.7 percent for white female South Africans.[29] Colored and Asian women had higher unemployment rates than white women but considerably lower than black women.

In 2013, grants from the government were the primary source of income for a black female head of a household. In contrast, for a white female head of household, the primary sources of income were salaries, wages, and commissions. Black female heads of households were by far the largest group to receive grants. [30]

While all race groups have experienced an increase in unemployment across the years, unemployment rates are highest among younger people, women, and black South Africans. The unemployment rate for black male "born frees" aged 15–24 is now as high as 53 percent; for black female "born frees," it runs even higher at 61 percent. [31]

Moreover, such employment rates tell only part of the story. A look at different industry sectors in the formal economy shows that women continue to be employed in what are viewed as traditionally female industries, or the "caring industries." Women are also more likely to be employed in low-skilled occupations, with just 11.7 percent of employed women in high-skilled ones. And it is important to note that, of women employed in professional jobs, only 16 percent of black women occupy those positions compared to 42.6 percent of white women.[32] (See Box "Women's Employment by the Numbers" for more data on women's employment.)

What is particularly puzzling is that, while close to half of college graduates are women, the percentage of women in management occupations are extremely low and has actually declined to lower levels than those between 2004 and 2014. In contrast, the percentage of men in management occupations is almost double that of women.[33] This statistic is rather baffling because female undergraduate students make up the majority of South Africans in the higher education system.

Perhaps one reason for the dearth of female managers is that women continue to enroll in what are considered traditionally female programs such as education, nursing, psychology, and the humanities—which often don't have the same type of managerial positions as corporations.[34] At the same time, as discussed in Chapter 8, the number of women studying business has increased over the years. For example, Kerrin Myers, former director of the Centre for Entrepreneurship at Wits Business School and now CEO of Resonance Consulting, has seen women's enrollment increase steadily over the years at the business school at the UCT and been surprised to see the number of women in management positions decrease over the years:

> Probably 40 to 50 percent of every class is female at the moment. It hasn't been that high always. But, of course, most of those women would go into corporate jobs. Still, the gender commission's recent report shows that the number of women in top management positions in South Africa is actually going down. I think an enormous amount of implicit sort of sexism is occurring.[35]

That sexism is the key problem may be true, as women tend to make less than their male counterparts in the same jobs.[36] For example, 23 percent of male senior executives are paid in the upper quartile of the market whereas only 2.3 percent of women in these positions are paid in this quartile.[37]

Thus, the likelihood of a woman securing a job after graduation, assuming she has demonstrated that she has the skills and capability, is good because, as mentioned, affirmative-action policies encourage organizations to employ women. But because a huge amount of sexism and nepotism remains, jobs often will go to men because of whom they know.[38] As Trevor Sehoole, assistant professor of higher education policy at the University of Pretoria and former department minister of higher education in the South Africa Department of Education, comments:

> The economy is a boys club, mainly led by men. South Africa has been very proactive in terms of promoting the interests of women and getting them to be part of the economy. There have been a lot of opportunities for their participation in the economy. But as you know, the nature of capitalism is such that there is access but not open access to everybody. So we have had a number of women in empowerment schemes that have been made available for women in the economy, but the results have been mixed.[39]

Women's Employment by the Numbers

When looking at employment by occupation, it appears women continue to hold occupations considered traditionally female (due to rounding, numbers do not necessarily add up to totals):

- 21 percent of women are in elementary occupations[40];
- 17 percent are clerks;
- 14.6 percent are domestic workers;
- 14.8 percent are in sales and services;
- 14.1 percent are technicians;
- 6.1 percent are managers;
- 6 percent are professionals;
- 4 percent work in crafts and related trades;
- 2.9 percent are plant and machine operators; and
- 0.03 percent works in skilled agriculture.[41]

Of all those employed within the community and social-services sector, 61 percent are women, with black women accounting for 45 percent of all those employed in the sector, compared to just 8 percent of white women. And, while women account for 48 percent of all jobs held in the wholesale, retail, and trade sector, 34 percent are black women versus 6 percent white women. [42] These two sectors account for more than half of female employment. [43] Thus, racial divisions prevail: 56.5 percent of white women compared to 17.1 percent of black women are in skilled occupations, whereas 42.4 percent of black women compared to 1.3 percent of white women are in low-skilled occupations.[44]

The Continuing Debate Over Affirmative Action

In recent years, South Africans have debated the necessity of continuing affirmative action. On the antiaffirmative action side, because of the shortage of qualified black women, many companies often hire those who are less than qualified just to fill their quotas. The other side of the argument is that, in the past, even highly qualified women would never have been offered a chance in the corporate world. Some people also believe that, given an opportunity, women will usually rise to the occasion and quickly fill any gap in their skill set.[45]

A case in point is Nadine Petersen, a faculty member in the department of education at the University of Johannesburg who was a beneficiary of affirmative action. When she was just starting out in higher education, the university where she worked recognized the need to hire black employees. Petersen readily admits she was not qualified to teach and was only halfway through her honors degree when she was offered a job. "I think at that stage, there was also a paucity of black women, particularly those who could speak both languages and had the potential to be able to be nurtured as future academics," she recalls. [46] In the end, both Petersen and the university benefited.

Of course, when an institution hires someone who is not qualified, it can create resentment in the workplace. According to Yvonne Shapiro, former director of the SAQA:

> I do sometimes worry that people are—I don't know what term to use—they are sort of getting into things just on the basis of being women or being black. What I'm really trying to say is sometimes there's a huge amount of unfairness because people are applying quota systems and setting people up for failure.[47]

Shuray Bux, director of manufacturing industry development at the Department of Economic Development & Tourism for the Provincial Government of the Western Cape, experienced the frustration of being under pressure to employ a woman because there were too many men in the organization. He has also been in the situation where posts have been left unfilled because not enough women have had the education, skills, or experience to fill them. He speaks of those situations as the "side effects" of affirmative action that "nobody is willing to discuss."[48]

The question for South Africans is whether to put people in jobs when they are not qualified or only hire qualified candidates, knowing that a significant portion of the population is still trying to catch up from the inequalities suffered under apartheid rule. There are no easy answers.

What is clear is that unqualified people are obtaining positions and spending too little time becoming proficient at their jobs. Once they are in the door, another company often recruits them, at a higher position, within a short time. Even though they may actually not have developed the skills that are required in that time to do the job at the next level, affirmative-action quotas create pressure to recruit them regardless.[49]

The issue of putting people in jobs without the necessary skill levels also plays out in the civil service. During apartheid, white Afrikaners filled most civil-service posts. Once affirmative action was introduced, black staff replaced a large portion of those jobs—yet without any training. The new workers lacked the skills to handle a civil-service bureaucracy, and today the system is in disarray.[50]

According to Nadine Petersen:

> That's another sector of our society that's falling apart. In the last year or two, we have developed massive social problems and unrest, and they were around issues of no service delivery. It's easy to give people jobs, but if you don't give them the prerequisite training, people fall flat. Our civil service is imploding.[51]

Those people who agree affirmative action has run its course believe that black South Africans are getting opportunities and top jobs without merit—that the main priority is simply hiring the right number of people with the right color of skin.[52]

However, white women have also benefitted from affirmative action, as can be seen in the employment statistics. That phenomenon has led to discussions as to whether or not white women should continue to be covered under affirmative action. Thus far, the answer has been yes. The 2013 amendment to the Employment Equity Act of 1998 did not exclude white women as one the "designated groups" that are protected under affirmative action. Instead, it clarified that members of those designated groups must be citizens of South Africa by birth or naturalization prior to April 27, 1994.[53]

Policies related to professional employment have also come under scrutiny. As Harold Herman, emeritus professor of education at University of the Western Cape, puts it:

> That's going to come to an end because it's already counterproductive. Because you must remember, we're (black South Africans) a firm majority here, unlike the United States, where you're a firm minority. So it has to come to an end. Otherwise, we're going to have a complete culture of entitlement of because I'm black, I'm entitled to this.[54]

Some people argue, too, that affirmative action is having a negative impact on the economy. An unqualified workforce is costly for organizations, as it can result in lost productivity, customers and innovation, and in the case of the civil service, civil unrest.[55]

Unfortunately, such affirmative-action controversies have left some negative impressions about gender equality and the empowerment of women.[56] In many ways, however, the policies have produced positive results and have been needed to correct the inequalities of the past. It is true that some women have been promoted into positions for which they have not been prepared, but many are not to blame, as they have not had the chance to acquire the necessary knowledge or skills to perform in the formal economy. The question is not about women's ability to do the work but whether the system can give them the education, skills, and experience necessary to perform well.

Indeed, certain groups should continue to be empowered through affirmative-action policies. Working-class and rural black people, particularly women, are deserving of additional attention. The opportunities available to poor black women are still very limited, and they continue to represent over 50 percent of all those who live in poverty.[57] There is no doubt they must be affirmed.

Women in Government

When discussing women's progress in South Africa, the representation of women in government is often cited as a great example of their advancement. Yet, even there, the results have been mixed. After the 2009 national elections, women made up 44.5 percent of the lower house of Parliament and 29.6 percent of the upper house.[58] But after the 2014 national election, the percentage of women within all levels of government, both national and provincial, fell—except at the cabinet level, where the percentage remained the same. And of the two main political parties, the ANC and the DA, it was within the ANC that women's representation dropped.[59]

One position, however has been, but for a brief period of time, firmly held by a woman. From 1994 to 2009, the speaker of Parliament was female: first Frene Ginwala, next Baleka Mbete, and then Gwen Mahlangu-Nkabinde [60] The first male speaker of the post-apartheid period was Max Sisulu who was elected to the post in May 2009. Elaine Salo, former director of gender studies at the University of Pretoria, recalled a conversation she had with Mr. Sisulu's wife, noting, "She was saying, just to indicate how the gender of that position had become institutionalized, that people are asking, 'Well, do we still address you as madam speaker?'"[61] And, in 2014, another woman, Baleka Mbete, once again became speaker.

From a long-term perspective, the progress and contribution of women in government in post-apartheid South Africa has been significant—especially considering the underrepresentation of women during apartheid rule. The story of Helen Suzman illustrates just how far women have come. Gillian Godsell, an associate research fellow at Wits University's Graduate School of Public and Development Management, wrote a high school textbook based on the story of Suzman's life. Suzman became a member of Parliament in 1953 when just three women served in that body; soon it dwindled down to only her. For long periods of time, she was the sole female representative in Parliament. Godsell thinks the number of women coming forward and serving in Parliament since Helen first did so is extraordinary.[62] SAQA's Yvonne Shapiro agrees:

> I do remember all those years ago—I was quite young at the time. There was one and only woman in Parliament in South Africa, and her name was Helen Suzman. And it was quite astonishing. There she was, and she was in the

> opposition party, and she was all alone. And if you compare that to what we have now, and to the speaker, and all of those kinds of things, it's absolutely fantastic.[63]

The visible presence of women in government—as a result of specific efforts by the ANC to help achieve that—has been extraordinary.[64] Yet some people are concerned that, while a significant number of women are now in Parliament, some of those women may not have the consciousness to take up what University of Pretoria's Elaine Salo calls the "disempowered women issues." Salo, like others, worries that Parliament may just become "a means to self enrichment" and "just a system of party patronage" for some women.[65] But she also observes that "the presence of women in our political systems means there won't be one person, like Helen Suzman, being the lone moaner and shouter about injustice towards women and other historically marginalized groups."[66]

As a result of the efforts of the government and the women who were involved in the creation of a new constitution and gender-specific policies, Parliament, government departments, and the Office of the Presidency—places that used to have almost no women—are now populated with a significant number of women.[67] In addition to Nkosazana Dlamini Zuma, Chair of the African Union Commission, and Thuli Madonsela, who until October 2016 served as Public Protector, several other prominent and influential women work in government today.

For example, Helen Zille is a major force in South African politics, having started her career in the 19070s as a political journalist and anti-apartheid activist. She has worked in all levels of government—first as a member of the Executive Council (MEC) in the Western Cape, then as Mayor of Cape Town, and since 2009, as the Premier of the Western Cape. She is a member of the DA, the leading opposition to the ANC. She continues to be a major political force, despite her decision in April 2015 to not seek reelection for congress in the DA. She will remain Premier of the Western Cape until 2019. [68]

Another important figure in South African politics is Patricia de Lille. In 1974, de Lille became active in trade union politics and, over the years, was elected to various leadership positions. She served in Parliament from 1994 to 2010, and during her time there, she established her own political party: the Independence Democrats, which merged with the DA in 2010. In 2011, de Lille became the 33rd Mayor of Cape Town and was recently elected leader of the Western Cape Democratic Alliance (DA) provincial congress, replacing Helen Zille.[69]

Trade Unions and Provincial Government Posts

The rise of these women in government and political positions has had a beneficial influence on the national psyche. Having female or black female officials addressing the public, making decisions, and giving direction has helped raise awareness of the rights of women.[70]

But awareness does not equal acceptance or approval. And many challenges remain in terms of women's representation in leadership roles in the government and other organizations that influence the government—such as COSATU, the DA, and the ANC. For example, the trade union COSATU criticized DA leader Helen Zille for not appointing any women to her cabinet after the DA won majority rule in the Western Cape during the April 2009 elections. Five months later, COSATU admitted, as it was opening its congress, that it too had a lack of female leadership. The majority of women in that organization still occupy junior administrative positions, in spite of a 50 percent equity target. COSATU acknowledged, "Male comrades deny their female counterparts an opportunity to rise through the ranks."[71] The most senior woman in the organization was appointed Minister for Women, Youth, Children, and People with Disabilities.

The latest figures that COSATU released on women are from a 1997 report which showed they represented 11 percent of branch or regional secretaries; 12 percent of organizers; 25 percent of legal, media, and research positions; 10 percent of education officers; and 94 percent of administrative support.[72] Those data, along with the fact that the COSATU has not bothered to measure women's roles in the organization since 1997, is troubling for an organization that describes itself as politically progressive. In many ways, COSATU encapsulates the continuing power imbalance in the country and the disconnect between making policy and implementing it. It will be interesting to see what, if anything, COSATU does to create gender equity within its organization.

The ANC also has a way to go when it comes to women in leadership positions. Before the April 2009 elections, President Jacob Zuma spoke with journalists about his potential presidency and what his administration might look like. He admitted that internal divisions within the ANC had resulted in women being overlooked for provincial chairperson positions. He was concerned that, at that point, the ANC had not come up with one woman as a potential chairperson of a province. He shared his belief that the ANC should consider gender when the provincial and national executive committee selects chairpersons and premiers, commenting that the ANC Women's Committee needs "at least four women premiers."[73]

After the 2009 elections, four of the eight provinces the ANC runs had a female premier. But in the 2014 elections, only one female premier won office. [74] Despite the fact that women represent a majority of ANC's membership, they continue to be excluded or denied leadership positions, particularly at the provincial level.

Influencing Factors: Engrained Attitudes and Norms

A variety of factors have made it difficult for women to progress and to leverage the opportunities that have been created as a result of the gender equality and women's empowerment initiatives that the government has established since 1994. The degree to which such factors influence or hinder a woman's ability to advance depends on her race, socioeconomic status, level of education, and where she lives. Many of those factors are closely intertwined with each other and deeply rooted in South African culture. That, in turn, makes it difficult to minimize their influence on women's lives. Some of the key factors are outlined below.

Attitudes of Male Government Leaders

Leaders are expected to behave in ways that reflect the laws, policies, and culture of a particular organization, government, or country. Their individual behavior, informally as well as formally, signals to others what is and is not acceptable and sets an example for others to follow. Many South Africans worry that President Zuma's behavior and public comments related to women have given South African men permission to behave in ways that are counter to the principles of gender parity set forth in the constitution and established in the country's laws and policies.

Richard Lapper of the *Financial Times* began his review of a biography of South Africa's then president-to-be Jacob Zuma thus: "a corrupt careerist, a veteran womanizer and a puppet of the left whose trademark song is 'Bring Me My Machine Gun,' the leader of South Africa's governing ANC and very likely the country's next president, has earned a most unfortunate reputation."[75] Was that reputation well earned? The answer depends on to whom you speak. But without a doubt, Zuma has engaged in some highly questionable behavior.

For instance, Zuma went on trial in 2006 for the alleged rape of a 31-year-old family friend who was HIV positive. Zuma's remarks during the trial were appalling, given the record of rape and incidence of HIV/AIDS in the country. The trial provided a glimpse into the often-conflicting attitudes that South Africans have toward women, sex, and power, as well as the role of patriarchal norms and practices in South African society.

During his trial, Zuma stated that the way in which he had sexual intercourse with the defendant was in accordance with Zulu cultural norms. He testified that the accuser had given him signs, such as wearing a knee-length skirt and going without underwear beneath her kanga (wrap), which in Zulu custom signifies sexual arousal. Based on that, he claimed, the sex was consensual. He admitted during the trial that he had not used a condom but had taken a shower afterwards. He did all that knowing she was HIV positive. Zuma was then president of the South African National AIDS Commission.[76]

The courtroom proceedings, particularly the defense attorney's line of questioning and reasoning, spoke volumes about the attitudes toward women and dispelled any illusions about the ease of following through on constitutional commitments to gender equality and the empowerment of women. As it was known that the accuser had been raped several times as a child, the defense attorney suggested during the trial that she should have developed the skills and ability necessary to resist rape—that she could have defended herself had she really wanted to.[77] Outside the courtroom crowds burned photographs of the accuser, and crowds shouted, "Burn the bitch, burn her" and "How much did they pay you, bitch?"[78]

Surprisingly, women were in this crowd, as well as men. And throughout the trial, Zuma's wives sat in silence.[79] Women supporters of Zuma believed that since he was a chief, the woman had no right to bring disgrace on him, even though he may have raped her. It was her responsibility to remain silent. She had broken a norm; she had accused a Zulu man, and a national leader, of rape.[80]

In the end, Zuma was acquitted. The woman, whose home was broken into and ransacked several times during the trial, now lives in exile as a result of threats on her life. Meanwhile, Zuma is president of South Africa.[81]

Zuma is a Zulu, and the practice of polygamy is part of Zulu traditional practice.[82] In January 2010, he married his fourth wife at his homestead in KwaZulu Natal. It was actually his fifth marriage, as one wife committed suicide in 2000 due to alleged trauma in the relationship. Zuma is also divorced from Home Affairs Minister Nkosazana Dlamini-Zuma. Then, in 2012, Zuma married Gloria Bongi Ngema, making her his fifth wife. Zuma has paid ilobolo (dowry) to her family, and she brought umbondo (wedding gifts) to the Zuma family, which is the last traditional event before the wedding.

The fact is that, while the government supports women's rights within all types of marriage, it also recognizes customary marriage under the 1998 Recognition of Customary Marriage Act[83] and legally accepts polygamous marriages performed under Customary Law. [84] Thus, the public's response to Zuma's marriages has been mixed; some people defend the practice, while others believe it has no place in a modern society. The controversy over it embodies the continuing struggle between South Africa's progressive concept of nation building, as articulated in it's constitution, and the pull of traditional practices, as demonstrated in 2008 when Parliament approved the establishment of a ministry of traditional affairs.

At the World Economic Forum in Davos, Switzerland, just a month after taking his third wife, journalists asked President Zuma if his belief in traditional practices, including polygamy, had divided South Africans. He responded by saying:

> There are many people who say that symbolically it is a great step backward for the leader of South Africa to be embracing a practice that they say is inherently unfair to women. That's my culture. It does not take anything from me, from my political beliefs, including the belief in the equality of women.[85]

Another Zuma exploit became public when he admitted in February 2010 that he was the father of a baby girl born out of wedlock that previous October—his 20th child. He released a statement saying he remains committed to the government campaigns to eradicate HIV and AIDS, and he blasted the news media for revealing the names of his new daughter and the mother.[86] Yet Zuma's personal behavior undermines his own comments and the government's campaign against unprotected sex and multiple partners.

Zuma's rape trial was particularly upsetting for women. Many were appalled by the statements that he made about women, the line of questioning permitted in the courtroom, and the antics outside it. Women felt as if they lost something during the trial. In the words of Jenni Case, associate professor of engineering and former director of undergraduate studies at the University of Cape Town (UCT):

> It was a hard year for so many of us. There is a sense of loss–a loss of faith in ANC. I resigned from it. I had joined the ANC in recent years and had been supporting it. The statements on women are what pushed me totally over the edge. It was the Zuma things that flipped me.[87]

A question in many people's minds is whether the president has any respect for women at all and what message he is sending to men across the country. Indeed, women are detecting a "new sexism"[88] emerging in South Africa. It is creeping into discussions, the news media, and other organizations.[89] It stands in contradiction to all the legislative requirements, employment-equity targets, and other gender-specific initiatives—including a constitution based on nonsexism. How can these initiatives coexist, let along succeed, with a president whose public comments and private life run so counter to gender equality?[90]

The South African group Gender Links[91] called on President Zuma, in wake of his comments on gender-related issues before and during the campaign, to demonstrate his commitment to the "principles of gender equality enshrined in the Constitution"[92] by encouraging an open discussion about women's rights and whether polygamy has a place in a country where gender equality is a "cornerstone of its democracy." The organization found Zuma's conduct and remarks highly "worrisome" and characterize him as a polygamist. Although the practice is not outlawed, Gender Links describes it as "self evidently patriarchal, unfair, and in all likelihood unconstitutional."[93]

It is an understatement to say women are concerned about Zuma's presidency. His public comments about women, his acquittal on rape charges, his comments about HIV/AIDS, the marriage to his fourth and fifth wife and the disclosure of his fathering his 20th child with a mistress —they all run counter to the country's movement toward responsible sexual practices, gender equality, and the empowerment of women. Zuma's remarks and behavior convey the message that men can do as they please when it comes to women. They suggest that, in their personal behavior, people need not adhere to national laws and policies. As Nadine Petersen, professor of education at the University of Johannesburg, asks:

> What kind of message does this send out to black youth? It's okay to have the gendered attitudes? It doesn't matter what the constitution says?[94]

Another example of questionable attitudes and actions toward women involves Julius Malema, until 2013 the ANC Youth League president and today the commander in chief of the Economic Freedom Fighters (EFF), who publicly supported Zuma's sexist practices. Malema is an important person in South Africa, as the Youth League is a powerful organization that has considerable influence within and outside the ANC. Nelson Mandela was once its president, a position that many people believe Malema will hold in the future, as well. But Malema's remarks regarding Zuma's rape case have been the source of contention. He suggested that the woman who accused President Zuma of rape must have had a "nice time" because she stayed for breakfast and asked for money for a taxi.[95]

The Sonke Gender Justice NGO filed a hate speech complaint against Malema over his claims that Zuma's rape accuser enjoyed herself with Zuma. In addition, the Equality Court found Malema guilty and ordered him to make a public apology within two weeks of the decision in March 2010, as well as to pay R50,000 within a month to a shelter for abused women. He made a public apology 15 months after the verdict yet continues to refuse to pay the shelter.[96]

Malema also accused Helen Zille, the leader of the DA and a former antiapartheid activist as being a racist and "colonist." When she announced the appointments to her cabinet in the Western Cape province after the DA election victory in April 2009, Malema posted the following on his Facebook account: "this bitch must get a life—it's an all-male cabinet, maybe she wants to do more porn movies!!!" [97] He has also been quoted as saying the Youth League was "prepared to take up arms and kill for Zuma."[98] Those remarks caused such a strong public reaction that the ANC took the unprecedented step of beginning disciplinary procedures against him.

Other high-ranking government officials have shown their colors with regard to their attitudes toward women. Manala Manzini, a respected ANC government leader, was South Africa's National Intelligence Agency director-general until the end of August last year. In 2007, he left his wife Myakayaka-Manzini, chief director at the Department of

International Relations and former deputy president of the ANC Women's League. Although he was still legally married to Myakayaka, Manzini was planning at that time to marry another woman. Myakayaka accused her husband of domestic violence and abuse. It wasn't until Myakayaka expressed her shock and outrage at Manzini's future plans to marry that Manzini confessed to the abuse. He defended his behavior by saying, "She refused to cook or iron my clothes. She was so powerful in her work position and refused to cook."[99]

This high-profile story of domestic abuse and patriarchal attitudes about women's roles is yet another example of the continuing disconnect between what government leaders say about gender equality and women's empowerment and their actual attitudes and behavior. Elaine Salo, former associate professor of political science and international relations and of women and gender studies at the University of Delaware, shared her thoughts about the incident:

> This woman was beaten up by her husband, who was Intelligence Chief in the past government, because he thought she was too arrogant to want to cook for him or iron his clothes. Now bloody hell, she's a professional. What did you think? You know, you go, 'Huh, what planet are you from? Why can't you do it yourself? Don't you have hands at the end of your arms?' She was beaten up, beaten up. And now, he's gone into another relationship, using the cultural notion of polygamy to justify this relationship.[100]

The degree to which patriarchal attitudes and behaviors—like those of Zuma, Malema, and Manzini—influence a woman's life varies across South Africa. There are women who are in a family or an environment where they are treated as equals, and then there are women who are still in the older, traditional cultural environment.[101]

Orly Stern, a former human rights lawyer from the Sonke Gender Justice Network and now an independent consultant, comes from an upper-middle-class family in Cape Town. She describes life for a woman like her as "absolutely perfect." She has never felt disadvantaged and notes that women are highly valued in her family. Yet she realizes from her experience working at Sonke Gender Network that women in other parts of the population would tell a very different story. [102] She has worked on gender practices throughout the nation and knows a significant portion of women live in patriarchal environments where domestic abuse is prevalent. Those women have little to no control in relationships or their families.[103]

According to Stern:

> The man heads the household. He makes decisions from economic issues to running the family to sexual positions and safe sex—which is a very big issue in South Africa with the HIV pandemic. So it's seen as the man is the head, and the woman is supposed to be obedient and listen to her man, and if she doesn't, this hurts the man." [104]

Thus, women in patriarchal families and communities do not have control over their own bodies. And as the UCT's Jenni Case notes, attitudes about rape are disturbing:

> A woman who says she's being raped will be seen as the offender. And the men will be seen as doing what men should do. I mean, we don't have a way of thinking about sex in this country. I don't see an easy change. Its kind of one woman's life at a time right now."[105]

The reality is that women aren't empowered to speak out against these attitudes and offenses. According to Nadine Petersen at the University of Johannesburg:

> Women do not have the authority—particularly black, African women—to negotiate safe sex. It's just not possible. It's under the banner of culture. Every single year in my English class, the African male students will tell me, "That's my culture." How do you change attitudes around that? I have no clue. I can't do it in one little course in a semester.[106]

Men's sense of entitlement in the sexual arena means that they give little thought to safe sex or not having multiple partners—which makes women extremely vulnerable.[107]

Given the prevalence of patriarchal attitudes and behavior in the country, the creation of a Ministry of Traditional Affairs in March 2008 is a particular cause for concern. While some people argue that the ministry was created to monitor and evaluate the implementation of Customary Law and hence push it toward modernity, little to nothing has been communicated publicly as to the role, function, or purpose of the ministry.[108]

It is particularly worrisome because in the rural areas where Customary Law applies more than anywhere else in South Africa, access to the judicial system is extremely uneven already, and people are concerned it will be pushed completely to the side in favor of archaic tribal customs. For example, there is evidence that traditional practices of virginity testing and abduction for forced marriage are still taking place throughout the country.[109]

Today, South Africa relies on the rule of law to give substantive meaning to citizenship, but if the Ministry of Traditional Affairs allows for even more latitude than is already given to chiefs, then women in the rural areas will have little to no recourse.[110] The fear that the ministry may be pushing laws backwards is legitimate—especially given Zuma's comments about traditional laws and practices, coupled with a general sense that conservatism is creeping back into the public discourse.[111]

Ultimately, when it comes to women's progress in South Africa, some of the most fundamental questions become: Will women's efforts to uplift themselves always result in a rash of accusations and derogatory comments? Are men willing to accommodate the possibility of their female partners and bosses holding power over them? And if people who are making policy are themselves guilty of gendered attitudes, how likely are they to ensure that policies to support women are implemented?

Many women are nervous about what the answers to those questions may be.

HIV/AIDS and Women

A discussion of the factors influencing women's prospects would be incomplete without a conversation about AIDS, which has been cited as the major cause of premature deaths in South Africa. In 2013, about 6.3 million people were estimated to be living with HIV in South Africa, or about 19 percent of the adult population aged 15–49. The mortality rates jumped 79 percent between 1997 and 2004, with women experiencing a higher increase than men.

Indeed, women have been the greatest victims of the disease. They account for approximately 54 percent of the South African population that is HIV positive. Women between 25 and 29 years old have been affected the most—up to 36 percent—and have eight times the infection rate of their male counterparts.[112] Children are especially vulnerable, as well, given the high rates of mother-to-child transmission as well as the likelihood of becoming orphans.[113]

The 2007–2011 South African National Strategic Plan (NSP) on HIV and AIDS has as its primary goals the reduction of the number of new

HIV infections by 50 percent and the expansion of access to appropriate treatment, care, and support to 80 percent of all people diagnosed with those infections. By achieving these goals, the impact of HIV and AIDS on individuals, families, communities, and society will decrease.[114]

The NSP has acknowledge the role that unprotected sexual intercourse and multiple sexual partnerships plays, but it has stated that "the fundamental drivers of this epidemic in South Africa are the more deep rooted institutional problems of poverty, underdevelopment, and the low status of women, including gender-based violence, in society."[115] The NSP also recognizes that cultural attitudes and practices increase South Africans exposure to HIV infections. It cites the gender inequalities that are inherent in patriarchal cultures as a contributing factor since women's lower status significantly limits the choices that they can make about sexual intercourse. According to the NSP, "Such decisions are frequently constrained by coercion and violence in the women's relationships with men. In particular, male partners either have sex with sex workers or engage in multiple relationships, and their female partners or spouses are unable to insist on the use of condoms during sexual intercourse for fear of losing their main source of livelihood."[116]

HIV infection is also believed to occur during some of the rituals that traditional healers conduct. One such practice recommends sex with a virgin as part as a treatment for disease.[117] According to the NSP, other cultural beliefs and practices increase exposure to infection:

> Young men's rites of passage to adulthood, rites of marriage such as premarital sex, virginity testing, fertility and virility testing, early or arranged marriages, fertility obligations, polygamy, and prohibition of post-partum sex and also during breastfeeding, and rites related to death such as levirate (or spouse inheritance) and sororate (a widower or sometimes a husband of a barren woman marries his wife's sister) are also believed to spread HIV infection.[118]

The HIV/AIDS pandemic in South Africa is placing enormous physical, economic, and emotional burdens on those who care for the sick and needy. Women in South Africa are carrying a disproportionate amount of those burdens. A national survey shows women provide eight times more care related to all illnesses than men and over two-thirds of the care for people living with AIDS.[119] In fact, care is seen as a woman's job in the country, so they really have no choice in the matter. For many women, such caretaking is a full-time job that keeps them from earning money outside of the home—even though many people don't think that a woman is actually doing work when she is caring for the ill.[120] Some nongovernmental organizations are making efforts to get men more involved in HIV/AIDS care work.[121]

The main challenge is the loss of women's lives to the pandemic. But with so many infected, women often have a sense of hopelessness toward HIV/AIDS. They view the situation with a fatalistic attitude, believing that it's impossible to stem the spread of the disease. Maria Phalime recalls the time when she was practicing medicine and working at a day hospital in the Western Cape:

> The number of times I've spoken to women who say, 'Well, we're all gonna get it at some point.' The sense of acceptance of it was overwhelming. I felt like shaking so many people. It's like, 'Your test results have come back, and show that you're HIV positive.' And their attitude would be 'Oh, that's the way it is. It's God's will,' or 'What can I do about it now?' or 'I'll just tell my boyfriend," or I'll just tell my husband.' I think this could really pull back gains that women have made. [122]

On World AIDS Day, December 1, 2009, Jacob Zuma introduced South Africa's new policy on pregnant women to prevent mother-to-child transmission (PMTCT). The new policy allowed pregnant HIV patients to begin receiving drugs 14 weeks into their pregnancy versus 28 weeks under the previous policy. In an effort to keep both male and female HIV patients healthy and active, he also announced that they could receive drugs before they became sick, allowing those infected to live longer and reducing death rates. In addition, state health facilities began to provide free male circumcisions in an effort to reduce the risk of transmission.

By 2011, advances had been made: 95 percent of infected pregnant women were receiving antiretroviral drugs to PMTCT, and more children were receiving AIDS treatment.[123] But despite that progress, AIDS remains South Africa's leading cause of death today.

Of course, Zuma's own risky behavior has not gone unnoticed. During his speech, the South African leader promised to get another HIV test and urged the nation "to use condoms consistently and correctly during every sexual encounter."[124] It is difficult to say which message South Africans, especially male South Africans, will take to heart—the one that emerged from his rape trial or the one spoken on World AIDS Day. Actions typically speak louder than words.

Issues of Empowerment

Given the patriarchal and sometimes abusive attitudes toward women, it is not surprising to hear that South Africa owns an unfortunate world statistic: it has the highest number of rapes reported to police, with a likelihood that only a fraction are reported.[125] Of those that are, 30 percent involve gang rape and 58 percent result in injuries.[126] And any woman raped by a man over the age of 25 has a one in four chance of her attacker being HIV-positive.[127]

What's more, of the estimated 500,000 rapes committed annually in South Africa, only one in six reported rapes reach court with just 6 percent ending in a conviction.[128] Rape cases typically have long delays, rape kits are frequently misplaced, there aren't enough prosecutors, and those who are assigned these cases are overworked. And due to patriarchal attitudes, the burden of proof typically falls on the victim. Such factors contribute to a high number of women dropping charges.[129]

In response to some of these issues, the government established six dedicated sexual offense courts throughout the country in 2013. The facilities include, among other things, court preparation rooms and closed- caption television rooms for victims.[130] In a survey of just under 2,000 men between the ages of 18 and 49 from all race groups and across the socioeconomic ladder, the South African Medical Research Council found that more than 25 percent of those responding said they had committed rape and 50 percent of those said they had raped more than once. They also admitted to raping their partner and participating in gang rapes. Some raped other men and boys. Most of the men surveyed said they raped before they were 20 years old.

Some traits have been identified as being more prevalent among men who rape. Men who were age 20–24 were more likely to have raped than younger or older men. Men who had raped were also better educated, although they were not likely to have graduated from the university. Men who raped were less likely to have never worked and more likely to have occasional work. There were also racial differences in those who raped: colored men raped more than those of any other racial group.

In addition the men who admitted to having committed rape were more likely to be violent toward women, have multiple sex partners, engage in transactional sex with prostitutes, and drink heavily. The director of the Council's Gender and Health Research Unit, Rachel Jewkes, cites South Africa's overwhelmingly patriarchal culture again as a factor:

> We certainly have a dominant view/idea of masculinity that is really rooted in our overall patriarchal society. That idea is based on the fact that men are superior to women—that men should be leading women. And one way in which men demonstrate the control is through the idea they should be able to get any women they want as a girlfriend or for sex.[131]

The high prevalence of rape and HIV in South Africa can be attributed to the ideas of manhood, which includes the belief in men's sexual entitlement and power over women.[132] That belief runs counter to all the gender equality initiatives and women's empowerment laws and policies, as well as the constitution.

And, in fact, in direct conflict to that view, women who have benefited from the opportunities made available to them post-apartheid act from a sense of empowerment and control over their lives. As Kerrin Myers at Wits University explains:

> I think that when democracy came, the group that was most profoundly empowered was women. At the time, I was running a market research business and producing social research reports, and I did a report on women. And one of the things that I picked up was that women were feeling really, really strong and empowered by the fact that there was a constitution, and their rights were guaranteed, and they were going to change the world.[133]

These women are feeling strong and full of possibility, and increasingly choosing not to marry. According to Elaine Salo:

> I think a lot of women have often personally made a choice, in terms of saying, OK, I'm going to stay single because my career trajectory is more important, and I don't want all the other issues in terms of the diversions that families and dependents bring with them. A lot of women have made those kinds of choices.[134]

Sometimes, however, although these women want to remain single, they also want to have children. Maria Phalime notes, "I think what women are saying is, 'I don't want the hassle of a man, but I still want to have the experience of being a mother.'"[135] The number of single women in the country with children is rising, although it is difficult to know what percentage has chosen to be a single parent and what percentage has had no choice.[136] If a rural woman is a single parent, it is not usually by choice.[137]

Women who have benefited from the new laws and policies pose a challenge to traditional concepts of masculinity, and many men have difficulty dealing with a woman who is not obedient and wants to lead her own life.[138] As Crain Soudien, acting vice chancellor of UCT, says:

> I think that there are huge, unarticulated issues around masculinity, and women are, unfortunately, at the receiving end of those experiences. And the increases in the levels of rape are related to this idea of what it takes to be a man. I think this thing about what it takes to be a man is in such turmoil and such fluidity in the country right now.[139]

Soudien adds: "There's such a high level of gender-based violence in this society for both historical and structural reasons. And, when you start opening access, in terms of women, they are seen as proposing a challenge to men."[140]

In other words, women are paying a price for their advancement in the form of a backlash from men.[141] When opportunities open up, and suddenly one group—which was never perceived as a challenge before—becomes a competitor in the job market and at home, such a backlash occurs. And in South Africa that backlash is "visited upon" women's bodies.[142] In many ways, men are feeling humiliated—which fuels a deep-seated resentment that often manifests itself as a form of sexual violence and abuse of women.[143]

In response, women are finding new ways of surviving and protecting themselves. Yvonne Shapiro of SAQA says:

> If you're going to survive, you have to behave like a man in order to get forward. You don't behave like a woman, because people are just going to backlash you. And you will get a lot of abuse for being a woman, especially if you have a position of authority.[144]

The clash between new and old values concerning gender in South Africa has created a major crisis between men and women.[145] Although democracy has empowered both, women have sometimes advanced more rapidly than men. And some people view the competition for jobs and resources as a zero-sum game: one person's gain is another person's loss. If women advance in any capacity, men may feel threatened—as if somehow the push for women's advancement is taking away from their own rights.[146] That may be a contributing factor to the widespread abuse that is taking place, which has also found its way into the workplace as sexual harassment. According to Yvonne Shapiro:

> The woman now has the position that the man wants. Now, she's there, so he thinks the best way to bring her down, to discredit her, is to sexually harass her or to make sexual connotations about her and sexual remarks. It's such a common thing that's happening.[147]

The State of Things Today

The years after 1994 were filled with great promise of political freedom and economic advancement. Yet South Africa has yet to realize the economic gains for all of its citizens. With lingering inequalities and a difficult economy, it has become increasingly difficult to convince people that the pie is growing for everyone. After the end of apartheid, many historically disadvantaged South Africans, and many men in particular, viewed the next chapters of their lives as the age of possibility. As they now see this possibility fading, they may be looking for someone to blame.[148]

Of course black, rural women also anticipated an age of possibility and have been similarly disappointed. With hardship and turmoil all about them, women in South Africa have had to find their own way—to stake out their own ground. That ground is shaky, as they must reconcile their new, more empowered, role with how they feel about the men in their lives—their brothers, fathers, uncles, and grandfathers who may have attitudes toward women that run counter to their aspirations.[149]

As Nadine Petersen puts it:

> These are gendered socialization practices that come from growing up in particular homes within particular groupings within society. That picture hasn't changed. We can have all the policies that we want that are so progressive, all these commissions—whatever you like—but if the policy doesn't change for the people themselves, nothing will change.[150]

That leads into another key factor that is thwarting women's ability to progress: the fact that the constitution, laws, and policies of the country are ahead of the current social norms of a significant portion of the population. That means women must find ways to exercise these opportunities in the context of a conservative family and societal environments.[151] There is no doubt that the South African constitution and other government policies, have opened up opportunities for some women. What they haven't done is to change the national consciousness to one that is gender sensitive and nonpatriarchal.

Getting beyond such entrenched attitudes may be a matter of women occupying more positions of authority and having more power across society. Cameron Dugmore, former provincial minister of education and now minister of cultural affairs and sport at West Cape, believes, "When women have economic power they will gain social power, and I think when one reaches that stage, that's when attitudes start to shift because they then begin to reflect a new reality."[152]

While that may be true, it will take time for a critical mass of women to populate senior positions and exert enough influence to bring about the necessary change. And many poor, black, rural women have been waiting for several decades to see things improve. A more effective and proactive approach might be for the government to focus on the implementation and enforcement of its policies and to ensure that the comments and behavior of its leaders are consistent with national policy. As Kerrin Myers observes: "There's no shortage of policy frameworks and strategy, but on the ground, things are still very, very tough. If you talk to women who come from a township, their lives are very, very difficult. Something needs to be done."[153]

Despite the challenges that remain for women and the difficulties they have faced, it is important for them to continue on the path to gender equality and empowerment. Says Elaine Salo: "Look, thank God that change has come, because the aspirations of especially young, black women have just opened up wide, and the role models are out there. It's just still too small a number of women."[154]

Profiles of South African Women

Phuti Malabie

Phuti Malabie is considered one of the most influential women in government and business in South Africa, having been CEO (2010–2015) of Shaduka Group, a leading investment holding company. *The Wall Street Journal* named her one of the "Top 50 Women in the World to Watch" in 2008, and *Forbes* has called her one of the 20 youngest powerful people in Africa and named her "Africa Business Woman of the Year" in 2014.

Malabie was born in Soweto, Johannesburg, South Africa, in 1971. Her father was a successful businessman and cofounder of National Sorghum Breweries. In 1976, as the country was in political turmoil, her parents moved her and her younger sister to Lesotho. She graduated with a degree in economics from Rutgers University in New Jersey and earned her M.B. A. from De Montfort University in Great Britain, where she studied the impact of international trade on black economic power.

During her 10 years at Shanduka, Malabie was responsible for bringing the Chinese Investment Corporation (CIC) into South Africa and getting it to make its first direct investment in the country, including a 25 percent ownership in Shanduka. She also brokered other powerful partnerships that expanded the company's portfolio and skills in the electrical power sector.

Malabie decided it was time to leave Shanduka in 2015, when the company merged with Pembani—a private equity firm that invests in the energy sector, mineral resources, and infrastructure industries—and Cyril Ramaphosa, Shanduka's founder, resigned. Malabie started her own investment firm, Sigma Capital.

In a 2013 interview, Malabie was asked about her hopes for the future. She responded by saying that she hoped the government would find ways to successfully deal with the high unemployment rates and lack of skills of young people. She also said she hoped that the growth in black-owned companies translated into sustainable businesses that in turn contributed to society.

Sources:

Lihle Mtshali, *But home is where Phuti Malabie's heart is and South Africa remains her country of choice*, Sowetan Live, Johannesburg, South Africa, May 07, 2007,

http://www.sowetanlive.co.za/sowetan/archive/2007/05/07/but-home-is-where-phuti-malabie_s-heart-is-and-south-africa-remains-her-country-of-choice

(accessed November 7, 2016)

Destiny.com, *Phuti Malabie*, May 13, 2011

https://www.destinyman.com/2011/05/13/pmalabie-2011-05-13/(accessed November 7, 2016)

Martin Creamer, *Mining Personality Phuti Mahanyele,*

Mining Weekly, May 3, 2013, London, UK

http://www.miningweekly.com/article/phuti-mahanyele-2013-05-03(accessed November 7, 2016)

CNBC Africa, *Phuti Mahanyele quits after a decade at Shanduka*

February 23, 2015
http://www.cnbcafrica.com/news/southern-africa/2015/02/23/shanduka-mahanyele-resignation/(accessed November 7, 2016)

Baleka Mbete

A teacher, poet, and activist linked to the Black Consciousness Movement, Baleka Mbete has served the ANC and South Africa in a variety of roles and positions. She went into exile in 1976, leaving behind two young children. Upon her return to South Africa, Mbete was elected Secretary-General of the ANC Women's League and served on the party's National Executive Committee.

In 1994, she was elected to Parliament and participated in the selection of candidates to serve on the Truth and Reconciliation Commission. She became the deputy speaker of the National Assembly in 1996, serving in this role for eight years before becoming speaker for four years. In 2007, she was elected the first female ANC national chairperson holding that post until the 2014 national elections, when she returned as speaker.

Her service to the ANC and the country has not been without controversy. Allegations against her have ranged from obtaining an illegal driver's license; the Travelgate scandal, involving 40 members of Parliament accused of illegally using government travel vouchers to take expensive vacations for themselves and family, where she returned the money she received; throwing out a members of Parliament from an opposition party who questioned if a former ANC minister was guilty of theft; and accusations, while serving as ANC national chairwoman, of receiving a bribe in the form of R25 million in shares and dividends from Gold Fields. (For the latter, Parliament cleared her of any wrongdoing because she wasn't a member of that body when she received the shares and dividends.)

Mbete continues to be criticized, even by President Zuma, for the way Parliament is being run and her perceived partiality toward the ANC in her rulings and how she presides over the House. She stood down an attempted vote of no confidence in September 2014 by members of the opposition parties who accused her of losing control over Parliament proceedings.

In April 2016, in what has been described as one of the most "shameful events in Parliamentary history," police forcibly removed opposition leaders from the EFF while raising questions about allegations of corruption against President Zuma. Fists and bottles began to fly as the MPs were removed.

Mbete's tactics on the removal of the members of the EFF and her lack of control over the proceedings have led to increased criticism and a lack of confidence among many people in her ability to effectively run Parliament.

Yet despite those challenges, Baleka Mbete is poised to be the next ANC presidential candidate.

Sources:

Ranjeni Munuanjen, *Baleka Mbete: Madam Speaker, Madam President?*, Daily Maverick, April 20, 2016, Benmore, South Africa

http://www.dailymaverick.co.za/article/2016-04-20-baleka-mbete-madam-speaker-madam-president/#.WCHSfOErJBw

(accessed November 8, 2016)

Greg Nicolson, *Baleka Mbete: In the centre of the maelstrom*, Daily Maverick, April 20, 2016, Benmore, South Africa

http://www.dailymaverick.co.za/article/2015-02-17-baleka-mbete-in-the-centre-of-the-maelstrom/#.WCHVEeErJBw

(accessed November 8, 2016)

Crystal Orderson, *South Africa's opposition reject an 'utterly discredited and illegitimate president,'"* The Africa Report, May 6, 2016, Paris, France

http://www.theafricareport.com/Southern-Africa/south-africas-opposition-reject-an-utterly-discredited-and-illegitimate-president.html

(accessed November 8, 2016)

Notes

1. South Africa Department of Trade and Industry, "Black Economic Empowerment," http://www.southafrica.info/business/trends/empowerment/bee.htm (accessed November 30, 2009).
2. Salukazi Dakile-Hlongwane, Chief Executive of Nozala Investments, helped establish the women's investment firm in 1996. Its goal is to ensure the economic advancement of women. She is also the Chief Executive Officer of Eqstra Holdings Limited, board member of MultiChoice Africa, and has worked for the African Development Bank; the Southern African Development Corporation; and FirstCorp Merchant Bank.

   http://www.wbsjournal.co.za/articles/south-africas-30-wonder-women-948.html (accessed June 24, 2015).
3. Phuti Malabie, Chief Executive Officer of Shanduka, a black-owned and managed investment company started by businessman and politician Cyril Ramaphosa. She joined Shanduka in 2004 and became managing director of Shanduka Energy until 2010 before becoming CEO. Malabie is a board

member of the Vodacom Group and the Black Management Forum. In 2008 she made the Wall Street Journal's list of "Top 50 women in the world to watch," in 2012 was selected as the "Leading African Women in Business" by Africa Investors, and in 2014 was Forbes "Africa Business Woman of the Year." http://www.wbsjournal.co.za/articles/south-africas-30-wonder-women-948.html (accessed June 24, 2015).

4. Nonkululeko Nyembezi-Heita was CEO of Arcelor Mittal South Africa Limited from 2008–2014. She began her career in 1984 with IBM in the United States and South Africa and left in 1998 to become the CEO of Alliance Capital Management and from there to Vodacom as head of the mergers and acquisition division. She is the 2011 winner of the Wits Business School Management Excellence Award. http://www.wbsjournal.co.za/articles/south-africas-30-wonder-women-948.html (accessed June 24, 2015)
5. Nkosazana Dlamini-Zuma was a student activist in the 1970s until she went into exile in Britain in 1976. When the ANC was unbanned in 1990 she returned to South Africa and became a leading member of the Gender Advisory Committee. For the next 18 years she led various ministries: 1994–1999 Minister of Health; 1999–2009 Minister of Foreign Affairs; and 2009–2012 Minister of Home Affairs. In 2012 she was elected Chair of the African Union becoming the first woman to do so. http://www.theguardian.com/commentisfree/2012/jul/18/african-union-nkosazana-dlamini-zuma (accessed June 29, 2015); http://www.wbsjournal.co.za/articles/south-africas-30-wonder-women-948.html (accessed June 24, 2015).
6. Thuli Madonsela has been South Africa's Public Protector since 2009. She is a human rights lawyer and expert on equality and policy having served on the team that drafted the country's constitution in 1996 after giving up her scholarship to study at Harvard University. Madonsela was also instrumental in creating the policy framework that established the foundation for the Ministry for Women, Children and People with Disabilities. In 2012 the National Press Club of South Africa named her Newsmaker of the Year. http://www.nationalpressclub.co.za/releases/20120122.php (accessed June 29, 2015). http://www.wbsjournal.co.za/articles/south-africas-30-wonder-women-948.html (accessed June 24, 2015),
7. Eynon, "Interpreting the Economic Growth and Development PoliciesOf Post-Apartheid South Africa: Its Influence on Higher Education and Prospects for Women" 200.
8. Ibid.
9. Ibid., 201.
10. Ibid., 202.
11. Ibid., 201.

12. Ibid.
13. Ibid.
14. Ibid.
15. Ibid.
16. Ibid.
17. Ibid.
18. Ibid., 202.
19. Ibid., 201
20. Ibid., 206.
21. Ibid.
22. Ibid., 207.
23. Ibid.
24. Ibid.
25. Ibid.
26. Ibid.
27. Faranaaz Parker. "Women Still Struggle for Equality," *Mail & Guardian Online*, September 2, 2009, http://mg.co.za/article/2009-09-01-women-still-struggle-for-equality (accessed November 17, 2009).
28. Statistics South Africa, *Quarterly Labour Force Survey*, Statistical Release PO211, Quarter 4, 2014, Pretoria, South Africa (February10, 2014), Appendix,1.
29. Ibid.
30. Statistics South Africa, *General Household Survey 2014*, July 2015, Pretoria, South Africa, 165.
31. Kane-Berman, J. *Born Free But Still in Chains: South Africa's First Post-apartheid Generation* (Johannesburg, South Africa: South African Institute of Race Relations, 2015), 9.
32. Statistics South Africa, South African Statistics 2015, Pretoria, South Africa, 2.13.
33. International Labor Organization, *More Women Needed at Top Management Positions in Africa*, January 12, 2015, http://www.ilo.org/addisababa/media-centre/pr/WCMS_335704/lang–en/index.htm (accessed November 06, 2016).
34. Eynon, 210.
35. Ibid.
36. Parker, "Women Still Struggle for Equality."
37. PWC South Africa, *SA Has to Build Pipeline of Female Leaders*, July 2014. http://www.pwc.co.za/en/press-room/corporate-women.html (accessed November 06, 2015).
38. Eynon, 210.
39. Ibid.

40. The International Labour Organizations International Standard Classifications of Occupations defines elementary occupations as those that "consist of simple and routine tasks which mainly require the use of hand-held tools and often some physical effort."

Tasks performed by workers in elementary occupations usually include selling goods in streets and public places, or from door to door; providing various street services; cleaning, washing, pressing; taking care of apartment houses, hotels, offices and other buildings; washing windows and other glass surfaces of buildings; delivering messages or goods; carrying luggage; door-keeping and property watching; stocking vending machines or reading and emptying meters; collecting garbage; sweeping streets and similar places; performing various simple farming, fishing, hunting or trapping tasks performing simple tasks connected with mining, construction and manufacturing including product-sorting and simple hand-assembling of components; packing by hand; freight handling; pedaling or hand-guiding vehicles to transport passengers and goods; driving animal-drawn vehicles or machinery. International Labour Organization, http://www.ilo.org/public/english/bureau/stat/isco/isco88/9.htm (accessed January 3, 2010).
41. Statistics South Africa, *Gender Statistics in South Africa, 2011*, Pretoria, South Africa, 2012, 37.
42. Statistics South Africa, *South African Statistics 2015*, Pretoria, South Africa, 2.17.
43. Government of South Africa, *The Status of Women in the South African Economy*, August 2015, Pretoria, South Africa, 57.
44. Statistics South Africa, appendix, 1.
45. Eynon, 202.
46. Ibid., 203.
47. Ibid.
48. Ibid.
49. Ibid., 204.
50. Ibid.
51. Ibid.
52. Ibid.
53. Government Gazette, January 16, 2014, Volume 583, no. 37238, Republic of South Africa, Cape Town, South Africa, http://www.labour.gov.za/DOL/downloads/legislation/acts/employment-equity/eea_amend2014.pdf
54. Eynon, 205.
55. Ibid.
56. Ibid.
57. Stats South Africa, Poverty trends in South Africa: An examination of absolute poverty between 2006 and 2011, 2014, Pretoria, South Africa, 41.

58. Women in National Parliaments, http://www.ipu.org/wmn-e/classif.htm#1 (accessed November 20, 2009).
59. Gender Links for Equality and Justice, South Africa misses the mark on women in politics, October 28, 2014, http://genderlinks.org.za/programme-web-menu/a-press-releases/sckvr-elections-2014-05-26/ (accessed November 06, 2016).
60. All Africa, "Sisulu Elected as First Male Speaker in Parliament," May 6, 2009, www.allafrica.com/stories/200905060888.html (accessed November 21, 2009).
61. Eynon, 211.
62. Ibid.
63. Ibid.
64. Ibid., 212.
65. Ibid.
66. Ibid.
67. Ibid.
68. *QUARTZ*, "Helen Zille, the woman who exposed a major apartheid-era coverup, is leaving South African politics," April 14, 2015, http://qz.com/382255/helen-zilles-relationship-with-the-media-is-the-most-important-confusing-part-of-her-legacy/ (accessed June 30, 2015).
69. *South Africa History Online*, http://www.sahistory.org.za/people/patricia-de-lille (accessed June 29, 2015); *Mail & Guardian*, "De Lille crowned new Western Cape DA Leader,"April 18, 2015, http://mg.co.za/article/2015-04-18-de-lille-crowned-new-western-cape-da-leader (accessed July 1, 2015).
70. Eynon, 212.
71. Carien du Plessis, "Cosatu to Focus on Gender Equity after Criticising Zille's Male Cabinet," *Business Day*, September 19, 2009, 4.
72. Ibid.
73. Originally published by *The Sunday Independent*, "Zuma: Loafers Must Go, but Women are Welcome," April 12, 2009, posted on www.iol.co.za (accessed April 14, 2009).
74. *News 24*, Duarte lambastes ANC over single female premier, May 20, 2014, http://www.news24.com/elections/news/one-female-premier-unacceptable-duarte-20140520 (accessed July 1, 2015).
75. Richard Lapper, "A Canny Leader with a Chequered Past," *Financial Times*, January 4, 2009, http://www.ft.com/cms/s/2/23652f16-da82-11dd-8c28-000077b07658.html (accessed January 30, 2009).
76. Alec Russell, "The next president of South Africa," *Financial Times*, April 17, 2009, http://www.ft.com/cms/s/2/f4f4b2ec-288c-11de-8dbf-00144feabdc0.html?ftcamp=rss (accessed April 21, 2009); *The Economist*, "Africa's Next Big Man," April 18–24, 2009, 11; Nolwazi Mkhwanazi,

"Miniskirts and Kangas: The Use of Culture in Constituting Postcolonial Sexuality," *Dark Matter,* May 2, 2008, http://darkmatter101.org/site/2008/05/02/miniskirts-andkagas-the-use-of-culture-in-constituting-post colonial-sexuality (accessed December 12, 2009).

77. Preg Govender, "Our Power, Our Choices: Loyalty, Silence and Women's Lives," Women's Day Speech, Pretoria, South Africa, August 9, 2006, 2. www.sangonet.org.za/portal/images/stories/ . . . /pregsgovender1.pdf.
78. Govender, "Our Power, Our Choices: Loyalty, Silence and Women's Lives," 3; Mkhwanazi, "Miniskirts and Kangas: The Use of Culture in Constituting Postcolonial Sexuality."
79. Mkhwanazi, "Miniskirts and Kangas: The Use of Culture in Constituting Postcolonial Sexuality."
80. Russell, "The Next President of South Africa;" *The Economist,* "Africa's Next Big Man,"11.
81. Ibid.
82. *BBC News*, "South Africa's Zuma to Marry Third Wife," January 4, 2010, http://bbc.co.uk/go/pr/fr/-/2/hi/africa/8434865.stm (accessed January 4, 2010); Don Scrooby, "Wedding of South Africa's President Challenges Concept of Nation Building," *Name of Publication,* January 5, 2010, http://technorati.com/politics/article/wedding-of-south-africas-president-challenges/ (accessed January, 7, 2010).
83. The Presidency of the Republic of South Africa (2008), 140–141; Recognition of Customary Marriages Act 1998 (No. 120); CEDAW (2010), 143.
84. Ibid., 145.
85. *BBC News*, "Polygamy Defended by South Africa President." January 28, 2010, http://news.bbc.co.uk/go/pr/fr/-/2/hi/africa/8485730.stm (accessed January 29, 2010).
86. Barry Bearak, "South Africa: Zuma Acknowledges Paternity," February 3, 2010, *New York Times,* http://www.nytimes.com/2010/02/04/world/africa/04briefs-ZUMAACKNOWLEDGE_BRF.html (accessed February 4, 2010)
87. Eynon, 217.
88. Ibid.
89. Ibid.
90. Ibid., 218.
91. Gender Links is an organization focused on bringing about equal participation of men and women in all aspects of public and private life. In order to do this the organization focuses on three linked programs: media, governance, and gender justice. Gender Links work on a local, national, regional, and international level. The organization's goals are to promote gender equality in and through the media; conductive effective campaigns to end gender violence, HIV, and AIDS; and to build the capacity for women and

men to engage in democratic processes that advance equality and justice. http://www.genderlinks.org.za/page/mission-and-vision (accessed November 9, 2009).

92. *IOL South Africa*, "Zuma Must Commit to Gender Equality," April 28, 2009, http://iol.co.za/general/news/newsprint.php?art_id=nw20090428122703282C798748&sf (accessed April 29, 2009).
93. Ibid.
94. Eynon, 218.
95. *The Economist*, "Briefing South Africa's Elections: Voting for the People's Man," April 18–24, 2009, 24.
96. *AllAfrica.com*, "Malema is a Human Rights Activist – Lawyer," June 6, 2009, http://allafrica.com/stories/200906080073.html (accessed December 10, 2009); Sonke Gender Justice Network, "Sonke Staff Member Takes Julius Malema to Court," November 29, 2009, http://www.genderjustice.org.za/advocacy/sonke-staff-member-takes-julius-malema-to-court (accessed December 10, 2009); Sonke Gender Justice Network, "Sonke Staff Member Takes Julius Malema to Court," June 22, 2011, http://www.genderjustice.org.za/project-archive/sonke-takes-julius-malema-to-court/ (accessed July 1, 2015).
97. IOL, "Zille Attacked on Facebook!!!" May 20, 2009, http://www.iol.co.za/index.php?set_id=1&click_id=13&art_id=vn20090519111653731C146923 (accessed April 20, 2009).
98. *The Economist*, "Briefing South Africa's Elections: Voting for the People's Man," 24.
99. Moipone Malefane, "Intelligence Boss's Shock Admission: "I beat My Wife Because She Would Not Cook," *Sunday Times, South Africa*, September 20, 2009, http://www.timeslive.co.za/sundaytimes/article121923.ece (accessed November 30, 2009).
100. Eynon, 220.
101. Ibid., 221.
102. Ibid.
103. Ibid.
104. Ibid.
105. Ibid., 222.
106. Ibid.
107. Ibid.
108. Ibid.
109. Ibid., 164.
110. Ibid.
111. Eynon, 223.
112. Office of the Deputy President of South Africa, *The HIV & AIDS and STI Strategic Plan for South Africa 2007–2011*, Unveiled by the at the National

Consultation Conference, March 14, 2007, www.doh.gov.za/docs/misc/stratplan/2007-2011/part1.pdf, *9; UN Aids*, http://www.unaids.org/en/regionscountries/countries/southafrica (accessed July 1, 2015); *Mail & Guardian*, "South Africa has the highest number of new HIV infections worldwide-survey," April 01, 2014,http://mg.co.za/article/2014-04-01-sa-holds-highest-number-of-new-hiv-infections-worldwide-survey (accessed July 1, 2015).

113. Ibid., 10.
114. Ibid., 12.
115. Ibid., 10.
116. Ibid., 33.
117. Ibid.
118. Ibid.
119. Dean Peacock, "Tshabalala-Msimang's Statements at Commission on the Status of Women Undermine South Africa Credibility," *NGO Pulse*, March 2, 2009. http://ngopulse.org/article/tshabalala-msimang%E2%80%99s-statements-csw-undermine-sa-credibility (accessed November 30, 2009).
120. Eynon, 225.
121. Ibid.
122. Ibid., 226.
123. Pumza Fihlani, "Is South Africa's Aids Program Working?," *BBC News*, November 30, 2011. http://www.bbc.com/news/world-africa-15854793 (accessed November 24, 2016)
124. Celia W. Dugger, "Breaking with the Past, South Africa Issues Broad AIDS Policy," New *York Times,* December 1, 2009, http://www.nytimes.com/2009/12/02/world/africa/02safrica.html (accessed December 1, 2009).
125. Rachel Jewkes, Yandisa Sikweyiya, Robert Morrell, and Kristin Dunkle. "Understanding Men's Health and Use of Violence: Interface of Rape and HIV in South Africa," Gender and Health Research Unit, Medical Research Council, Pretoria, South Africa, June 2009, 1; David Smith, "Quarter of Men in South Africa Admit Rape, Survey Finds," *Guardian,* June 17, 2009, http://www.guardian.co.uk/world/2009/jun/17/south-africa-rape-survey (accessed December 14, 2009).
126. Jewkes et al., 3.
127. Smith, "Quarter of Men in South Africa Admit Rape, Survey Finds."
128. Organization of Economic Co-Operation and Development (OECD), *Social Institutions and Gender Index South Africa* (Paris, France, 2014, 3.
129. United Nations Office for Coordination of Humanitarian Affairs, "South Africa: One in Four Men Rape."
130. OECD, 3.
131. Delia Robertson, "Study Finds Shocking Incidence of Rape in South Africa," Voice *of America,* June 19, 2009, http://www1.voanews.com/

english/news/a-13-2009-06-19-voa25-68826272.html (accessed June 19, 2009).

132. Jewkes, et al., 3; Smith, "Quarter of Men in South Africa Admit Rape, Survey Finds;" United Nations Office for Coordination of Humanitarian Affairs, "South Africa: One in Four Men Rape."
133. Eynon, 228.
134. Ibid., 229.
135. Ibid.
136. Ibid.
137. Ibid.
138. Ibid.
139. Ibid.
140. Ibid., 230.
141. Ibid.
142. Ibid.
143. Ibid.
144. Ibid.
145. Ibid.
146. Ibid.
147. Ibid.
148. Ibid., 231.
149. Ibid.
150. Ibid., 223.
151. Ibid.
152. Ibid.
153. Ibid., 224.
154. Ibid., 231.

CHAPTER 9

Closing Thoughts on the Future

This book has examined how the post-apartheid government has influenced the prospects of South African women through its policies regarding macroeconomic growth and development, higher education, gender equality, and women's empowerment. Each strategy has been considered a key driver in the creation of a new, democratic South Africa. As has been explored in previous chapters, the results have been mixed. So where does it all leave South Africa when it comes to moving forward? Where should the nation go in the future?

Future Prospects for Women in South Africa

In just a little more than two decades, South Africa has rewritten its constitution, revised its macroeconomic growth and development policies, restructured its higher education system, and made a commitment to providing opportunity for all its citizens—specifically those who have historically been marginalized, such as women and blacks. No other country has undertaken such transformation in such a relatively short period of time. As a result of such ambitious plans, many South Africans have looked to the future with hope and a sense of possibility for themselves and their families.

Yet 23 years after apartheid, that optimistic view is beginning to give way to frustration and anger. Many poor black South Africans still live in abject poverty, are unemployed, lack proper housing and other basic

© The Author(s) 2017

D.E. Eynon, *Women, Economic Development, and Higher Education*,
DOI 10.1007/978-3-319-53144-1_9

services, and only continue to lose ground as the disparity between the rich and poor grows ever wider. The results of their frustration and anger can be seen in the escalating crime rates and daily public protests—as well as in the results of recent elections, which brought a shift in the political landscape and demands for new economic and social approaches.

There is a growing sense among South Africans that it is time for the government to stop talking about the promises of the constitution, laws, policies, and initiatives that it has put in place and to begin delivering on the basics—like decent housing and jobs. COSATU and the Communist Party were instrumental in Jacob Zuma's elections—both in 2009 and most recently—and they continue to put pressure on the government to reconsider its macroeconomic growth and development policies.

In 2009, Trevor Sehoole, then department minister of higher education in South Africa's Department of Education, stated, "There is a lot of expectation from the masses, from the working class, from the labor movement, and from the Communist Party that government should do away with some of the policies that were in place over the past 15 years and adopt new policies."[1] It still isn't clear today what, if any, substantive changes have occurred during that period to make the country's economic growth and development policies work for the masses.

A growing number of people are also concerned that Zuma is bringing a new conservatism to South Africa, in part based on his and his supporters' behavior during presidential campaigns. For example, in the 2008 campaign, many viewed Zuma's offering of prayers to ancestors, defense of polygamy as "African," denouncement of same-sex marriage as a "disgrace to God," and promise to bring back the death penalty as signs that he would move the country back to tribalism—and turn away from the concept of nation-building as defined in the country's progressive constitution and laws.[2] A shift to conservatism and tribalism could have significant ramifications for women, pushing back many of the advancements they have made in recent years and making it nearly impossible for black rural women to progress.

Moreover, as research repeatedly shows, South Africa continues to define and understand itself through a mostly racial lens, which limits the country's ability to look at issues like gender, poverty, and class in a multidimensional way. To address the problems that South Africa faces, the country must find new ways of evaluating how they have occurred—making it clear that race isn't the only source of tension in the country. For example, a gendered view of poverty, unemployment, and violence would help create a more comprehensive and nuanced understanding of the complexity and challenges that the country faces today.

Perhaps South Africans continue to define and understand themselves in racial terms because it is a familiar—and therefore comfortable—worldview. Achieving true transformation will require all South Africans to be the drivers of change, a position many have not been in before. As Elaine Salo, former director of gender studies at the University of Pretoria, explains it:

> It's having the willingness to confront the fear that challenge and growth brings. All of us, as South Africans, face that because our comfort zones are shifting. And change and transformation induces large-scale anxiety. It was bad before, and you didn't like it, but at least you knew what it was. You knew what the parameters and borders were. But this, you don't know what it is, and now you're responsible for it. That can be scary.[3]

Any discussion about South Africa's future must include the topic of HIV/AIDS. As the number of those infected only increases, the disease is taking an ever-growing toll on the country. The good news is that the Zuma and the ANC are now taking an aggressive approach to combat the pandemic after years of neglect and denial. Much work must be done, and organizations like the Ubuntu Education Fund are on the ground working to reverse the rate of infection through education, distribution of antiretroviral drugs, and new forums for people to discuss cultural attitudes about sex. Jacob Lief, the fund's president, explains:

> We quickly realized that the crucial question is how you keep the young mothers alive. The minute the mother dies, the child becomes that much more vulnerable—things lead to transactional sex, robbery, whatever it takes to survive, which is natural. We realized it was important to stabilize the home environment, and in our case, that was keeping a young mother alive. A generation of mothers has been wiped out by HIV, so we got into HIV testing, treatment, and education.[4]

South Africa's future will be influenced by how well the country is able to control the rate of infection and increase the number of people who can live with the virus. If current trends continue, the country may find the social, economic, and emotional toll too heavy to carry as current and future generations will pay with their lives. Such issues are certain to have an influence on South Africa in the near term.

Yet despite anxiety about such deep-seated problems and what the future may bring, people do remain cautiously optimistic. Says Nadine Petersen, professor of education at the University of Johannesburg:

> I wouldn't be in this country if I weren't hopeful. I love my country. I love what I do. I love the contribution that I can make as a black woman teaching other students. Despite the gloomy picture I may have painted, I still think there are enormous possibilities in this country if we work toward achieving a particular goal. I see the hope that women carry at all levels of society and across all class levels. That gives me hope that we have the ability to force change, if necessary, where it needs to happen. Maybe that sounds idealistic. Things are not good, not by a long shot. It's our responsibility to create that critical mass.[5]

Suggestions for Moving Forward

This book has focused on how women's prospects and lives have changed since the end of apartheid rule. And one thing that the research has made abundantly clear is that—whether one is discussing access to higher education or employment opportunities—poor, rural, black South African women represent a significant portion of the population and have not benefited from the opportunities that have become available to women as a whole.

The 2016 Global Gender Gap Report by the World Economic Forum was a matter of particular puzzlement and frustration. It ranks countries based on how well they have decreased gender disparities related to economic participation and opportunity, educational attainment, health and survival, and political empowerment. Inexplicably, it ranked South Africa the 15th best country in the world. The country received a relatively high score of 0.764, with 1.0 representing complete equality between genders.[6]

That is difficult to accept in a country where polygamy is allowed, rape and sexual abuse against women are the norm, violence against women is on the increase, women are underrepresented in professional and management positions, and a significant percentage of them continue to live in poverty and lack access to basic resources. While it is helpful to attempt quantitative measurement of countries' progress in decreasing gender disparity, the report's numbers are clearly skewed and should not be held up as evidence that all is well with South African gender relations. That is why it is so important to conduct qualitative studies about women in South Africa that create a more accurate, nuanced, and clear picture of what is happening.

It is also vital to examine different groupings of women in the country. In a nation as complex as South Africa, and in one with a history of such bitter racial division, putting all women in just one category distorts the picture of their lives. The opportunities for white South African women differ significantly from those of black South African or Indian women, just as the lives of women in rural areas greatly contrast with those of women in urban ones. That holds true for enrollment and graduation rates in higher education, employment opportunities, and safety and health issues. Examining different groups of women allows for a far better understanding of the challenges they each face—as well as for the development of much more targeted and effective responses to those challenges.

Perhaps most important, greater dialogue between the men and women of South Africa must occur. In conducting the interviews highlighted in this book, a pattern would develop. Each interviewee would begin on an optimistic note, saying that women were making progress—that, while not all women were advancing, in general things were moving ahead in the right direction. Then the conversation would shift toward a discussion of men's attitudes. Interviewees would linger over issues of violence, sexual abuse, rape, HIV/AIDS, and the difficulty of living in a patriarchal society. As shared by Harold Herman, emeritus professor of comparative and international education at the University of Western Cape, "Just as apartheid has created this huge disparity between white and black, so the social system, the religious practices, and the tribal culture, have created disadvantages for women."[7]

It's apparent that it's impossible to talk about women's opportunities without talking about—and with—men. Unfortunately, for many women, men can have a negative influence on their lives and make it difficult to move ahead. And often, the more women progress, the more some men become abusive and patriarchal in their attitudes.

That cycle needs to be broken. Two things must happen to start working toward a solution: first, men should be engaged and a part of the process, and, second, a national dialogue should begin between men and women on how to end the abuse and violence. Orly Stern, former human rights lawyer for the Sonke Gender Justice Network, feels strongly about the need to work with men:

> There's a lot of work done in empowering woman, but if you want to stop rape and gender violence, and if you want to work towards gender equality, you need to target the men. So my organization works with men and boys to try and end their silence. We do a lot of work around HIV/AIDS, advising men to get tested, not to have concurrent partners. And we discuss violence and abuse against women.[8]

Starting a national dialogue about such challenges will be difficult, Stern adds, noting:

> We're afraid. People are afraid to talk about it. People are embarrassed. But it's happening. Understanding why it's happening, I don't know—that's so complex.[9]

As South Africa prepared for the 2010 World Cup, the issues of violence, rape, HIV/AIDS, and crime in South Africa appeared in international headlines. In response, government officials and World Cup organizers worked hard to convince the world that South Africa was a safe place to come to enjoy the event. The occasion provided a perfect opportunity for the government to begin a national dialogue about violence and abuse against women. While it was doubtful Jacob Zuma would spearhead such a dialogue, given his personal life and the comments he made about women during his rape trial, what about the women in government? Did they use their voice and speak up about these issues?

Sadly, both Zuma and women in government remained silent. As Jacob Lief, president of the Ubuntu Education Fund, observed:

> Why aren't we talking about this? I'm not talking about the community voice. There are a lot of community activists. I'm asking, where are the members of Parliament? Where's the first lady? Where are the people standing up and saying "Stop"? We talk about a national crisis that is happening to our young girls, and until we have leadership, we're fighting a fight that we can't win. And it needs to happen at the top. Strong leadership is the key. I'm not saying we can't push, and we'll continue doing what we do, but we need to see someone else step up. Do you know the deputy president of our

country is a woman, and she didn't utter one word about this? It's inexcusable.[10]

So what must be done? Leaders, both male and female, in positions of political and economic influence in South African should pursue four key steps. They should:

Work to change practices that have hindered women's access to basic services, education, and economic advancement, as well as their opportunity to play a role in personal and political decision-making.

Many of those practices remain rooted in deeply entrenched cultural and traditional norms. Thus, it is vital that women in a position of power and authority speak up on behalf of other women and advocate for changes. In addition, men should be actively engaged in the process to help create new approaches, so any such advances are encouraged and supported by both genders. One way to begin the process—a first step in creating pathways for understanding, common ground, and shared interests—is to find and create opportunities for men and women to engage in meaningful dialogue.That, in turn, can be used to build the foundation for shared interest and action.

Establish a structure at the local level to ensure gender policies and laws are implemented and obeyed.

A majority of women still live in rural areas where their local government and chiefs have the most influence on everyone's daily life. A structure must be put in place at the local level, and in both public and private organizations, to ensure policies and laws support gender equality and women's empowerment. The difficulty in rural areas is the lack of resources and infrastructure for the implementation and enforcement of these laws and policies. The South African government should allocate additional resources to rural areas to ensure women have access to the judicial system and the necessary legal services to bring a case or complaint to and through the legal system. This will also require an investment in more police, judges, and attorneys in rural areas.

Subordinate customary and cultural practices to the right of equality for women.

Women's equality should always take precedent over customary and cultural practices. As is, traditional customs too often trump the law in rural areas. The rights of women, as defined in the constitution and laws, must be recognized, implemented, and enforced—regardless of traditional customs. When customary practices and laws conflict with women's constitutional rights, the courts can play a critical role in resolving these potential conflicts by overturning such practices and laws which discriminate against women.

> Promote and support women's economic empowerment and active engagement in the formal economy.

As has been discussed at length, most South African women are still engaged in the informal economy and continue to live in poverty. The government, private sector, and higher education system should work together to design a comprehensive plan that identifies and creates opportunities for women to actively participate in the formal economy. In addition, micro-financing, a tool that has been used extensively in India and in several African countries, has yet to take hold in South Africa. The creation of a micro-financing program in South Africa is just one example of how women could become more economically empowered and engaged.

> Focus especially on women who live in rural areas and are significantly disadvantaged.

Since women's bargaining power in households comes from empowerment in education, income, legal rights, and religious or social validation, women who live in rural areas, who are at a significant disadvantage and should be targeted. For example, rural women should be encouraged and helped to complete their education at all levels, as each additional year of schooling increases their potential for future wages and delays the need to get married. In addition, they must be given access to financial resources, public services, and land. And rural women, who make up few elected representatives in most rural councils or serve as party chairs or heads in rural councils, should be invited to run for such positions and supported in those efforts.

South Africa, while economically ahead of other African countries, has yet to fully benefit from the promise of the global economy even though it has adopted neo-liberal economic growth and development initiatives, restructured its higher education system, and created legislation and initiatives aimed at bringing women into the educational system, formal economy, and government. The country has experienced economic growth but not necessarily development. The unemployment rate has risen since 1994, as has the number of people living in poverty. Although higher education enrollment rates have increased, relatively few poor South Africans, especially black South African women, have enrolled in and graduated from college. And women are still underrepresented in higher education programs and jobs in the global, knowledge-based economy.

Debates continue as to whether South Africa should have embraced the neo-liberal economic practices of the West or stayed on course with the redistribution and equity approach that the incoming government of the ANC first introduced in 1994. South Africa's experience suggests that economic growth and development policies of an emerging country must fit its cultural, social, and political context—and not merely replicate the Western model—if that country is to engage in the global economy and bring prosperity to its people.

Meanwhile, it still appears that higher education and the engagement of women can contribute significantly to the advancement of an emerging country like South Africa. There is no doubt that the constitution, as well as other legislation and government policies, have opened up opportunities for some women. What they haven't done is to change the consciousness of the South African society to be a gender sensitive and nonpatriarchal society. That may be a matter of women becoming economically empowered and occupying more positions of authority across society. Yet it will take time for a critical mass of women to populate those positions and exert enough influence to bring about the necessary improvements that many poor, black, rural women have been waiting for over two decades to see. And that will not just automatically occur.

Thus, renewed efforts are required among government leaders, policy makers, and others—in particular, those related to pursuing some of the recommendations outlined in this chapter. By exploring these recommendations, it is my hope that women will be able to continue on a path of progress, and that those who have thus far been left behind will have the opportunity to pursue and realize their promise.

Notes

1. Eynon, "Interpreting the Economic Growth and Development Policies of Post-Apartheid South Africa: Its Influence on Higher Education and Prospects for Women" 239.
2. Farouk Chothia, "Will Zuma Bring Tribalism to South Africa?" *BBC News*, April 23, 2009, http://news.bbc.co.uk/2/hi/africa/8012903.stm (accessed April 23, 2009).
3. Eynon, 241.
4. Ibid.
5. Ibid., 242.
6. Richard Samans and Saadia Zahidi, *The Global Gender Gap Report 2016* (Geneva, Switzerland: World Economic Forum, 2016), 10.
7. Eynon, 244.
8. Ibid.
9. Ibid.
10. Ibid., 245.

Bibliography

African National Congress. *RDP White Paper*. Accessed November 21, 2009. http://www.anc.org.za/content/rdp-white-paper-discussion-document.

African National Congress. "The State and Social Transformation." Discussion document, 1996. Accessed October 22, 2009. http://www.anc.org.za/content/state-and-social-transformation.

Allen, Michael H. *Globalization, Negotiation, and the Failure of Transformation in South Africa: Revolution at a Bargain?* New York, NY: Palgrave Macmillan, 2006.

Assie-Lumumba, N'Dri T. "Educational and Economic Reforms, Gender Equity, and Access to Schooling in Africa." *International Journal of Comparative Sociology* 41, no. 1 (2000): 89–120.

Assie-Lumumba, N'Dri T., ed. *Women and Higher Education in Africa: Reconceptualizing Gender-based Human Capabilities and Upgrading Human Rights to Knowledge*. Ithaca, New York: CEPARRED, 2008.

Baden, Sally, Shireen Hasim, and Shelia Meintjes. *Country Gender Profile: South Africa*. Brighton, UK: Bridge Development, Institute of Development Studies, University of Sussex, 1998.

Becker, Gary. *Human Capital: A Theoretical and Empirical Analysis, with Special Reference to Education*. 3rd ed. Chicago: University of Chicago Press, 1993.

Benson, Bruce. *The Enterprise of Law: Justice Without the State*. San Francisco: Pacific Institute for Public Policy Research, 1990.

Billson, Janet M., and Carolyn Fluehr-Lobban. *Female Well-being: Toward a Global Theory of Social Change*. New York: Zed Books, 2005.

Blackden, Mark, Sudharshan Canagarajah, Stephen Klasen, and David Lawson. "Gender and Growth in Sub-Saharan Africa: Issues and Evidence." In *Advancing Development: Core Themes in Global Economics*, edited by George

© The Author(s) 2017

D.E. Eynon, *Women, Economic Development, and Higher Education*,
DOI 10.1007/978-3-319-53144-1

Mavrotas and Anthony Shorrocks, 349–370. New York: Palgrave Macmillan in association with the United Nations University-World Institute for Development Economics Research, 2007.

Bloom, David, David Canning, and Kevin Chan. *Higher Education and Economic Development in Africa*. Washington, DC: World Bank, 2006.

Boko, Sylvain, Mina Baliamoune-Lutz, and Sitawa R. Kimuna, eds. *Women in African Development: The Challenge of Globalization and Liberalization in the 21st Century*. Trenton, NJ: Africa World Press, 2005.

Budeli, Mpfariseni. "Employment Equity and Affirmative Action in South Africa: A Review of the Jurisprudence of the Courts since 1994." Paper presented at the Twenty Years of South African Constitutionalism conference, New York University. http://www.nylslawreview.com/wp-content/uploads/sites/16/2014/11/Budeli1.pdf

Bunting I., C. Sheppard, N. Cloete, and L. Belding. *Performance Indicators in South African Higher Education 2000–2008 Summary Report*. Cape Town, SA: Center for Higher Education Trust.

Campbell, John. "Slow Progress for South Africa's 'Born-Free' Generation." Council on Foreign Relations, 2015. Accessed June 15, 2016. http://www.cfr.org/south-africa/slow-progress-south-africas-born-free-generation/p37393

Cloete, Nico. *Free Higher Education: Another Self-Destructive South African Policy*. Cape Town, SA: Center for Higher Education Trust, January 2016. http://www.chet.org.za/papers/free-higher-education

Council on Higher Education. *Higher Education Monitor: The State of Higher Education in South Africa*, no.8 Tshwane: Council on Higher Education, (October 2009).

Council on Higher Education. *A Proposal for Undergraduate Curriculum Reform in South Africa: The Case for a Flexible Curriculum Structure*. Pretoria, SA: Council on Higher Education, 2013.

Council on Higher Education. *South Africa Higher Education in the First Decade of Democracy*. Pretoria, SA: The Council on Higher Education, 2004.

Council on Higher Education. *Vital Stats, 2013*. Pretoria, SA: Council on Higher Education, 2015.

Department of Education. *Information on the State Budget for Higher Education 2007*. Pretoria: Department of Education, 2007.

Department of Education. *Monitoring and Evaluation Report on the Impact and Outcomes of the Education System on South Africa's Population: Evidence from Household Surveys*. Pretoria, SA: Department of Education, 2006.

Deputy President of South Africa. *JIPSA Report on Activities in 2007*. Pretoria: SA April, 2008.

Dickow, Helga, and Valerie Moller. "South Africa's Rainbow People National Pride and Optimism: A Trend Study." *Social Indicators Research* 59, no. 2 (2002): 180.

Edigheji, Omano. *The Emerging South African Democratic Development State and the People's Contract.* Research Report 108. Johannesburg, SA: Center for Policy Studies, 2007.

Edigheji, Omano. "Globalization and the Paradox of Participatory Governance in South Africa: The Case of the New South Africa." *African Journal of International Affairs* 7, no. 1& 2 (2004): 1–20.

Eynon, Diane. "Interpreting the Economic Growth and Development Policies of Post-Apartheid South Africa: Its Influence on Higher Education and Prospects for Women." Doctoral diss., University of Pennsylvania, 2010.

Federici, Silvia, George Caffentzis, and Ousseina Alidous. *A Thousand Flowers: Social Struggles Against Structural Adjustment in African Universities.* Trenton, NJ: Africa World Press, 2000.

Freund, Bill, and Vishnu Padayachee. "Post-apartheid South Africa: The key patterns emerge." *Economic and Political Weekly* 33, no. 20 (May 16–22, 1998): 1173–1180.

Geisler, Gisela. *Women and the Remaking of Politics in South Africa.* Uppsala, Sweden: Nordiska Afrikainstitutet, 2004.

Giliomee, Herman. *The Afrikaners: Biography of a People.* Charlottesville, Virginia: University of Virginia Press, 2003.

Ginwala, Frene, Maureen Mackintosh, and Doreen Massey. "Gender and Economic Policy in a Democratic South Africa." Ann Marie Wolpe Papers, A 14, 9, 1991, University of Cape Town Library Archives, University of Cape Town, Cape Town, SA.

Government of South Africa. *The Status of Women in the South African Economy.* Pretoria, SA Republic of South Africa, Department of Women, August 2015. http://www.gov.za/sites/www.gov.za/files/Status_of_women_in_SA_economy.pdf

Govender, Pregs. *Love and Courage: A Story of Insubordination.* Auckland Park, SA: Jacana Media Ltd, 2007.

Govender, Preg. "Our Power, Our Choices: Loyalty, Silence and Women's Lives." Women's Day Speech, Pretoria, SA, August 9, 2006.

Habib, Adam. "South Africa: The Rainbow Nation and Prospects for Consolidating Democracy." *African Journal of Political Science* 2, no. 2 (1997): 211–215.

Habib, Adam, and Vishnu Padayachee. "Economic Policy and Power Relations in South Africa's Transition to Democracy." *World Development* 28, no. 2 (2000), 245–263.

Handley, Antoinette. "Business, Government and Economic Policymaking in the New South Africa, 1990–2000." *Journal of Modern African Studies* 43, no. 2 (2005): 211–239.

Hassen, Ebrahim-Khali. *South Africa: Budget* 2009: *Great Transformation or Illusion Leading to Delusion.* Johannesburg, SA: The South African Civil

Society Information Service, 2009. Accessed November 17, 2009. http://allafrica.com/stories/200902120773.html

Hendrickse, Rozenda. "Reshaping Power South Africa's Gender Machinery Reviewed." Paper prepared for presentation at the International Political Science Association 22nd World Congress of Political Science: Reshaping Power, Shifting Boundaries Universidad Complutense de Madrid, Madrid, Spain, July 12, 2012.

Herbst, Marissa, and Willemien du Plessis. "Customary Law v. Common Law Marriages: A Hybrid Approach in South Africa." *Electronic Journal of Comparative Law* 12, no. 1 (2008). http://www.ejcl.org/121/art121-28.pdf

Higgs, Philip. "Current Status of, and Legislation to Redress, Gender Inequalities in South Africa." In *Women and Higher Education in Africa: Reconceptualizing Gender-based Human Capabilities and Upgrading Human Rights to Knowledge*, edited by N'Dri T. Assie-Lumumba., New York: CEPARRED, 2007.

Hirsch, Alan. *Season of Hope: Economic Reform Under Mandela and Mbeki.* Scottsville: University of KwaZulu-Natal Press, South African and International Development Research Centre, 2005.

Human Sciences Research Council. "Fact Sheet: Poverty in South Africa." Accessed October 17, 2009. http://www.sarpn.org/documents/d0000990/

International Monetary Fund. *Post-Apartheid South Africa: The First Ten Years.* Washington, DC: IMF Publication Services, 2005.

Jaffee, Georgina, and Collette Caine. "The Incorporation of Women Into the Industrial Workforce: Its Implications for the Women's Question in South Africa." Paper presented at the University of York Centre for Southern African Studies, Social Dynamics Q1, no. 10, September 29-October 2, 1986.

Jewkes, Rachel, Yandisa Sikweyiya, Robert Morrell, and Kristin Dunkle. "Understanding Men's Health and Use of Violence: Interface of Rape and HIV in South Africa." Pretoria, SA: Gender and Health Research Unit, Medical Research Council, June 2009.

Johnson R. W. *South Africa's Brave New World: The Beloved Country Since the End of Apartheid.* New York: Penguin Group, 2009.

Kabemba, Claude, and Tobias Schmitz. *Understanding Policy Implementation: An Exploration of Research Areas Surrounding the Reconstruction and Development Programme.* Research report no. 73. Johannesburg, SA: Centre for Policy Studies, 2001.

Kane-Berman, J. *Born Free But Still in Chains: South Africa's First Post-Apartheid Generation.* Johannesburg, SA: South African Institute of Race Relations, 2015.

Knight, Richard. *South Africa 2006: Challenges for the Future.* South Africa Delegation Briefing Paper. New York: Shared Interest, 2006. Accessed on January 14, 2009. http://richardknight.homestead.com/files/SouthAfrica2006-ChallengesfortheFuture.pdf

Kunnie, Julian. *A Comprehensive History of South Africa's Struggle*. Oxford: Westview Press, 2000.

Kunnie, Julian. *Is Apartheid Really Dead? Why Apartheid Changed Its Character in 1990*. Oxford, UK: Westview Press, 2000.

Lawson, Sandra. "Women Hold up Half the Sky." Goldman Sachs Global Economics Paper no. 164, March 4, 2008. http://www.goldmansachs.com/our-thinking/investing-in-women/bios-pdfs/women-half-sky-pdf.pdf

Lulat, Y. G.-M. *A History of Higher Education from Antiquity to the Present: A Critical Synthesis*. Westport, Connecticut: Prager, 2005.

Mabokela, Reitumetse, and Kaluke Mawila. "The Impact of Race, Gender and Culture in South African Higher Education." *Comparative Education Review* 48, no. 4 (2004): 396–416.

Ministry of Higher Education and Training, Republic of South Africa, "Reflections on Higher Education Transformation." Paper prepared for the second National Higher Education Transformation Summit, October 17, 2015.

Ministry of Higher Education and Training, Republic of South Africa. *Report of the Ministerial Committee on Transformation and Social Cohesion and the Elimination of Discrimination in Public Higher Education Institutions*. November 30, 2008.

Mama, Amina. "Feminism or Femocracy? State Feminism and Democratisation in Nigeria." *Africa Development* 20, no. 1 (1995): 37–58.

Mandela, Nelson. *Long Walk to Freedom*. Boston: Little, Brown and Company, 1994.

Mavrotas, George, and Anthony Shorrocks, eds. *Advancing Development: Core Themes in Global Economics*. New York: Palgrave Macmillan, 2005.

Meier, Gerald, and James Rauch. *Leading Issues in Economic Development*. 8th ed. New York: Oxford University Press, 2005.

Melander, Erik. "The Limits of Manipulation Theory: The Apartheid Third Force and the ANC-Inkatha Conflict in South Africa." *Peace Economics, Peace Science and Public Policy* 8, no. 4 (2002): 3–5.

Morley, Louise, Fiona Leach, and Rosemary Lugg. "Democratising Higher Education in Ghana and Tanzania: Opportunity Structures and Social Inequalities." *International Journal of Educational Development* 29, no. 1 (2009): 56–64.

National Student Financial Aid Scheme. *2014/2015 Annual Report: NSFAS Toward a Student Centered Approach*. Cape Town, SA. http://www.nsfas.org.za/content/reports/NSFAS AR 2014-15.pdf

Nowak, Michael, and Luca Antonio Ricci, eds. *Post-Apartheid South Africa: The First Ten Years*. Washington, DC: International Monetary Fund, 2005.

Nzimande, Blade. "The Post-School Education and Training System: Some Issues of Policy." Public lecture by the Minister of Higher Education and Training,

Wits School of Public and Development Management, Pretoria, South Africa, July 23, 2009.

Office on the Status of Women. *South Africa's National Policy Framework for Women's Empowerment and Gender Equality*. Pretoria, SA: South Africa Government, 2000.

Organisation for Economic Co-Operation and Development. *Country Background Report: South African Education*. Paris: OECD, 2008.

Organization of Economic Co-Operation and Development. "Development in Non-Member Economies." In *OECD Economic Outlook 2008*, 221–223. Paris: OECD, 2008.

Organisation for Economic Co-Operation and Development. *Economic Surveys, South Africa Overview*. Paris: OECD, 2015.

Organisation for Economic Co-Operation and Development. *Education at a Glance* 2014: *OECD Indicators*. Paris: OECD, 2014. Accessed on June 10, 2016. http://dx.doi.org/10.1787/eag-2014-en

Organization of Economic Co-Operation and Development. *Reviews of National Policies for Education: South Africa*. Paris: OECD, 2008.

Organization of Economic Co-Operation and Development. *Social Institutions and Gender Index South Africa*. Paris: OECD, 2014.

Peacock, Dean. "Tshabalala-Msimang's Statements at Commission on the Status of Women Undermine South Africa Credibility." *NGO Pulse*, March 2, 2009. Accessed November 30, 2009. http://ngopulse.org/article/tshabalala-msimang's-statements-csw-undermine-sa-credibility

Pillay, Punday. "The Political Economy of Higher Education in South Africa." *International Journal Educational Development* 10, no. 2/3 (1990): 211–215.

Program on Action on Women's Empowerment and Gender Equality. *Report on National Gender Machinery*. Pretoria, South Africa, 2005.

Purfield, Catriona Mary, Marek Hanusch, Yashvir Algu, Tania Priscilla Begazo Gomez, Martha Martinez Licetti, and Sara Nyman. *South Africa Economic Update: Promoting Faster Growth and Poverty Alleviation Through Competition*. Washington, D.C.: World Bank Group, 2016.

Reconstruction and Development Programme. *Key Indicators of Poverty in South Africa*. Pretoria: Ministry in the Office of the President, 1995.

Reddy, Thiven. *Higher Education and Social Transformation: South Africa Case Study*. Pretoria, SA: Council on Higher Education, 2004. http://www.che.ac.za/sites/default/files/publications/HEandSocialTransformationReport_25Feb2004.pdf

Republic of South Africa. *A Basic Guide to the Reconstruction and Development Program*. Accessed January 12, 2009. http://www.africa.upenn.edu/Govern_Political/ANC_Recon.html

Republic of South Africa. *Growth, Employment and Redistribution: A Macroeconomic Strategy*. Pretoria: Department of Finance, Republic of South Africa, 2000. www.treasury.gov.za/publications/other/gear/chapters.pdf

Republic of South Africa Ministry of Education. *National Plan for Higher Education in South Africa*, 2001. Accessed February 18, 2009. http://www.education.gov.za/Documents/policies/NationalPlanHE2001.pdf

Romalis, John. "Factor Proportions and the Structure of Commodity Trade." *American Economic Review* 94, no. 1 (2004): 67–97.

Samans, Richard, and Saadia Zahidi. *The Global Gender Gap Report 2016*. Geneva, Switzerland: World Economic Forum, 2016.

Scott, Ian, Nan Yeld, and Jane Herdy. "A Case Study for Improving Teaching and Learning in South African Higher Education." In *Higher Education Monitor* no. 6. Cape Town, SA: Centre for Higher Education Development, University of Cape Town, 2007.

Sehoole, Trevor C. *Democratizing Higher Education Policy: Constraints of Reform in Post-apartheid South Africa*. New York: Routledge, 2005.

Shavit, Yossi, Richard Arum, and Adam Gamoran, eds. *Stratification in Higher Education: A Comparative Study*. Stanford, California: Stanford University Press, 2007.

Shisana, O., T. Rehle, L. Simbayi, W. Parker, K. Zuma, A. Bhana, C. Connoly, and V. Pillay, eds. *South African National HIV Prevalence, HIV Incidence, Behaviour and Communication Survey*. Cape Town: HSRC Press, 2005.

Simons, Ray. *Women in Urban and Rural Areas*. Lusaka, Zambia, February 1989, AL2517. The Original South Africa History Archives Collection, South Africa History Archives, Wits University, Pretoria, South Africa.

South Africa Council on Higher Education. *The State of Higher Education in South Africa: Higher Education Monitor no. 8* (2009). A report of the CHE Advice and Monitoring Directorate. http://www.che.ac.za/sites/default/files/publications/Higher_Education_Monitor_8.pdf

South African Police Service. *Annual Report 2014/2015*. Accessed June 10, 2016. http://www.saps.gov.za/about/stratframework/annual_report/2014_2015/SAPS_AR_2014-15_for_viewing.pdf

Taylor, Viviene, and Ina Conradie. *We Have Been Taught by Life Itself: Empowering Women as Leaders-The Role of Development Education*. Pretoria: HSRC, 1997.

Teboho Moja, T. "Politics of Exclusion in Higher Education: The Inadequacy of Gender Issues in the Globalization Debates." In *Women and Higher Education in Africa: Reconceptualizing Gender-based Human Capabilities and Upgrading Human Rights to Knowledge*, edited by N. T. Assie-Lumumba, 70. New York: CEPARRED, 2007.

Tshoaedi, Malehoko. "In the Union . . . Women Union Officials Speak Out." *South African Labour Bulletin* 22, no. 2 (2000): 55.

Weeks, John. "Stuck in Low GEAR? Macroeconomic Policy in South Africa, 1996–98." *Cambridge Journal of Economics*, 23, no. 6 (1999): 795–811.

Williams, Mariama. *Financing for Gender Equality and the Empowerment of Women: Some Theoretical and Practical Issues from a Trade and Macroeconomic Policies Perspective*. New York: United Nations Division for the Advancement of Women, 2007.

Wilson, Francis, and Mamphela Ramphele. *Uprooting Poverty: The South African Challenge*. Report for the Second Carnegie Inquiry into Poverty and Development in Southern Africa. Cape Town: David Phillip, 1989.

Worden, Nigel. *The Making of Modern South Africa*. Oxford: Blackwell Publishers, 1994.

World Bank. *Country Partnership Strategy for The Republic of South Africa for the Period 2008-2012*. Report no. 38156-ZA (2007). http://documents.worldbank.org/curated/en/591591468307149656/pdf/38156.pdf

World Bank. *South Africa Economic Update: Fiscal Policy and Redistribution in an Unequal Society*. Washington, D.C.: World Bank Group, 2014.

World Bank. "South Africa Economic Update: Promoting Faster Growth and Poverty Alleviation Through Competition" In *South Africa Economic Update*, 8th ed. World Bank Group, Washington, D.C.: World Bank Group, 2016.

World Bank. *Expanding the Possible in Sub-Saharan Africa: How Tertiary Institutions Can Increase Growth and Competitiveness*. Washington, D.C: World Bank, 2007.

The World Bank Southern African Department. *South Africa Economic Performances and Policies Overview*. Washington, D.C.: The World Bank, 1994.

World Bank Task Force on Higher Education and Society. *Higher Education in Developing Countries: Peril and Promise*. Washington, D.C.: World Bank, 2000.

Zarenda, H. *South Africa's National Development Plan and its implications for regional development*. Stellenbosch, SA: Tralac Trade Law Center, 2013.

Index

© The Author(s) 2017

D.E. Eynon, *Women, Economic Development, and Higher Education*,
DOI 10.1007/978-3-319-53144-1

CPSIA information can be obtained
at www.ICGtesting.com
Printed in the USA
LVOW13*2322301117
558172LV00017B/408/P

9 783319 531434